The Small Towns Book

show me the way to go home

James and Carolyn Robertson

Anchor Books

Anchor Press/Doubleday
Garden City, New York

1978

The Anchor Books edition is the first publication of *The Small Towns Book*.
Anchor Books edition: 1978

The Small Towns Book was developed and prepared for publication
at The Yolla Bolly Press, Covelo, California, under the supervision of
James and Carolyn Robertson during the spring and fall of 1977.
Production staff: Jay Stewart, Diana Fairbanks, Joyca Cunnan,
Gene Floyd, Loren Fisher.

Library of Congress Cataloging in Publication Data
Robertson, James, 1935-
The small towns book.
1. Cities and towns — United States — Case studies.
I. Robertson, Carolyn, joint author. II. Title.
HT123.R6   301.36'3'0973
ISBN 0-385-11012-X
Library of Congress Catalog Card Number 76-23813
Copyright © 1978 by The Yolla Bolly Press

*This book was funded in part
by a grant from the National Endowment for the Arts.
The findings and conclusions of this book do not necessarily represent
the view of the Endowment.*

This book is dedicated to
Paul Bruce Dowling
who showed us where the people live.

Table of Contents

Preface

Out of hundreds of photographs of small towns past and present, we chose this one of the town band of Oberlin, Ohio, to represent this book. More than any other single image, it signifies for us a devotion to local life and affairs that is the spirit of the small community at its best. The men in this municipal organization were almost certainly unpaid musicians who climbed into home-made — and probably excruciatingly hot — uniforms on Sundays and the Fourth of July to play in the town park. We guess they did this because they enjoyed their comrades, liked making music together, and because they were playing out a tradition — the townspeople expected them to be there.

We think it no accident that we could not find a contemporary image to represent this book. Most of the ideas that have moved us to write these pages are old ones. Most of the skills we seek, and the values we look for in rural life, are those that were left behind by our parents and grandparents years ago. It is our belief — and the principal thesis of this book — that in the not-too-distant future, we will find new uses for old ideas, and that homespun municipal improvements conjured by people who know how to take care of themselves will again be fashionable.

James and Carolyn Robertson
Covelo, California
June 23, 1977

There is a need for intimate human relationships,
for the security of settled home and associations,
for spiritual unity, and for
orderly transmission of the basic cultural inheritance.
These the small community at its best can supply.
Whoever keeps the small community alive
and at its best during this dark period,
whoever clarifies, refines, and strengthens
the vision of the small community,
may have more to do with the final emergence
of a great society than those
who dominate big industry and big government.

from the preface to the St. Johnsbury, Vermont, Town Plan

Acknowledgments

The authors are grateful to the following people for their parts in making this book happen: Robert H. McNulty of the National Endowment for the Arts, for understanding the need for this book and his patience; Jim Holliday, for his friendship and boundless energy; Robert Royston, Robertson Ward, and Rai Okamoto for their confidence in us and willingness to say so; Paul Bruce Dowling and Nanine Bilski Dowling for their loyalty and advice; Anne and Clayton Denman of the Small Towns Institute for their shared interest in small communities and their unflagging dedication to the people who live in them.

We also wish to thank: Harold Williams and Jane Schautz of the Institute on Man and Science for permission to reprint portions of two of their publications and for their cooperation in introducing us to the townspeople of Stump Creek; the people of Stump Creek for the use of their group photograph and for permission to reprint portions of *Stump Creek as Kramer* and the *Kramer Re-Mind;* The Town Forum for permission to reprint portions of several of their publications; the people of North Bonneville, Washington, and their planning consultants, Royston, Hanamoto, Beck, and Abey, for permission to reprint portions of *Town of North Bonneville Comprehensive Plan,* and for the use of several photographs.

Special thanks are in order to our editors, Harris Dienstfrey, whose friendship and steady support have kept us going, and Bill Strachan, who understood this book from the beginning and was willing to wait for it.

And finally we must thank the people themselves — those who live in the towns we visited and gave us their time and shared with us their dreams, and especially those who, for reasons of space or the peculiar evolution that this book has taken, will not find their towns in its pages. If we are successful, it is because of the contributions of all the people we met and talked to. Any oversights, omissions, or errors are our work alone.

Coming Home

INTRODUCTION

This book begins in August, 1972. We were somewhere in Kansas, heading west in a lumbering motor home on the last leg of an eight-week trip to the small towns of America. There were four of us: Carolyn and myself, my brother Alden, and his wife, Jean. We had been collecting material for a book on small town history and were exhausted. The moment is registered indelibly in my mind because a second book was just about the last thing any of us were likely to be thinking about — any of us, that is, except Carolyn. "I know!" she said, brightly. "Let's do a book on small towns, how they will be the place we all come home to — and how they deal with their problems." However badly timed, it was an innocent suggestion, and as events have proven, it was a good one. At the moment, however, the rest of us muttered and snarled resentfully. How could Carolyn be thinking of book number two while book number one lay all around us in a jumble of tape cassettes and undeveloped film? We tried not to think about it further.

But a good idea has a life of its own. And Carolyn's, being particularly good, was particularly adhesive. During the next year, as we wallowed in small town Americana, it kept sneaking up on us. Before long, it was generally understood that book number one would be followed by book number two.

About the same time, Carolyn and I decided to remove ourselves from the toney San Francisco suburb in which we had been living and move to the country. We bought an old homestead near a tiny town in the Coast Range, 175 miles north of San Francisco, and we began making plans to move our business there. We were vaguely aware of the fact that we were joining some kind of demographic shift, but were more concerned about making ends meet and remaining sane.

There were a number of pressures on us in our old location. Not unique ones, surely, but sufficient to cause us to make such a move. First there was (and still is) an inexorable and seemingly endless escalation of the value of real property in the Bay Area, driving up taxes, and sending renters like us scuttling elsewhere. But even if we had been able to afford the $90,000 to buy a two-bedroom house like the one we were occupying, we might have balked. The town we lived in, just across the Golden Gate Bridge from San Francisco, with Mt. Tamalpais at its back door, was changing in ways we had trouble adjusting to.

The town had started out (during our residence there) as a quiet corner for inveterate hikers, eccentric ladies with bizarre tendencies of dress, and book-heavy old gentlemen on intimate·terms with gray-muzzled mongrels. During our six-year tour there, however, it was seized by the barracudas of the Age of Aquarius: long-haired spec builders who swallowed up vacant lots and built fashionable homes for successful counterculture attorneys and rock stars whose rise had carried them into the six-figure bracket, smooth "investors" whose income sources were always mysterious, and any young San Francisco executive on the make who had discovered the chic of raw redwood, shingles, and stained glass. Children in the junior high school smoked dope because their parents permitted it or couldn't think of reasons why, in a liberated society, the young should not be exposed to the culture of grownups. Spoiled, bored, and smug, this progeny of the upper-middle class roamed the streets and the woods, as oblivious to their advantages as to the beauty of their setting, undoing municipal improvements and committing petty theft. It was depressing. There appeared to be no real community, but rather a huddle of strangers in the redwoods, locked and bolted in their $100,000 homes, and letting their dogs crap on each other's driveways.

The place certainly did not appeal much to us as an investment — monetary or otherwise. And it required an almost continuous process of desensitization, in order to avoid an emotional state of continually raging at one incursion or another. When we found forty acres with a barn and two little cabins in Mendocino County requiring as a down payment precisely the $5,000 nest egg we had scraped together, we leapt at the chance.

This is as good a place as any to state without qualification that what you are reading, and what is to follow in this book, is based on personal experience and observation, and nothing more. Neither of us has any business writing about small towns except that we have made them the subject of a kind of family study. Neither of us has any training in the subject or any remotely related professional qualifications. This rather shameless admission is bearable only because we have have found that we are in good company. We live in a society that is almost totally urban-oriented. Small communities have only just begun to attract the attention of academicians and planners, who, in our experience, still don't know what they are. The only real experts — long-time residents of small towns — don't write books about them. That makes us, it seems, as well-prepared as anyone else. At least we are personally involved in our subject and willing to assume full responsibility for our trespasses.

We set out, then, to write this book full of the frustration of urban and suburban life, sick at the senseless waste of a democracy run self-righteously amuck in Southeast Asia, frightened by the specter of the Third World (indignant at our greed) rising up to cut us off at the pump, and longing for a measure of quiet and self-determination in our lives.

In contrast to these feelings was the cargo of euphoria we transported across Kansas that August, fresh from the grassy streets of rural America. None of us had ever been across the continent except by freeway or airplane. And all of us realized then that until that trip, we had no idea whatever what our country was about. We drove over 8,000 miles that summer, sweltering in the heat, working without rest, tangled and scrapped among ourselves in the close quarters of our home-on-wheels — and we loved every minute of it. We avoided freeways, except when no other road presented itself, and entered no city of any size, except Annapolis, Maryland. We concentrated mainly on rural communities, interviewed hundreds of residents, and photographed even more. We learned that the strength of America still lives in the countryside. That strength is embodied in the people we met — tending their farms and businesses; concerned about their children; living purposefully and without excess; and comfortable with their lot. Amiable, honorable, and caring, these people taught us our first lesson: There is a "second" America, and it is something of which we can be very proud.

We came back from that trip convinced that the environmental and "back-to-the-land" movements of the sixties and early seventies were spreading through the middle class (many of those we interviewed were recent transplants from large communities); that America was going to come home; that the institutions against which we raged in the sixties would be rebuilt;.that we would learn how to live as neighbors once more; and that the small rural communities were the places to do all this.

That is the stuff out of which this book was first conceived.

THE SECOND LESSON

There is nothing wrong with the vision that we had, except that it is an enormous oversimplification. Having now spent three years in a rural community, witnessed the spectacle of an American President discredited, seen his successor voted out of office, and heard the voice of *his* successor telling us, in effect, that the age of surfeit is at an end, things appear somewhat changed. Or at least, we are perceiving them differently.

1. The population shift that we saw the first signs of back in 1972 has been confirmed: those who tinker with such matters now agree, Americans are redistributing themselves about the landscape and that the patterns are principally away from urban centers and toward smaller, mostly rural towns and cities. No one agrees on the significance of this trend. But it is unmistakable and shows no signs of weakening.

2. It is no longer possible for any of us to assume that the future is assured because technology or business or our government will somehow provide. Most of us, regardless of where we live, are dependent on a man-made, providence that has exceeded our grasp and shows every sign of coming to pieces. I have begun to believe that much of the frustration of our time is the panic of impotence — that we have frittered away our political and economic franchises to any who will promise to ease our burdens and that, as a people, we are both seducer and victim. Complacence has given way to its successors: fear and loathing. Unwilling to face our own culpability, we blame one or another of our own monsters for our plight and flee to the country, unaware that they follow us.

3. The rural environment of America is now in great danger. It is being threatened by any of us who have selected it as our habitat without changing our habits. The product of a much different era, rural America is, for all practical purposes, another culture. Lacking knowledge of its workings, we

17

tend to regard it with indifference while we absorb its virtues. Like a less "developed" society, it is largely passive, submitting to acculturation, and even seeking to speed the process. Unaware of our effect, we damn it for being backward and, then, for being corrupted.

4. Continued migration of urban populations to rural communities will speed the process of "suburbanization" in any rural setting. This is partly a product of simple numbers. But the change is made more secure by the process of acculturation described above. Acculturation takes place in any instance in which new residents make demands on their new surroundings that require the establishment of services or facilities not demanded by previous residents and not indigenous to the prevailing occupational and social patterns. A continued influx of urban or suburban residents to any small rural community, whether they are full-time residents or not, will eventually result in a continuous local pressure to urbanize the rural environment. This will occur even when residents (with or without urban experience) attempt to combat the trend because the source of the pressure is not concentrated in any group (such as real-estate developers) but is intrinsic to the expectations of many residents, particularly those who arrive in the countryside from urban origins.

5. Rural communities, regardless of their legal status, are essentially disenfranchised political entities. Ignored by the political and economic systems (except when they can provide a resource worth plundering), they are without influence and essentially without the access to it that generally accompanies urban experience, though this situation will change as the population shift progresses. The defense of rural integrity against the pressure for change is extremely difficult and must be undertaken at great odds.

6. The yearning for a simpler existence, which is often mistaken for a symptom of environmental distress, generally has little to do with environment and much more to do with values. Values can be affected by one's physical surroundings, but they are determined by more pervasive and unyielding forces. A change of one environment for another seldom has any lasting effect on the way one lives one's life, unless it is accompanied by other changes, much more difficult to make.

Though we are aware of the prejudices in modern American thought against stereotyped small town mentality (an attitude epitomized by Sinclair Lewis in *Main Street*), we do not share this view. We think human nature prevails in any situation. In small communities, it is often irritating. In larger communities, it is often institutionalized. By the same token, we now believe that the bucolic promise of rural life (largely invented by nonresidents) is vastly exaggerated. Rural communities are — to many ex-urbanites — boring, brutish places, requiring sacrifices and replacing the sensory overload of urban life with sensory deprivation. We have seen marriages collapse under the continuous strain of wood heat, rude surroundings, and hand-washed diapers. We have seen city people without rural skills trapped by the poverty they must endure in the country, adding immobility to their grievances.

Rural communities usually suffer, as we have suggested above, from political impotence and also from a level of chronic economic depression that would not be tolerated elsewhere. We believe it is possible to live in a rural setting and to undo the knots that sometimes accompany the pace and perplexities of city life — but we also think that it can only be accomplished at the expense of considerable sacrifice and extensive retraining. To some (like us), the sacrifices are easy to make. We weren't giving up that much. The retraining is another matter. Being willing to settle for less of everything is a conscious choice. Some deprivations, such as reduced income and restricted mobility, a limited choice of foods and clothing, or the lack of entertainment, are relatively easy to accept if one is prepared for them. Poorer schools, primitive municipal services (or none at all) are sometimes harder to bear. But we cannot shed our experience like a skin. My wife and I see our own rural community through the eyes of city people, and to understand in the fullest sense what this place is and what we are doing here, will take a lifetime. In the meantime, we are fully capable of wreaking a kind of cultural havoc in our own town in almost total ignorance of our effect. Though we have chosen this place for reasons that have everything to do with the fact that it *is* another culture, we didn't realize this at the time, and now we worry that we may be contributing to its permanent alteration.

It is quite correct that change is bound to occur in any case. But the change that occurs in rural communities is generally organic — by and large unaffected by the cycles and tempos of urban environments, and by virtue of being removed from them, it occurs slowly. What concerns us is that as the pressure of urban migrations mounts, rural communities will be forced to abandon the traditional qualities that we most seek in them. At the very moment we most need those who are trained culturally and occupationally to assist us in relearning the skills of self-sufficiency, we are obliterating them by assimilation.

Our initial Kansas euphoria about rural life has given way to a kind of grim determination to concern ourselves principally with our own town and the business of rectifying our conceptions of how we should live our lives in this setting. Were it not for our commitment to our publisher and a certain sense of duty to the issues, we would have been quite content to concentrate the energy that has produced this book on the local affairs of our town. We no longer think that the task of balancing our small town expectations against reality is as manageable as it once appeared, because it is now clear to us that the obstacles before us are of our own making. (It is always easier to deal with an enemy you don't carry around inside yourself.) It is no longer a matter of rushing to the country to free ourselves of some city-bound demon. We — the two of us specifically, and all of us generally — must change our ideas, or we are doomed to repeat in small communities, the very mistakes we made in larger ones.

We still believe that small communities may be the best places to learn how to reestablish a sense of direction in America. We do not necessarily believe that the only small communities in which this may be accomplished are rural ones. We just feel more comfortable there and have chosen rural communities as the subject of this book because we are especially concerned about their safety.

The number of towns that we initially selected and visited has been whittled down as we wrote the book. In the beginning, we sought rural communities in

19

which any number of indigenous problems were being treated with wit and native grace at the grassroots level. Later on, we revised our thinking, deciding to concentrate on those communities that were actively combating urban pressures, and in which the threats to rural life would be more fully revealed or the real nature of the rural culture could be seen most vividly.

That has given the book (we hope) a kind of concentration it lacked. But it also meant dropping a great deal of good material painstakingly assembled. It means that you will not read about Marshall, Michigan, for example, a town in which the subject of local history has been transformed from a hobby for the elderly into a municipal passion. Marshall is the home of one of the most active and politically adept historical societies it has ever been our good fortune to encounter. The people of that town have learned that you indeed cannot know where you are going unless you have a clear sense of where you have been. History in Marshall is the basis for community pride, a guiding mechanism for physical rehabilitation and development, and the training ground for those who are most vocal and informed about municipal affairs.

Likewise we can do no more than mention Corning, New York, where a major manufacturer in partnership with the government of this small city has embarked on a downtown rehabilitation project that would be the envy of any city in the land.

The workings of the local historians of Marshall and the downtown renovators of Corning would be instructive and interesting to anyone who is concerned with small town affairs because the problems, which both are solving so successfully, are typical. It happens, however, that both are communities somewhat larger than the others in this book, and neither can be considered rural for that reason. Additionally, while both are dealing with problems of significance, neither demonstrates the intense pressures felt by smaller communities affected by urban migrations.

We have departed from our criteria somewhat in one instance. The story in this book about Adrian, Pennsylvania, does not describe a community that is dealing with pressures for change, nor is it particularly revealing of the local culture, though it does meet that criterion to an extent. Instead, what we found there raises questions about the importance of local leadership which we felt justified its inclusion.

One of the most unsettling aspects of this project has been the continuous development of affairs in each town that makes any story woefully incomplete by the time a process as Byzantine as writing and printing a book is finally ended. As of this writing, our own community is threatened simultaneously by (a) a new state park which is literally in our backyard, (b) a proposed highway extension that would radically alter the character of this remote valley, and (c) legislation in the state government that would pave the way to building a major dam within a few miles or less of our home. We are aware of additional developments in most of the other towns about which we have written, that while perhaps not so dramatic, are equally important. We have had to content ourselves with the above admission, and hope that our readers will understand that the stories in this book are meant to represent a set of conditions that are approximately the same, regardless of variations over time. In spite of their necessarily unfinished state, we hope each contains information that is both interesting and useful.

I think our last words in this somewhat extended beginning should be directed to those who now live in cities and are thinking about their place in the country. It is for such people that we have special feeling and to whom this book is particularly addressed.

There is an enormous temptation, when you move to the country, to shut the door behind you. We see it continuously in ourselves — that secret wish to be the last aboard and keep everyone else away. Though we have tried to distinguish between that emotion and the real problems of small rural towns, we are sure that you will find traces of it in this book and we apologize for that. We admit to that transgression only because we think we now understand that what is sometimes said or done in the name of preservation is also sometimes an unacknowledged confession of guilt for the damage we may have caused. But there is no need to feel contrite over the way in which we trample the countryside — providing that as we trample it, we are continuously seeking to understand what is underfoot, and how to tread more lightly. It is said that the Indians could move along the forest floor without making a sound. It is perhaps no accident that they also were sensitive to the smallest nuances of life around them and felt themselves inextricably bound to all of it.

Living in the country is a skill, just like living anywhere else. Living well, in the fullest sense of that phrase, is perhaps the highest attainment we can seek. The evidence so far is that a few of us have excelled in that department. There is much work to be done in any rural town. Hard work. Any who enter such a place unmindful of their actions and seeking short cuts to a provident and comfortable existence will be disappointed in the end, and will contribute to the unnecessary deterioration of what might otherwise be a healthy and productive environment.

The best advice we can give is to come with a mind as open as you can make it, and a mouth that is carefully closed. Listen to the voices around you — particularly to those who speak of the land and times past. Be suspicious of anyone or anything that does not grow locally. Strengthen that which does. Speak when you must, but remember that the cities breed a kind of easy arrogance that sometimes passes for intelligence in the countryside. There is more wisdom in a backwoods farmer than any of us will ever know.

JR
Covelo, California
April 1977

Part One
Fighters and Keepers

Time Out of Mind and Change

A friend of ours has just returned from a visit, after almost twenty years, to his hometown in Ohio. He came back amazed. "They remembered me!" he announced. "Not only that, they remembered things about my family that I didn't even know!" That's the way things still are in Middletown, Ohio, or any other small town in rural America. We are not talking about the small towns that are busy becoming cities. We are not talking about suburbs. We are talking about small communities in rural settings — isolated from urban areas and with populations between 100 and 10,000. The classic Small Town. America is full of them. They are the kind of places where change moves like the hour hand on the clock — too slow to be seen by the human eye. Even after twenty years more things are the same than are changed. These are places with memories that go back generations. They have always been there. It's just that until recently, no one paid much attention to them.

Our own town is similar. At almost anytime, you are apt to overhear a conversation in which someone is telling a story about what happened to an uncle, or how some family conflict was settled — fifty years ago. And you listen, because chances are, the descendants of the main characters in the story are people you know. A strange car drives into town. It and the occupants are noticed. There is speculation about who they might be coming to see and for what purpose. Any lapse of public etiquette is instantaneous news. There are no secrets. What isn't public fact is the subject of endless speculation. It is all terribly fusty. Sometimes it is a damned nuisance. It is at least stable. And for reasons that can be felt better than they can be described, a place of stability in these times is attractive.

Increasingly, change of a magnitude for which there is no precedent is overtaking many small rural communities. As the machinery of commerce and government uses up the resources most easily tapped and most readily convertible, those farther away will be looked at for the first time. As the decentralization of American business continues, more and more people will be released from urban populations to find their way into smaller communities.

The people who sit on the front porch swings in Middletown have seen them coming. The city has had its day. Times are changing. Small towns across the country are beginning to feel the pressure.

Traditionally the small town has resisted change by passive means. Either it had little of value to interest bringers of change, or it simply subdued — by absorbing — those few upstarts who would have things a different way. But the pressure of large numbers or of large institutions is another matter. And increasingly, the changes threatening to alter small rural communities are massive ones.

Since most small towns lack the resources or the trained people to effectively cope with large scale pressures from outside, they must either succumb or invent their own defenses. Though we are sure that the failures probably outnumber the successes, the successes are often spectacular and can give encouragement to the most discouraged. Consistently the towns that have been most effective in deflecting unwanted changes are those that have found their defenses at the very heart of the community — in the strengths and imaginations of individuals. It is not as though these places shunned assistance from outside, as you will see in the two instances which follow. But they were guided by an understanding of what it is that brings community members together and permits them to cherish what they share. Though invisible, it is the raw material out of which the most impregnable defenses are made.

We'll Do It Ourselves, Thanks

NORTH BONNEVILLE, WASHINGTON

The U. S. Army Corps of Engineers is a huge enterprise. Like most federal agencies, its size alone makes it incapable of tendering sympathy down to the scale of individuals. But the Corps is cursed by two additional handicaps when it comes to public relations. The first is that it is a military agency, which means that discipline, indifference to individuals, and a predilection for organizing itself around specific, well-defined objectives are part of its basic nature. Though compelled by the absence of a state of war to set aside commando tactics, the Corps is run by military men trained to approach problems in an adversary role, who believe that firepower wins battles. As if that weren't enough, the Corps is also comprised of engineers, preoccupied with how *things* work or can be made to work — an enterprise in which the vagaries of human behavior have no place.

It is the nature of bureaucracies to do away with willful individual responsibility. Designed like machinery (one machine, one task), they function smoothly only when each component individual minds his own business. Situations that do not fit in a designated place are referred elsewhere. Decisions that require any amount of interpretation of rules are *always* referred elsewhere — in an upward direction. By definition, bureaucracies work well only when the tasks they are given are uniform and entirely predictable. They are models of conservative behavior. When the material with which they work does not match the design according to which they were built, they stall, like any good machine.

Given the nature of the U. S. Army Corps of Engineers, it is no wonder that it treated the town of North Bonneville alternately as a beachhead occupied by enemy guerrillas and as an unwilling cog in an otherwise smoothly designed piece of equipment. It is no reflection on the Corps that the task set before it included work for which it is fundamentally unsuited. Nor is it any reflection on the people of North Bonneville that they saw the officers of the Corps with their decorated shoulders and straight trouser creases as renegade warriors set loose with the single purpose of destroying them. The people of North Bonneville were looking at the Corps as if it were a body of individual people — a fact technically correct but operationally irrelevant.

As a matter of fact, it was only when a couple of people began to see the Corps as the piece of governmental machinery that it is, that the town began to make any progress at all in its defense. But that's getting ahead of the story.

It is safe to say that before all this started, no one at the state capitol in Olympia or in Washington, D. C., including congressmen from the state of Washington, ever had any cause to think about the town of North Bonneville. It just wasn't the kind of town politicians paid any attention to. Six hundred people. Mostly woods and mill workers. A kind of lackluster place just a stone's throw from the whistling turbines of the Bonneville Power Administration's powerhouse at the head of the Columbia River tidewater. To some people, that powerhouse was the only important thing about North Bonneville.

And then all hell broke loose. Suddenly state agencies in Olympia, even the governor himself, together with senators and congressmen in Washington, D. C., were being sucked into a fracas over the building of a second powerhouse at Bonneville Dam. It seems that the town was lying in the way of the construction, and it wasn't happy about it. Somebody there was putting up one hell of a fight, sending ripples up through the ranks of the Corps of Engineers, and making waves all the way back to Washington. Whoever it was knew how to do it right. It looked like trouble. Real trouble.

It was. Just how real it was — and still is — can be seen by looking back twenty-eight years to the history behind it. Though the town predates the dam, it was the building of the dam and powerhouse in the thirties that brought fortune, both good and ill, to North Bonneville. The good fortune was obvious. The ill fortune was that the powerhouse was only the first of a projected two. At the time the dam was completed in 1938, newspapers carried an artist's conception of the yet-to-be-completed complex. The drawing showed a second powerhouse exactly where the town sat. On August 20 of the preceding year, the Seventy-fifth Congress had authorized the maintenance and operation of Bonneville Dam — and its eventual completion.

The drawing in the paper was nothing but an artist's conception. But the plan was on file somewhere in Washington, D. C., and it cast one long shadow over the town, down through the years. The people felt it on their lives.

"There are a lot of people who have died here waiting for the Corps to buy them out. You can look around and see all the houses that need paint."

Newcomers would look all up and down the Columbia River Gorge and find real estate scarce. But there was always something available at a good price in North Bonneville. Eventually they'd learn why. "It was only after they'd bought a place that people who knew would say, 'What'd you buy down there for? Don't you know they're going to tear that town down someday?' "

Business people in the community couldn't plan on growth. "How can you plan anything when you don't know if you're going to be here next year?" There were no major improvements made in the town. The banks wouldn't loan money on property in North Bonneville. The town sagged. And the bitterness grew.

Never official, the Corps' plans were all the more poisonous because they couldn't be fought. "How can you fight an artist's conception?" Yet it was every bit as damaging as a sure thing — only slower. Each time the talk of the dam expansion faded, something would bring it back. It was never clear what.

This is downtown North Bonneville. The highway that follows the Columbia River on the Washington side runs smack through town and becomes the main street. What keeps the place from being just another strip town is the spectacular surroundings — conifers that grow right down to the street and mountains all around.

When we were there, the town was half shut down. Every other building on the main street seemed to be empty. That's the way the Corps wanted it. The folks in town had other ideas. Jerry's Cafe and the Roosevelt Tavern (next to the barbershop) were two of the town's most active gathering places. From inside you could watch the Corps' black pickup trucks cruise up and down the main street outside.

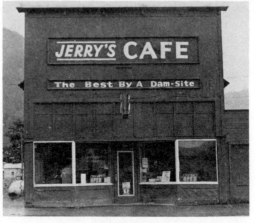

In 1971, local people, alarmed at the deteriorated state of their town, put together something called NOBLE, an acronym for North Bonneville Life Effort. Determined to shake the Corps' curse of the projected powerhouse, they started community development work. In June, a comprehensive sewer plan for the town was completed by a Vancouver engineering firm. The county completed the construction of a new water system for the town about the same time. The people began to think they could rebuild their town.

Then on August 3, 1971, officers from the Portland district office of the U. S. Army Corps of Engineers held a meeting with town officials. The purpose of the meeting was to announce that, from a set of alternatives, a site had been chosen for the second powerhouse at Bonneville Dam. The site was on the Washington shore of the river — just as the artist had pictured it back in 1938 — and its selection would require that the town of North Bonneville either disperse or relocate. The Corps did not say when it would begin constructing the powerhouse.

TRIPLOG. *Driving into North Bonneville. One main street. About a half mile long. Appears tired. Half the storefronts are closed up, some with signs still in place as though they might flicker back to life at any moment. None are grand. Concrete block with false fronts. Some older wood frames that look like they might have once been homes. Jerry's Cafe, "Best By a Damsite." Beauty Shop. Bait Shop. Gas Station. Post Office. The Town Hall. Big Douglas firs growing down the slope above the town right to the street's edge.*

DIVIDE AND CONQUER

They're all so young. David Hussell, administrative assistant to Mayor Ernie Skala; Pollard Dickson, the town's planning coordinator; Mike Mills and Gill Kelly, the two interns. David Hussell is tall, but he has a baby face and curly hair — makes him look like a high-school chess team member. Flat voice. Quiet. He tends to stay in the background, but it becomes clear that he knows exactly what he's about. Pollard Dickson is the front man. He speaks easily with a big voice and a good sense of timing. He is comfortable with himself and it's contagious. The group exudes confidence.

On August 24, 1971, the town held a public hearing on the powerhouse site selection, and the mayor submitted a brief that included statistics gathered during an earlier NOBLE survey. The survey showed that a majority of residents and businesses, given a choice, would relocate to a new town site. It also stated that the city government's position would be to expect the Corps of Engineers to pay the entire cost of relocation, and that only the town would have the authority to determine what was and was not acceptable — a position that the town stoutly maintained during the four years of ensuing controversy and negotiations. In other words, the town wanted to relocate (rather than just disperse), intended to do what was necessary so that it could relocate, and expected the Corps to shoulder the cost.

The Corps maintained that it was prevented by law from doing anything more than replace certain civic facilities, and that such replacement was at the discretion of the Chief of Engineers in Washington, D. C. Under the Federal Relocation Act of 1970, its only direct responsibility was to individual owners.

In December 1971, the town hired David Hussell, an ex-Navy pilot to assist the mayor and city council as they went from agency to agency seeking financial help. It was grim. The position of the Corps was that it had no responsibility or authorization to assist the town in relocating itself. Hussell describes the situation:

"The town was told, by the Corps, that we had the complete responsibility for all the planning, the purchase of land, the building of the town itself, and everything. And here we were sitting with a population of five hundred people, none of us with any money — yet we had the responsibility of putting the whole package together ourselves and paying for it. It was the city council's belief that it should have been the Corps' responsibility, because they were imparting the impact on the community."

Through the early part of 1972, the city council scoured the state of Washington and Washington, D. C., for any help they could get. Initially, they didn't get much except sympathy. By the middle of the year, and with the help of the Washington State Department of Commerce and Economic Development, most of the state and federal agencies which could be of assistance knew about the town's plight. In June of 1972, the state governor, Daniel J. Evans, in response to a formal request from the town, appointed the state Planning and Community Affairs Agency as the state's representative in the affair, and contacted Senators Magnuson and Jackson, requesting funding to help the town prepare for its relocation. They were told that federal assistance could not be assured and that in any case the matter would have to wait until fiscal 1974. So much for the federal government.

At the end of 1972, the town asked for help from Russell Fox, a planner and faculty member at Evergreen State College, some three hundred miles away. Fox was running an unusual urban planning project with a group of students who worked in the field under a "contract" arrangement with the college. Pollard Dickson was one of those students. He had shut down his design and contracting business in eastern Washington and had gone back to school at Evergreen State College because he felt he needed more planning experience. When North Bonneville asked for planning help, it was Dickson and a handful of fellow students who took on the assignment.

"There were twenty of us to begin with. We were doing a lot of projects simultaneously. But as we got into them, they became more specific and more concentrated in their direction. In February of 1973, some of us decided to spend full time on this project. A group of twelve of us came down to the city council and indicated to them what we could do. We outlined a complete planning program which we would undertake with them, but we would do it only if we could live in the town. And we committed ourselves to live in the town three days a week."

From the beginning, Dickson and the other students saw the political as well as the design implications of what they were getting into. "There were a number of people in the group who were interested in the physical design and in the researching of technical information that would be used as design deter-

31

minants for the new town. There were also a lot of people who were extremely interested in the political implications of relocation. So we got into politics. Boy, did we ever!"

Fox and his students also realized that there was no way they were ever going to be useful to the town or be able to do what the town wanted them to do unless they got to know the people. And to do that, they would have to live there.

"You've got to understand that this county is very much of an insider's county. Even Dave, after two years here, was still considered very much an 'outsider'. And of course the Evergreen students were nothing but a bunch of street hippies. A couple of local citizens even bought newspaper space to complain about us. They said the city didn't know what it was doing bringing those Evergreen students in here. Instead, they should go down and talk to Colonel Triem at the Portland district office of the Corps of Engineers if they wanted any help with relocation. This is a small town, just like any other. It took a lot of patience on both sides before either side could accept the other."

Though the townsfolk were suspicious, a hard-pressed city council, grateful for the pledge of help from the young people, voted to make available $1,000 from a depleted city treasury to house them at a local motel and feed them for the three days a week they were in North Bonneville. The students were stunned by this display of confidence.

"I could not believe that," says Dickson. "It was a unanimous vote. We just all sat there shaking our heads. And after that we got $700 worth of OEO money from Evergreen to get us here and back." The students moved in and set up shop in a back room of the town hall. The town, then, had no money and twelve students. It didn't look like much at the time, but for the town it was a turning point in the battle for its life.

"The whole momentum changed after Evergreen came in," explains Hussell. "We found self-help. We were doing things for ourselves because the students were in the community and were a part of it. The town began doing its own planning."

During all this time, the Corps of Engineers still had made no formal announcement of an intent to build the powerhouse. Their announcement back in 1971 had simply been that they had selected a site on the Washington shore and that the town would have to go. They hadn't said when for one reason: they didn't know. Congress had yet to appropriate funds for construction. It still had not done so in the spring of 1973 when Evergreen students started to work in the town.

Still, the Corps had done its best to continually discourage all efforts by the town to save itself. As the Corps originally explained, the Federal Relocation Act does not provide for saving towns or relocating them. It provides only for the purchase of property from individual owners. If the Corps could purchase the land from enough individuals, those people would find somewhere else to live, and the Corps would not be obliged to deal with the town of North Bonneville, because it would no longer exist. This strategy of dispersal, and a continual effort to block or divert the town's struggle to plan for its own survival, would characterize future Corps' actions. It would also be the cause of much frustration and bitterness on both sides.

The fight began to take on the qualities of a race against time: the Corps hurrying to get congressional appropriation in order to buy up land and disperse the people; the town hurrying to do the planning necessary to build an entire new town from scratch, and at the same time trying to keep its people together.

A STICK OF OUR OWN

"We began to put the pieces together," says Dickson. "And as we worked, it was obvious to the city council that we were serious. We were not by any manner of means professionals in this kind of ball game, because nobody is. There's not a person — I don't care how professional they are — who's qualified to do this kind of work. There's just nobody who has any kind of experience like this."

There also wasn't much data to start with. Dickson complains bitterly about the fact that there wasn't an accurate land parcel map in the whole county. The student planners had to create what they needed. Though some data on the town itself had been generated by NOBLE, much more was needed: history; condition of property and improvements; attitudes of the people; public utilities and facilities; existing land-use patterns; traffic circulation; existing land values — it all had to be gathered. In order to know what was needed in the new town, the planners had to know what the old one already had.

But there still wasn't money. So in addition to gathering data, Dickson, Hussell, and the others had to look for funds. The original work program outlined by the students, a relocation planning study, would be completed at the end of that school year, June 1973. If the program were to continue to the next step, money would have to be found to pay the planning staff starting in June. Russell Fox, from Evergreen, found it. The college applied for and received a Title I Higher Education Assistance Grant good for one year, to continue the planning work. The work program was expanded so that Dickson and some of the other Evergreen students could be hired at the end of the school year to continue working.

"As Pollard says, 'We began to put the pieces together,' " recalls Hussell. "As a matter of fact, we started piecing so many things together so quickly that the Corps of Engineers came in here on April 4, 1973, and said that *they* would plan the town *for* us! They came floating in here and said, 'We'll do it for you. In fact, we are right now signing a contract with a firm in Portland to do the job.' That's exactly what they told the people — we were sitting right here and heard it: 'We are already signing a contract.'

"The only question we asked at that meeting was, 'Who is going to do the planning?' And they said, 'Well, *we* are. We're going to hire the firm and they're going to work for us. We'll do it for you. We'll give you a nice town.' And the town council, after all of this, and all those old bills that were hanging out — that $6,000 they had refused to pay back in 1971 — the town council said, 'Good afternoon, gentlemen!' And very bluntly let them know that the *town* was going to be the client in every sense of the word. If the Corps could

34

hire a firm to do planning *for* the town, why the hell couldn't they pay for a firm to do the planning *with* the town?

"Of course," Hussell adds, "the Corps had thought that we didn't have it in us or couldn't find the resources to do any of this work. Then when Evergreen got involved and things got moving, the Corps saw that the town wasn't going to stand by and be destroyed. When they came in and said, 'We'll do it for you,' the town council said, 'Baloney. We won't have it. We'll do it for ourselves. We've seen some of the towns you've planned, and we don't like them.'"

Dickson takes up the story and adds grimly, "They didn't want an Army camp." He goes on to say that all their planning would have been nothing more than an exercise if the townspeople hadn't been determined to fight the Corps, and willing to get directly involved in the work of saving the town.

"I think the Corps very badly misjudged the persistence of the townspeople to wait it out. It wasn't just all this high-level stuff we talk about. We concentrate on that because we're immersed in it up to our eyebrows. But we're also living here. And our office is open on a day-to-day basis. We have found ourselves very inefficient as an office when it comes to paperwork because we have *people* coming in all the time." Dickson emphasizes the word as a way of making clear its importance.

"We find out that's really the only success of this project. Because these people have direct access to us. Even when we're on the phone talking to someone in Olympia or Washington, the local citizens walk right into the office and hear us talking. They know what's going on. That's a very important aspect of this project." He makes the point again and again: the involvement of townspeople in the whole process, and their support, was what kept the planners going at the pace required. They knew they were needed. As the townspeople saw how the students worked, and the level of their commitment, the suspicion and talk of "hippies" evaporated. From then on, it was the students' town too.

But there was still a question of time. And for Pollard Dickson, there was a question of how many townspeople they would lose to the Corps' land-acquisition tactics: "In November 1973, the Corps held a public meeting to announce that the powerhouse would be built, that the people would be moved, and that the Corps would begin immediate appraisals of their land.

"Previous to that," he continues, "the town, through the Relocation Advisory Board [an interagency advisory council which the town had set up during the summer], with the Corps sitting at the table, had tried to get the Corps to institute a series of three or four meetings with the general public to explain their relocation benefits as provided by law: how fair-market acquisition of their property works, how the base from which fair-market value is determined, what their options would be in terms of a new town, and so forth. Instead, the Corps called one public meeting without the involvement of the town government. They explained everything once. Gave each person a little brochure. That was it. The people understood their rights, they understood all the procedures, they understood everything. Uh-huh. Sure they did!

"So a lot of residents petitioned the town to act as their agent for the establishment of processes for determination of fair-market value, and for acquisi-

35

tion procedures. What we were doing was confronting the Corps with the fact that they had to deal with the town as a *unit,* and not as individuals; because the individuals were telling the Corps that they wanted the town to help them.

"The Corps ignored those petitions completely. Instead, they came in and began immediate appraisals of property and started waving checks in front of people's noses. And they started buying property."

Apparently, the Corps had promised to give a scheduling of their acquisition program, and had told the town that they would only need thirteen parcels at the east end of town in order to begin work on the initial phase of construction.

"But we found out after they bought a couple up there, that they were also buying a house over here, and another one over there — that they were buying houses all over town. You know what they were doing — they were block-busting. They were trying to get people stirred up, get emotion going. Somebody'd say, 'Did you hear? They got $10,000 for that little shack!' Then they'd run right down and say, 'I'll take it too!' Remember that at this time none of the people had an option to go to a new town. And the Corps wasn't yielding on anything."

People in the town were beginning to feel the pressure. The question of the day on any street corner was, "Who's going to sell out next?" It wasn't a stampede, but it was enough to make the town fathers worry.

With little more to go on than a proposed new town site and a great deal of study data which Hussel and Dickson and company had gathered on the present town, a huge public meeting was called by the town on January 10, 1974. Dickson describes it with obvious relish: "We did a crash program. We drew up some crude town relocation plans. We relocated a railroad that runs through the site, we put in some trees. We showed a residential area, a central business district, the highway. We scheduled a great big public meeting and sent notices out to all agencies. We put up great big maps, and we printed up five hundred copies of our drawing with all the analyses we went through and handed one to everyone who came."

The Corps had apparently been saying that they could not recognize a new town since there was no site. So the meeting was called partly to help the townspeople see they had some alternative to dispersing, and partly to put the Corps on the defensive about the site. It might be pointed out here that the site chosen was one of the few feasible places for a new town in the Columbia River Gorge — a flat bench about a half mile downstream from the present town. The choice, aside from being an obvious one, was particularly painful for the Corps, who had designated the space to receive 18 million cubic yards of fill to be dug from the new powerhouse site, and had plans to use the site as a public park. Dickson and his planners had taken the fill into account. Their drawings showed how it could be used to create low hills to help shield the town from the winds which whistle up the gorge. They also had the soils analyses to prove that the site would accommodate the impact of a new town.

"So we said, 'There's our town,' and we put it right in the middle of their day-use area. We confronted the Corps with all this at that public meeting and demanded that they give us a written recommendation and documentation of response in accordance with our plan. And this happened, of course, right about the time the Water Resources Development Act was to be signed. Well, it just blew those guys right off their rockers."

The Water Resources Development Act which would be signed into public law by President Nixon on March 7, contained some very interesting grassroots legislation, the original language of which was the work of the people of North Bonneville.

The story of the Water Resources Development Act, in brief, is this: Since the Corps maintained all along that it could not pay the town to do its own planning, Pollard Dickson, David Hussell, and the Skamania County Prosecuting Attorney had made a pilgrimage, at the town's expense, to Washington, D. C., in the early summer of 1973, to help their elected representatives in Congress draft legislation that would authorize the Corps to do just what it said it could not. During the previous year, contact had been maintained with the offices of Senators Jackson and Magnuson, and Congressman McCormack, all of whom had reasons of their own for wanting to help the town.

Pollard Dickson admits: "We have been very very lucky to have their support. It's amazing how much power Magnuson wields. He's second, I think, in seniority in the Senate — he is Mister Senate Appropriations. And when the generals meet back in Washington at the Corps' headquarters, it isn't some staff member who shows up, it's Senator Magnuson. You just don't have meetings with senators unless they're interested. That sort of thing doesn't happen very often for a small town. But not very many small towns have a $500 million hydroelectric plant being built right downtown either. Those people back in Congress don't want that powerhouse delayed; and the only way to be sure that doesn't happen is to make damn sure that town is taken care of. So you see, we have kind of a stick of our own. It helps keep our congressmen's and our senators' attention too. Somehow there's that stinkin' little town still down there. And somehow it's awful hard to build a great big powerhouse in the middle of a little tiny town. We just won't give 'em a building permit!"

Though the original language of the portion of the Water Resources Development Act that would apply to North Bonneville was significantly changed as a result of later pressure from the Corps, Section 83 of the law specifically authorized the Corps to provide financial and technical assistance to help the town with relocation. And the officers in the Portland district office knew that as soon as it was signed into law, they would be hearing from North Bonneville. What they hadn't expected was the town site meeting in January.

The town's move forced the Corps to call a public hearing of its own in order to take testimony from all agencies on the utilization of powerhouse project lands for the new town. These same agencies had been to the town's public meeting in January and were supplied by the town's planners with all the support data the town had at its disposal to prove its case.

"By that time," Dickson adds, "we had so much information available, and so much of it was coming from other agencies, that the Corps found itself forced to approve that site for planning. It didn't mean they accepted the idea. But they had to approve it for *planning*. And since the Water Resources

Development Act had just been signed into law, we immediately began negotiations to get a cost-reimbursable contract with the Corps that would enable
the town to go out and get the design team it wanted."

And, after months of haggling, that's exactly what it got.

THEY DON'T MINCE WORDS

TRIPLOG. *Morning at the town hall. It's Saturday, but Mayor Ernie Skala is
here early. He's smoking a long, thin, brown cigarette. He has one of those
lined faces with bright, kind eyes. You can tell he works at being fair to everyone. His job is full-time. The pay ($30 a month) isn't. Pollard has explained
that he does it just because he really cares about the people. They love to tell
the story about the time the mayor was asked to testify along with a bunch of
Corps officers. Each was asked his rank. When the mayor's turn came he said,
"Just put down Ernie Skala, mayor, painter, retired." He speaks softly about
the people — how some of them hate the Corps:*

"You can't hardly blame them, y'know; they've been messed around with for
so many years. Some of them really aren't getting what they should be getting
in relocation benefits. The bitterness, mainly, is from the business people.
They're the ones that are the hardest hit. See, take an ordinary homeowner:
the Corps will pay them a fair-market value, and give 'em a subsidy of up to
$15,000 to buy a new home. Well, they're not in too bad shape. But the
business people, they don't get that. The best they can get, beyond the value of
inventory and building, is $2,500 for 'loss of business'. Nothing for good will.
And nothing to rebuild with. So they're really in bad shape. At today's prices,
who can afford to build a new store?"

We ask him about the tight bond we sense among the people of the town.
We ask if that was always there.

"For a certain amount of 'em — about half of 'em. The faint-hearted left.
[Laughs] But we've had quite a problem holding them together. We try to
keep their spirits up. We always come up with some sort of victory, you might
say — buoys them up to a certain extent. But you know, these people know
what they want. They know where they want to live. And they're not about to
be run out. There's a certain stubbornness, I'd say. . . . You can't blame them
for not wanting to scatter out. We've been getting reports from many of those
that left and are planning on coming back as soon as the new town is laid out.
The place just kind grows on 'em I guess."

We've heard oblique references of deaths clearly attributable to the Corps'
tactics. We ask the mayor. He's not eager to talk about it, but he tells us about
the Lauterbachs: "It just happened that the Corps wanted to build a tower
right where their house was [this was before the November 1973 announcement that the powerhouse would be built], so they bought 'em out. And they
moved over a hundred yards or so and built another beautiful home — with
the assurance from the Corps that they wouldn't have to move. Then a year
after they'd moved in, the Corps came along and said, 'We're going to have to

Faye Lauterbach is standing
on the north bank of the
Columbia River (which also
happens to be her backyard)
and is looking toward her new
home — the one the U. S. Army
Corps of Engineers has told her
is in the way of the new powerhouse. Behind her about 100
yards is the site of her old house
— the one the U. S. Army
Corps of Engineers told her was
in the way of a power transmission pole. To her left and
across the river is the present
generating facility of the
Bonneville Power Adminis-
tration.

Marian and Bud Rhode,
owners of the Gardens Tavern,
and the tavern itself with Mayor
Skala at the counter for a draft.

move you out.' So they were in their new home only a year. Well, that got Henry down pretty bad, and he just keeled over and died a couple of weeks later. She's quite bitter about it."

TRIPLOG. *Faye Lauterbach. Nice modern house downstream from the town, right along the river on a piece of flat land. Good view of the dam and power-house. Daughter, son-in-law, and grandkids next door. Huge tower beyond that where their first house stood. She waves at us from inside her living room as we approach, a nice welcoming gesture. She is in her sixties. Close-cut gray hair. A redhead's skin, very fair, lots of freckles. Gold-rimmed glasses, intelligent eyes. Her house is large and carefully ordered. A color photograph of her dead husband on the table next to the fireplace. She has said she is will-ing to talk to us. We ask her if she is bitter about what happened. She is gentle about it.*

"No. I think that someplace back in Washington, D. C., someone sits there and decides, 'We'll build it there,' and they don't take into consideration what it's going to do to the people. Maybe they take a few aerial views. They could probably drive through this town of North Bonneville and say, 'It's just a shack town. It'd be good riddance. We'll just scoop it out.' I think their land-acquisi-tion program leaves a lot to be desired. They should consider the people. They consider the *fish!* So there should be more consideration given to the problems of the people."

We ask her to describe the effect the news that they would have to move a second time in twelve months had on her husband.

"It was disastrous. He was putting on a good front. He wouldn't admit to friends that he was upset. But he didn't sleep. Night after night he was up prowling around, and he said to me a thousand times, 'I know this shouldn't bother me. I shouldn't get so upset over it. But I can't help it. To think that we have to leave this nice home.' "

She shows us the picture from the table. Tells us it's a passport photo. She had planned to get him abroad on a trip to take his mind off the news, but he died before they could leave.

"He was just so upset, that it was too much for him. His heart just couldn't take it. Of course, he had a history of heart trouble, but I know he would be alive today if this hadn't happened."

Her husband isn't the only casualty.

"People who thought that it wasn't disturbing them at all would go in for a physical and find their blood pressure was way out of bounds. And they weren't high blood pressure people, either. It's something you can't control. Especially when you get our age, I think. When you're all set for retirement, and think you have the rest of your life mapped out, to have it all swept out from under you — it is a blow, and you can't help it."

We ask her how the first move affected her own feelings. And she tells us that, for her, the shock was felt only when she saw all the trees they had planted, and watched grow, in a tangled heap on the ground, their leaves just beginning to wilt. She says she wept.

40

TRIPLOG. *Bud and Marian Rhode, owners of Gardens Tavern. A tiny kitchen and parlor behind the tavern. Two dogs, a Siamese cat, and a box of ginger snaps. We just woke Rhode up from a Saturday afternoon nap. Bud Rhode wears a T-shirt, tinted glasses, has curly hair. Tough but friendly. He is a member of the town council. He's been through it all. Marian Rhode is Ernie Skala's stepdaughter. We ask her what it feels like to live in a doomed town. She doesn't mince words.*

"Well, I'll tell you. I said that if I ever got an ulcer over this damn thing — because I've been through about everything there is to be through in my life — that I was gonna sue the Corps of Engineers. I ought to sue 'em for two of them, because I got two of 'em. You eat, sleep, talk, and live it."

Bud Rhode adds: "For the last two — almost the last three — years now, they've almost completely changed my life here. I used to hunt all the time, and fish, pick mushrooms, picnic, or do whatever we wanted to do, on a Saturday, or on Sunday at least, when we had a day off. But in the last three years, I haven't had time for any of that."

Marian: "What he means by that — you don't dare leave town. Those goddamned fools'll do something. And you can't miss a council meeting because they'll pull something over your eyes. They're the biggest bunch of crooks. They're either dumb or damn smart or they're big liars. I don't know which."

Bud tempers his wife's opinion of the Corps. He says he doesn't know if they're liars or if the right hand doesn't know what the left is doing. We ask his wife why she hates the idea of the move so much.

"I'll tell you, this is the funniest little town there is in the whole world. If everything's going good, if everything's just smooth — everybody's unhappier'n hell, bored to tears. But you let some catastrophe happen here, and the one who's the maddest of 'em all is the first to turn to and start getting something going."

She tells us about the feeling of closeness in the town.

"I just can't see me living in a new town or any place else but North Bonneville. I can run to a fire in my housecoat and nightgown and look around and see three or four more, just like me. Or stand out here callin' the dogs at two or three in the morning. And this is what everybody feels like."

Her husband explains: "The people who are here, like Larry Adams and his wife here on the corner, and Mrs. Holmes, Pat and us, and the people that have been here, lived around here — we're so much like a family. Anything goes. They're all of 'em in the family. Do just like you would if you were among family. You can run out in the streets with your shorts on if you want."

That reminds him of the story of Bud Davidson, the fireman who used to live in the neighborhood. They called him "Dave."

"Dave would get so enthusiastic about this fire department stuff that he got kind of carried away. Man, when that fire siren blows, they just go! Well, this time it blew at about five o'clock in the morning, and Dave jumped out of bed, pulled on his shirt, and run down the street. [Laughs] He got about halfway down there, realized he didn't have any pants on, and here come his wife, a-runnin' after him wavin' his pants."

41

Marian sits back and sighs. "They're just taking so much away from us. Maybe nothing of 'value' — just our whole life. I mean, it's something you'll never, never, never get back."

NORTH BONNEVILLE, INSIDE-OUT

There is little doubt now in anyone's mind that the new town will be built. When it is ready for occupancy, it should "fit well" on the people, for two reasons. The first is that it will include many things that the residents love about their present town. The second is that it will be the product of a four-year effort to listen to the people, to understand how they live, and to identify what they want and need if their way of life is to be preserved.

From the beginning, Hussell, Dickson, and friends seem to have understood the importance of giving the people of the town their rightful place in relocation planning. The patterns of interaction between the people themselves and with their physical surroundings were the center of the planning effort — the capacity of the new town to permit these patterns to continue is the measure by which it will be judged a success or failure. The following is excerpted from the Relocation Planning Study prepared back in 1973:

Relocation of North Bonneville is a process that will disrupt human lives, community patterns, social functions and economic activity. The maintenance of a strong identity as a community while being forced to sacrifice the town's physical place along the river is a monumental undertaking for any community. Disruption of human lives . . . will be minimized only if the citizens directly affected experience an understanding of their relocation through direct involvement. Planning information . . . must therefore be set forth in a manner that individual citizens will be provided the material needed to make decisions with respect to relocation options. If there is to be any hope of maintaining an identity as a community, direct involvement of the citizens in relocation planning must be the primary goal.

The study goes on to emphasize the importance of the town's physical setting on the life of the community:

The majority of the citizens of North Bonneville have expressed a desire to relocate as a town in the strongly identifiable geographic area extending from Beacon Rock State Park on the west to the Bridge of the Gods on the east. The fact that this area is the same one within which the present town exists illustrates the importance of how the citizens orient themselves to the physical terrain and the sense of place in the Columbia River Gorge. The selection of a planning area for relocation revolves around the community's desire to continue a conversation with the river they have related to most of their lives.

Dickson talks about the town's strong sense of "place." "Why did they want to relocate here and not somewhere else? Well, every single person that lives here relates to this place in a special way. If you go a little bit west of here and look back into these hills, there's a very definable space here. It's defined by the geographical features. And when the sun comes up in the morning, those red bluffs up there just glow — they're just absolutely as warm as toast — and you can see that at five o'clock in the morning. That defines their space for

The real magic of most small rural towns like North Bonneville is hard to put your finger on. If you like things neat, tidy, and brand new, it won't show you much. But somehow through the lives of people, time, and the accidents of circumstance, a tree full of blooms grows in front of a cottage or an old man in red suspenders walks down an alley of weathered wood — and it is just right. People have a way, if left to their own devices, of patching together their home places. As you walk the back streets of any small town, you will see the evidence: the garden plots where weeds and berry bushes tangle with each other to make a fence; the crazy, tacked-on sheds and outbuildings, built plain to serve a purpose and suddenly handsome because they were never expected to be. The best planners know all this. And when they move into a town like North Bonneville, they can only try to understand how it was created in the first place and hope to keep out of the way.

them; and, for us, it began to define a design territory. It was something that *they* told us about. This is their place in the Columbia River Gorge, and it became obvious that their personal sense of identity related to that. They as people associated very strongly with this single place. I felt that very deeply — I, personally, responded to that and felt an obligation to understand it."

What emerged from the early planning work was a firsthand and intimate knowledge of the town's insides, the stuff only a resident can know: how information is disseminated; where the gathering places are; how mothers, knowing the route from school across vacant lots, can make one call to a household along the way to see if their kids have passed by yet. They knew where the kids fished and where the old people fished. They knew the best places for picnics. They knew a little about a secret system of trails used by the children. And they knew the stories, the yarns that are swapped over and over whenever people gather, and that no one ever seems to tire of. They had compiled their inventories of "hard" physical data too. But they had made a special effort to understand, and to record in useful form, all the "soft" things, those invisible parts of the town that make it like no other — those things that are the unique product of the place and the people who live there.

"We plotted this stuff according to human use, and then we paralleled that with analyses for soils capability, for drainage, for wind, for land use, and showed how all these edges overlapped. That's pretty abstract stuff. But that's the kind of thing that these people responded to because it's *real*. It isn't a bunch of academic garbage. It's real because *their* kids are the ones we're taking pictures of while they're fishing for salmon or sturgeon. And so we made, I think, a monumental leap from academic rhetoric to the use of planning language that meant something to the people because they were the ones doing it, creating the very thing we were talking about."

When it came time to hire a team of professionals to plan the new town, Hussell, Dickson, and the planning commission pulled out a document they had assembled called a Scope of Work. It had been written over a period of four months, and it drew on everything they knew about the town, and established both criteria for the new town design and also guidelines for a planning effort that would involve every citizen.

Dickson continues, "When the team of planners came in here, the first thing they told us was they didn't know a damn thing about rural design or sociology. And they don't. Nobody does. So they really had to *look* at the community. And I know Barbara Lundburg and Bob Batterton from Royston's office climbed through the beaver ponds and up around the hills and back through everything. They lived here. They got to know the people. And difficult though the job was, they really *learned* about this place! I think that kind of learning is being translated into something that has meaning for the town now. When they build the new town, it's going to have the capability of accommodating the social flow patterns that this town has already generated over years and years and years. The kids are going to have somewhere to go to create their own private trails and secret places like they already have here. It'll happen because it's *allowed* to happen — because we've taken the trouble to find out about it."

44

TRIPLOG. *Mill Valley, California. Barbara Lundburg and Bob Royston. Mill Valley is a woodsy suburb of San Francisco, across the Golden Gate, about fifteen miles north. Royston's firm, along with a phalanx of consultant engineers and planners, has done North Bonneville's Comprehensive Relocation Plan. It was Barbara Lundburg's first town-planning job. She and Bob Batterton were assigned to live in the town for six months as Royston's resident staff. She is young and smart. Royston is a big, gentle old-timer. Looks like a smiling bear. Took a deep personal interest in the job and an active role in it. Flew back and forth on a regular beat. They have dragged out a huge pile of photos and drawings to show us, but the stuff sits on the big table for most of the conversation. Every now and then we hear the IBM typewriters going in the next room, and the telephone ringing with an electronic burble that doesn't sound like a phone. It's a big, modern office — and it feels like a long way from North Bonneville.*

Lundburg: "Going to a place like North Bonneville was very different for us. It's a lot more rural then we're used to planning for. It's not hard for us to plan a park for a suburb, like say Cupertino [south of San Francisco]; we have a lot of the same values, being within the same kind of a cultural atmosphere. But I'm totally a city girl. I had no point of view other than this one here. So I had to live there in order to find out what the other point of view was, so that I could apply all the data that I have to that point of view."

We ask, "Were you uncomfortable there?"

"No, not at all. That's the thing that really surprised me. I thought that I was going to be uncomfortable going there, just because I was from the city going to a small community. I thought I was going to be an outcast. But it wasn't that way at all. I found the people very friendly, very warm, and open. I did experience one thing that bothered me only for a slight period of time — I couldn't walk around. You can walk around a big city anonymously. You can't do that in North Bonneville. I mean, they know where you are, whom you're seeing, you know — I mean every minute! Everybody knows what's happening. You can't be anonymous!

Royston tells us he and his crew had just six months to complete a comprehensive plan according to the guidelines set out in the town's Scope of Work. It was a job several of the other planning firms had said was impossible. In December 1974, the group moved into the town and established an office and living quarters by hooking together a bunch of rooms at the local motel.

Lundburg: "We worked incredible schedules. I had one day off in two months, and we were working, like twelve-, fifteen-, sixteen-hour days, for six months. We each had a little room across the driveway from where the office was, and then we had a little house connected that we cooked in. Everything was intensified. We were working under heavy pressure, and, of course, we had the citizens coming in all the time. We did find it to be a burden on us at times, in that we had a lot of work to do, and were were madly trying to get things done, and we were stopping to take time to talk to people, which meant that we had to stay up to three o'clock in the morning rather than go to bed at midnight. But I'm sure, in the long run, doing it that way was much better."

45

The top photographs were taken by Pollard Dickson and his crew. They show a tiny fraction of the activity in town during the months that North Bonneville was trying to plan for its survival and at the same time convince the U. S. Army Corps of Engineers that it had a legal right to do so. (The Corps wanted to buy up private property a parcel at a time and simply disperse the community.) The town hall was also the office for the town's own planning efforts; Dickson and Hussell and their intern assistants kept it open day and night encouraging townspeople to look at and respond to town plan schemes. Robert Royston is at the microphone during one of the open planning sessions at which citizens were asked not simply to respond to schemes for the new town but to help evolve them. The photograph at the bottom of the page was taken from the railroad berm looking west and slightly south and shows the site of the new North Bonneville.

In December of 1974, the assembled team of planners: Dickson and the town's interns, Royston and his staff held the first of four workshops — the others to be spaced out over the next four months — for the purpose of arriving at a comprehensive relocation plan for the town. The planners would involve the people of North Bonneville in every aspect of the work, even some of the most technical. Nothing would be unavailable to citizens. They would consider a number of sites. Eventually, it would be the citizens who would select one. They would wrestle with land use and zoning. They would debate issues such as how far from the highway could they afford to put the town's central district without losing business. They would talk about form: what they wanted their town to look like, where the parks should be, the school, whether or not utilities would be underground. The workshops would not be two-hour coffee klatches. They would be day-or-two long affairs with sleeves rolled up and the drawings and maps and data spread all over the place. And the planners were sure they would be well attended; people in large numbers would come to all four. Between workshops, Royston's little motel office, and the town's planning office would both be open to all, night and day. There would be reviews with the town council and planning commission — all of them public meetings.

Looking back, the planners are uncertain as to who learned most — them or the "planees." Dickson puts it pretty simply: "We were all just goin' to school in it."

It didn't all go like clockwork. There were some initial difficulties in convincing townspeople that, as individuals, they had something the planners needed. The people had to be convinced. "So many times these 'take part' design efforts are so professional, and rely so heavily on professional experience or knowledge, that most average people are excluded or intimidated." Dickson worried about that. "The people who usually get involved are those with degrees, or those who have a more sophisticated outlook. These are country people. When they want to build a garage on their lot, or a house, they go out and build it. If they want to build it out of maple logs, they'll build it out of maple logs. They don't like planning. They don't like building codes. They don't like any kind of regulations. The people who pile up junk in their backyards, or fire up the chain saw and stack two cords of firewood in their yards, are not the ones that usually participate in the planning process. But these were the people we needed, and we got them.

"Some people were very shy. They didn't think they had anything to say. So we showed them they had a great deal to say. I think when they saw us asking the children questions, it helped. We actually asked the designers to come in and sketch the ideas of the children. We had the kids tell them what this community is all about. And that began to affect Royston's group after a while. When kids tell you about a certain spot, you have to go see it."

Dickson believes that Royston's own sensitivity to the natural setting of the town had much to do with getting people involved. Royston says that there isn't much that can recommend North Bonneville's main street as a thing of beauty, and all the people know that. "But there are some wonderful things that happen. You do step out on the main street, and you look up, and there is the mountain. And everybody has climbed Beacon Rock. Or, they all go swimming in the lake. They know the beaver ponds are only a five-minute walk. And all that lives in your memory. So everything else seems all right, because you know it's right there.

"We started right away with the idea that the landscape is important, that it should be the skeleton or the matrix of the town. And we found out early that the people understood that. They wanted that. And that kind of a framework already existed in the town. None of them could really identify these things at first. But they reacted very well when they began to see those ideas take form in the planning."

At the first workshop, the planners brought a collection of ideas about what an optimum town might be. And the people reacted. Representatives of state, federal, and other agencies described their specialized needs relating to the new town. The townspeople began to find a vocabulary for putting things they had taken for granted into an expression that the professionals could use. This interplay between the planner ("Is this what you mean?") and the town ("No, we had in mind something a little different") would characterize the entire planning effort. Gradually a form for the new town began to emerge.

The fourth, and last, workshop took place in April of 1975. Four comprehensive schemes, based on the sites previously selected, were presented. They were optimum town plans, each of which covered detailed design for town layout, circulation, lots, central business district, and detailed site description. Following the fourth workshop, the town council held a week-long review, during which townspeople were asked to vote for the site they wanted. At the end of the week, a public meeting was held to tally the votes. Royston describes it: "We had all the drawings up. They cast a vote at the town center for the site they wanted. They were trooping in there all week long, asking questions — good questions! Some of them would come and grunt and stomp out; others would come in and ask for an explanation of two or three things on each of the sited. And the wonderful thing was that they selected what I believe is the best site. They voted something like seven to one for that site. The Corps was there, and they couldn't believe it. That evening, the Colonel turned to me and said, 'D'you think they're trying to tell us something?'"

That same night, the town council voted unanimously to adopt the site selected by the vote. Their action was endorsed by the Corps' district engineer. The plan was done. And it belongs to the people of North Bonneville.

THE NEW TOWN

By the time this book appears, Robert Royston's firm will have published a thick, wide document entitled *Town of North Bonneville Comprehensive Plan*. It is a record of the town's planning process and a summary of the design criteria that came out of it. Though it is cast in that particularly deadly language familiar only to those who work in government, if you read between the lines it contains the germs of the life of the people of North Bonneville.

Plans extracted from *Town of North Bonneville Comprehensive Plan*. The top drawing shows the town form; below, the provision for pedestrian-bicycle pathways.

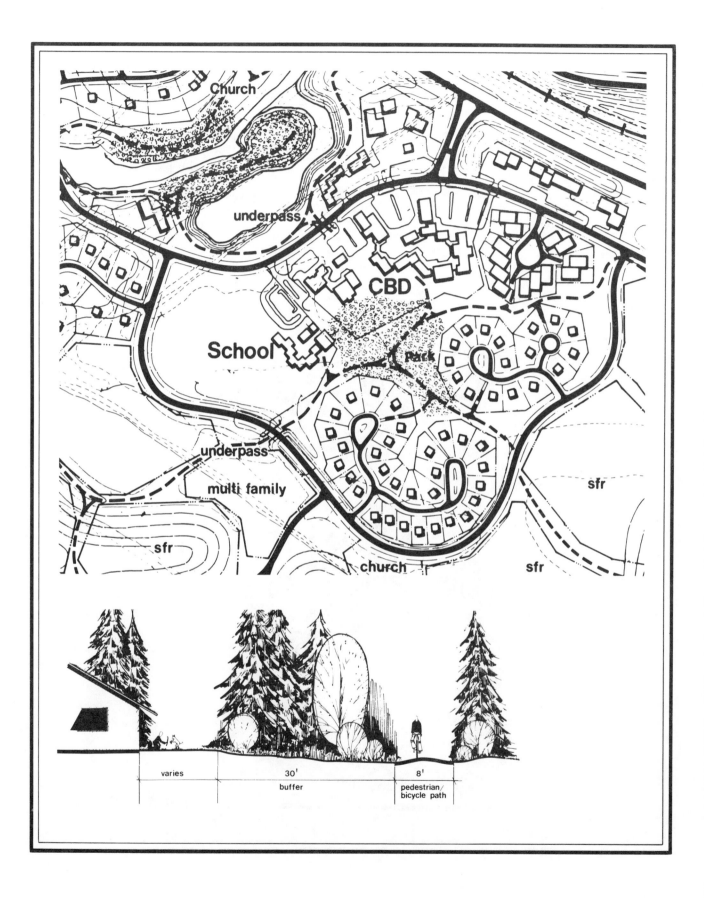

Church

underpass

CBD

School

Park

underpass

multi family

sfr

sfr

church

sfr

sfr

varies

30'
buffer

8'
pedestrian/
bicycle path

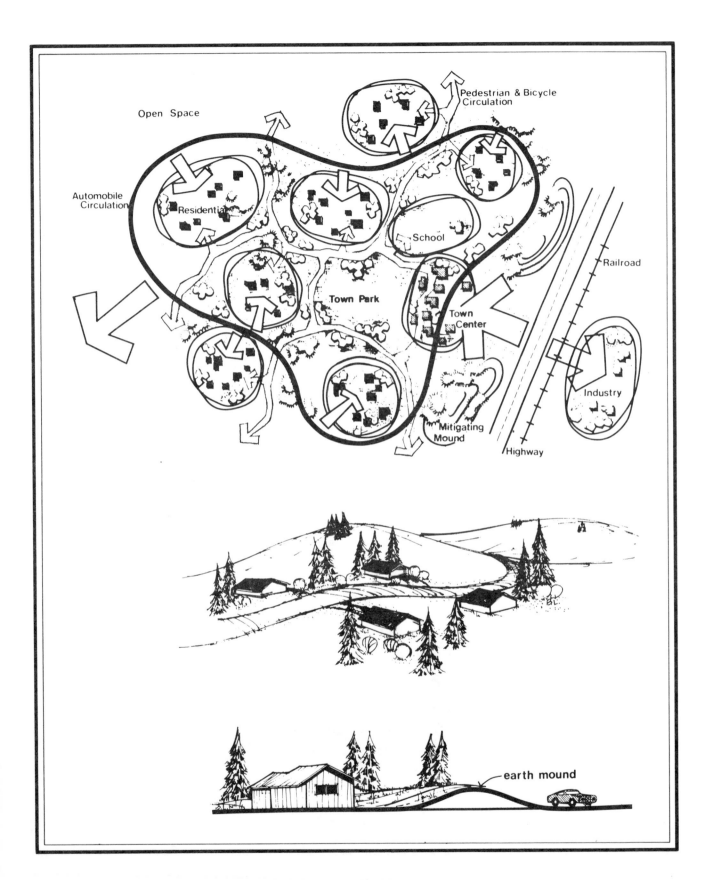

Plans showing circulation patterns; roadways built to follow the contours of the land; the use of mitigating mounds to shelter residences from noise and automobile exhaust fumes.

The new town will lie next to the Columbia River. Its western boundary will be at Beacon Rock State Park. It will be west (and downstream) from the present town. The town site will occupy 426.85 acres of flat, alluvial land. Its southern (riverside) boundary will be along the Corps' day-use area, which is intended to be a sculptured landform, to be constructed from 18 million cubic yards of fill taken from the new powerhouse excavation.

The town site will be bisected by Hamilton Creek, which drains nearby Greenleaf Lake. On the west side of the creek will be residential areas and an existing golf course which will be expanded to eighteen holes. To the east will be residential areas and the three principal focus points of the town: a park, the school, and the town center or business district. The north edge of the town proper will be formed by State Highway 14 and the tracks of the Burlington Northern Railroad. The townspeople's habits of using footpaths and trails as an important means of circulation is clearly evident. On the plan, buildings are clustered. The town park seems to extend long tendrils that separate and connect clusters. These tendrils are in fact natural areas intended to be used as a circulation network independent of streets. These "greenways," as they are called, will link all major town areas, making it possible for townspeople to get from any point to any other without using streets.

Residences will not face any major access or collector roads. Instead, they will be oriented toward the park network, making the movement of vehicles on residential streets a "backdoor" function. Fill that is not accommodated at the west and south edges of the town will be used to form mounds within the town site. These little hills will help protect the town from excessive wind and will create view corridors from the town to the river.

Aside from the plan itself, the building of a new town will be directed by a set of goals and policies that were based directly on the needs and stated preferences of the people of the town. The following is extracted from the *Comprehensive Plan*.

Landscaping will be primarily native and low maintenance in character. Tree cutting adjacent to and within the site will be controlled. A minimum setback of 200 feet will be required to protect the banks of all bodies of water. Pedestrian-bicycle pathways will not cross areas of environmental sensitivity.

The town's relationship to the dam and day-use area should reflect their importance as business-generators. The town's commercial center should be contained within a cohesive area oriented to the pedestrian. Business owners who wish to live in proximity to their places of business will be permitted to do so. Apartments and housing for the elderly will be located close to the commercial area. Pedestrian circulation is a basic element in the town transportation system. Bicycle access will be considered as an increasingly important form of transportation for the future and will be provided for.

The first housing priority should be to provide the widest possible choice in housing. The town should coordinate assistance that is required to provide low cost housing for low income people. Lot sizes should vary to provide maximum choice. However, minimum lot size should be 7,500 square feet. Mobile homes should be permitted in designated areas. Mobile home subdivisions should offer a range of lot sizes; however, the maximum mobile home density should not exceed eight units per acre. Though variety is desired, trailers, mobile homes, and apartments should not be mixed with detached, single family structures. Unoccupied travel trailers and campers should be permitted to be parked in screened areas on residential lots. The town should provide a clearinghouse of information on housing types and technologies.

Community facilities should be located within walking or bicycling distance of town residents. Staff for community facilities should serve more than one function to reduce cost. The town's school should be used secondarily as a multi-use community facility which should be a focal point of community activity. Churches should be located in or near residential areas. A medical clinic and nursing home should be important components of the town.

The town should own and operate a sewer treatment plant and sanitary system capable of serving the needs of the estimated optimum population. Public utility lines should be placed underground. Cable television service should be available to all residents.

As we write this, there is still no new town — except on paper — and the machines of the U. S. Army Corps of Engineers are eating up the east end of North Bonneville. That is where the coffer dam for the new powerhouse is to be located. Many buildings along the main street have been abandoned and bear stickers announcing to any passerby that the United States Government will tolerate no act of vandalism. Pollard Dickson, David Hussell, and the student interns, still at work, have turned their attention to questions of how the town will finance the purchase of lands, and how to make sure the Corps provides the interim housing that will be required. Preparation for the new town is about to enter another stage, in which engineers and designers will prepare drawings to direct the new town's builders. There will be more workshops. The town plan, fixed in concept only, will evolve further. Meanwhile, the black trucks of the Corps are everywhere. The engineers have a schedule. The nation is hungry for electric power. There is no time to lose. People in the town wonder whether their new homes will be ready before the wreckers reach them. The Corps is still buying property. The people are still selling it, but they're not moving. They're waiting for the new town.

North Bonneville's war against the U. S. Army Corps of Engineers is over. A kind of truce has been declared between them. In such conflicts, there are no real winners. And both sides have suffered losses. There is still a town to build. Whether there are larger lessons here about the real responsibilities of government for the well-being of people, remains to be seen. What we have found is that a handful of inexperienced people with no intrinsic resources other than their native intelligence and determination can accomplish whatever they believe is right.

There isn't much more that can be said about the new North Bonneville until it happens. But there is this to say about the people who will go there to live: You will have to look long and far to find a gathering of individuals who care more deeply about where they live, or know more about the reasons why.

Slaying the Dragon

ST. GEORGE, VERMONT

"You ask anyone in Burlington where St. George is, and I bet they tell you they don't know. I'll bet you. We're only ten miles from there, been here since 1763, and I'll bet you one in ten people don't know this place exists. No kidding. People at work know I'm a selectman and all, but they think I'm a selectman in Georgia which is another township up north of here. They ask me, 'How're things in Georgia?' Even when I tell 'em St. George, they forget. That's because no one really knows the place is here."

Armand Beliveau is one of three selectmen of the tiny township of St. George, Vermont, a few miles southeast of Vermont's largest town, Burlington (population 30,000). St. George is Vermont's smallest town with a population of about 500 and an area of only 2,200 acres. If you weren't certain it was there, you'd certainly believe it couldn't be. There is no town center. No post office. No public school. No churches. No business district. No natural resources of note, and no distinguishing physical features. But it has this to identify it: it is the source of some of the most imaginative work in land use and planning done in recent years. And it is work that is loaded with portent for any small rural community in the nation.

Armand Beliveau is the father of much of what is making St. George famous, though it is not fair or proper to suggest that he did it alone. Like any of the movers and shakers in this book (or elsewhere), he cared enough to invest himself deeply in his town — but knows enough to understand that he is effective only in so far as he shares the responsibility and the credit with his fellow townspeople. Though the ideas came from Armand Beliveau, it is the people of the township of St. George who had the good sense to recognize them and act accordingly. And that is no small accomplishment. The history of American small towns abounds with instances in which, given choices of equal importance, city fathers have opted for that which most closely approximates the status quo; when what was needed was a bit of responsible risk-taking.

Perhaps what has happened in the little township of St. George is the clearest evidence we have seen that in matters of highest urgency, it is wisest to place the decision directly in the hands of the people themselves. Or put in other words, the only business fit for a bureaucracy, or for those who make politics a career, is the most routine and least important.

It should be remembered — by anyone who isn't a New Englander — that the northeastern part of this country is still the land of the free and the home of the brave. Direct democracy is still practiced in some districts in the form of the Town Meeting, though we hear, with great misgiving, that in town after town, the press of business is forcing the citizenry to abandon this tradition for a more "modern" form of government.

Fortunately for its 500 residents, the town of St. George still conducts public business annually at the Town Meeting where all have an equal voice. When the pace of things requires it, special Town Meetings are held in addition. The three selectmen, none of whom is paid for his work, meanwhile carry out the wishes of the electorate, handling whatever administrative duties are required between meetings. In the state of Vermont (as is the case in much of the rest of New England), there is virtually no level of government between that of the town (or municipality) and the state. Counties exist primarily to administer the judicial system. Even roads are maintained either by the town or by the state. To some of us who live with a different system, there is something appealingly simple about this arrangement. Without the intervening structure of a county government, the state suddenly seems much more accessible, while the business of local government seems more solid and, somehow, more decisive.

We wonder if we would now be writing about St. George if what Armand Beliveau had in mind needed to be approved first by a County Board of Supervisors.

TRIPLOG. *St. George, Vermont. Armand Beliveau's living room. Armand Beliveau sounds like the name of a cabaret singer or a hair stylist or a magician who entertains at children's birthday parties. But the actual person is certainly none of those, though he does have two distinguishing characteristics. One is eyebrows like Bela Lugosi, great beetling affairs with long hairs that whip around in wild arabesques while the eyes go on about their business. The other is a voice something like Mickey Rooney's, though it should be said that when we spoke with Beliveau he was at home nursing the aftermath of flu and may not sound like this all the time. He also has a lively sense of humor and considerable aplomb, and will not be anything but amused at this description.*

Beliveau is a New Englander by birth, but a French Canadian by heritage. He was raised on a farm and had the great good fortune to have been educated in what must have been one of New England's first non-graded, move-at-your-own-speed public schools. The mayor, pastor, and school superintendent in his small town decided that Armand should go to college and, since his parents were depression-poor Vermont hard-rock farmers, took it upon themselves to see that he did. He needed a job to save for tuition. They got him one. He needed money for room and board at the University of Vermont. They helped him get a job there. He remembers with touching gratitude how his small town helped him get his start.

He studied engineering and worked in Virginia before joining IBM, his present employer. Then he lived in Poughkeepsie, New York, where he had his first tumble with the scourge of suburbia. He lost that one.

54

"When we lived outside Poughkeepsie, New York, in 1964, in a place called Wappingers Falls, my wife and I owned a chunk of about thirty acres that we bought years ago, way out in the country. There was a little dirt road that ran in front of the house that you could lay down on for twenty hours and never get run over. Well, by the time we moved out of there (in 1966) in back of our thirty acres was a development of half-acre lots, on one side of our thirty acres was a development of half-acre lots, on the other side was the same thing, and across the street was a brand new thousand-student central school. And the little dirt road had gotten to be three-laned blacktop that was some kind of a short cut for trailer trucks. I'd come there from Vermont, and I just couldn't stand the noise, day and night. Plus we couldn't enjoy our property. It was used as a recreational park by the people on all three sides of us. . . ."

Beliveau and his family moved to a rented house near Burlington, Vermont, while they built their house in St. George. This time they thought they would be enough off the beaten track in St. George to avoid the tract houses and the trailer trucks. But as it turned out, they themselves were part of the problem. For almost two hundred years, the population of St. George had held steady with a population of 80 to 120 souls. Then in the six years between 1964 and 1970, the population quadrupled. For a while, St. George achieved a measure of noteworthiness as the fastest growing town in Vermont. In the same period, all the farms in the township except for one, closed down for good.

At that time, the state had practically no controls on the conversion of open land to other uses. Zoning and environmental protection laws didn't come until later. As a result, St. George and the other rural townships around Burlington were exposed to the same haphazard development that was and still is taking place around small cities all over the country. In Burlington, it was stimulated by expansion of the local General Electric and IBM plants.

"You can see on the map exactly what happened. There is the city core where there are rental units available. In Burlington, they aren't necessarily very good rental units. Then just outside of that are the tracts built during the late forties and fifties. Then just outside of that ring, where there was land available, are the tracts built in the late fifties and early sixties. That's more expensive stuff. But when this great influx occurred in the late sixties, there was a need for housing, period, and the thing that wasn't always available was land. So developers looked all over for available pieces of land, and when they found one, they carved it up into half-acre lots and built houses. Or — because it wasn't just expensive housing that was needed — they built trailer parks. So development of this area happened by accident, more or less. No thought was given to anything except to the fact that it was developable land within reasonable (or in some cases, not-so-reasonable) commuting distance to the city. This outermost ring tends to be the cheapest housing — because the land was the cheapest and the commute the longest — or large country lots of twenty, thirty, or forty acres — or both. In St. George we got both. You can plot the trailer parks around Burlington and tell by the age of each park and its location about when each town got its zoning laws."

55

By 1966, when Armand Beliveau and his family moved into their new house, he knew that the thing that had dogged him in Poughkeepsie was already at work in St. George. There was this monster rummaging in the suburbs, devouring farms. He didn't say so, but we imagine Beliveau lay awake in bed in his new house and heard it snorting along the Interstate Highway as the trailer trucks shifted down in the small quiet hours of the morning.

For all we know, the noise doesn't drive him to distraction. But it does nibble away his peace of mind. Perhaps most people would learn to live with it. "So there's a dragon loose in the land. So he'll get acquainted with the neighbors. What else is new?" Armand Beliveau decided to do something. What did he do? He went to school. He enrolled in a course in land-use planning at the University of Vermont in Burlington. You might almost say that Armand Beliveau made the study of the use of rural land his hobby. In the intervening years, it has become one of his principal preoccupations.

As a part of his course in land-use planning, Beliveau made the acquaintance of members and staff of the local Regional Planning Commission, which had been set up in the state of Vermont a year or two earlier. He also convinced the town of St. George to contribute funds to support the commission's work, and to appoint a representative. He must have done his homework well because within a year, he was chairman of the commission, an office he held for two terms. By the time his second term had ended, in about 1968 or 1969, Armand Beliveau felt he was ready to go to work to help his own little town.

He didn't have to look very far to find an example of what could happen to St. George if nothing was done. Down the road about a mile from his own driveway is the St. George Estates, a residential development that was built around 1964. "Some guy from down Hudson Valley way in New York came up here and split up a hunk of land in the middle of St. George into twenty-five, one-acre lots. There were no regulations at that time. He just moved his bulldozer in and went to work. Didn't ask nobody nuthin." He points out that the entire site consists almost totally of a substance called Virginnes clay, and that it must have been obvious as soon as ground was broken that it was no place to build homes. "If you did a soil survey and tried to identify the worst possible place for a development, it would have to be the site of St. George Estates."

Virginnes clay is unstable. It is a substance that will absorb little moisture so that percolation is impossible. Worse, it behaves badly in freezing weather. None of the footings for the homes in St. George Estates went far enough down to escape the winter frosts. The result is that as the clay freezes and expands, it heaves, taking anything in the way along with it. Cracks developed in basement walls. Doors jammed shut. Windows broke as sills distorted. It was a nightmare. There was the usual spate of lawsuits. But litigation in such cases, even if successful, never undoes all the damage. The residents of St. George Estates were left with their houses and their cracks.

Armand Beliveau wasn't simply interested in preventing another such local disaster. He wanted more than that. The conventional approach to regulating land use is to try to write rules that prevent one person from harming another, or that discourage those who might do damage to the environment. Such a posture in the law creates adversary roles by definition. He wanted the people of St. George to direct development in the town, not simply set limitations on it.

Beliveau tells us that he had always felt that private enterprise should not be discouraged or somehow subverted by the law. He did not want to replace private developers and entrepreneurs with a public agency. On the other hand, it was clear to him that if private enterprise is left unfettered, there is no good way to sort out the villians from the heroes, until it is too late. He wanted somehow to join the energy and drive of private enterprise fueled by the urge for profits, and the deliberateness and the interest in the public welfare that are the hallmarks of the best public agency. The question was how?

His course in land-use planning had made him familiar with some of the new ideas that are being advanced cautiously in that field. One of these is something called "the transfer of development rights," or TDR in the land-use planners' trade. It is not an idea that has received widespread attention or use, partly because it is little understood, and partly because it requires developers and the public agencies that regulate them to work together in a positive or constructive frame of reference, and old ways are slow to change.

The idea is very simple. When it is employed, the owner of a piece of property relinquishes his or her right to develop that property in exchange for something else — usually money. It is a little like selling an easement. If you sell an easement on your property to a public utility for the purpose of running a power line through, you forfeit the right to do anything else along that easement in exchange for its price. You still own the land. But you are no longer free to do anything you please on that portion of it. The transaction is recorded on your deed in what is called a "restrictive covenant." The restriction stays with the property, regardless of who may own it later. In this form, the idea of an easement is very familiar and can be understood by anyone who has ever been involved in real-estate transactions. The transfer of development rights is essentially the same thing. It becomes somewhat more complex only in application.

Beliveau could see that the town of St. George, like any other town, had one thing in which developers could be enormously interested: land. But the town also represented a force that could easily discourage them. In these days of environmental legislation, developers are anxious not to be involved where an extended fight over a proposed development could amount to thousands of dollars in outright costs, not to mention lost sales due to delays. Once equipped with zoning laws and subdivision ordinances, the town of St. George would be a powerful opponent. Or, thought Beliveau, an equally powerful ally.

Beliveau believed that old attitudes about change and public responsibility needed to be shaken up, and then the town needed some tools with which to control or ward off unwanted development. These things had to exist before it would be possible even to discuss what to do with development rights. He feared that to Yankee ears, the notion of controlling development might smack too much of infringement of individual rights, but that it would be accepted later. Most important, the people of his town needed to believe that they could actually control their own future.

After spending almost a year in preparation, he made his pitch to the people of St. Goerge at a Town Meeting in March of 1968. He came prepared with the sketch of a zoning ordinance and with charts and tables to support his central thesis that if the people didn't move to take control of development within their town, someone else would do it for them. The following "Letter to the People" contains the gist of his argument, and was handed out at the meeting.

The growth of the County, the growth of the Greater Burlington area, the desire for rural living by more and more people, the effect of the Essex-Shelburne Beltline and the North-South Interstate with interchanges directly North of St. George or directly South or both, will force St. George to develop very fast and probably in the very near future.

We cannot stop the growth, but we do have two choices:

We can leave it to chance and to out-of-town land owners and contractors, some of whom care little for anything but the quick dollar. Or;

We can, in the spirit of a responsible community, with concern for our neighbors and our children, influence the development of this Town. We can arrange things so the opinions and desires of responsible citizens of the Town determine what happens here. We can do this now, *not after we get into more problems, by taking three steps.*

1. Get hold of our destiny by supporting this proposed Ordinance, *so that major changes in our Town have to come before the people (hearings) and so that the building that does occur, occurs in a way that will* benefit *most of the citizens of St. George present and future, not* ruin *it.*

2. Have your Planning Commission and your Selectmen . . . design a St. George of the future as responsible citizens of St. George would like to see it become. A comprehensive plan could be ready for presentation at the next Town Meeting.

3. Within the following year revise the Ordinance to fit the comprehensive plan, institute sub-division regulations, and other permissive by-laws that would attract responsible builders of homes, multifamily housing, and commercial and industrial establishments, to put this Town on a good fiscal base and assure reasonable services. . . .

Whether we like it or not we have to be a part of our society. We can no longer, in St. George at least, live without regard and concern for one another, without regard or concern for what happens here. Sometimes it's painful but good things do not happen by accident — they happen when people care.

The time is now.

In this "Letter," Beliveau and those who worked with him proposed, without actually saying so, that the town should be the developer in the sense that it should control what happens within its boundaries rather than waiting for an entrepreneur from out of town to come along and work his number on them. That approach is somewhat unorthodox in a large community. It is virtually unheard of in a rural town of 500 people. How would they accomplish such a thing? The entire town budget was less than $50,000, much of which was spent under contract to the nearby town of Hinesburg where St. George public school students were taught.

The first step was to pass the new zoning ordinance. Within months, it had been accomplished. At the same time, an effort was made to begin work on a comprehensive plan. Through the Department of Geology at the University of Vermont, arrangements were made for graduate students under faculty supervision to do, at no cost to the town, a detailed geological study of the entire township, according to Beliveau, the most comprehensive such study ever done for a Vermont municipality. From the resulting map, town planners could see where soils were most suited to the impact of intensive development.

Somewhere in this process, the people were asked how they wanted their town to accommodate growth, and the people decided it was time for St. George to have a town center. Part of the strategy of controlling development was to encourage it to take place where the people felt it would most benefit them. The center would incorporate municipal with commercial services, and high-density residential facilities. By concentrating the growth in a limited area around a center, it was believed that the rural character of the community could best be preserved.

On the basis of the geological survey conducted by the students from the University of Vermont, a soil types survey (done by the Soil Conservation District), and with the help of planners made available through the state's Regional Planning Commission, residents selected a site near the center of the township, on a small farm along Route 2A. Within six months, the owner of that farm died and the property came up for sale. Suddenly Beliveau and his friends were presented an opportunity to put their money where their mouths had been.

THE TOWN DEVELOPER

"We really weren't ready for this. It was about six months too early. But the opportunity might not be there when we were ready, so I talked to the selectmen. At that time, I had no official capacity in the town except my membership on the school board. Fortunately, two of the three selectmen could see a number of reasons why it might make sense for the town to get involved. So we had a special Town Meeting and a special vote to buy the property. The cost of the property was equivalent to one year's operating budget for the town. That was quite a commitment to ask from a little town. But it passed.

Before the meeting, Beliveau and one of the selectmen had shopped around to find financing for the purchase. Finally, after visiting six banks, they found one that was willing to advance the entire amount, $48,000, on a one-year renewable note at an interest rate of about 2%. "I immediately transferred all my business to that bank in gratitude. Of course it didn't make a damn bit of difference to them, but it sure made me feel good."

Now the town was the owner of forty-eight acres of what was designated in the town plan as the only available land for commercial or high-density residential development. The next task was to obtain the best possible design for the new town center. Here again, help from outside was available. The Vermont Chapter of the American Institute of Architects and the Vermont Council on the Arts jointly sponsored an architectural competition for the design. The competition was restricted to Vermont residents. Ten firms submitted entries, and in May of 1971, a panel of distinguished jurors chose the plan submitted by the Waitsfield firm of Burley Associates. A pamphlet prepared for public distribution by the local unit of the League of Women Voters describes the winning scheme:

The architects' plan calls for an internal pathway system which will enable people to walk or bicycle from any house in the planned-unit development area down to the Town Center without crossing a roadway. More detailed plans of the Center show shops separating the parking from the pedestrian space . . . and a school and town hall that will permit full community use of library resources, cafeteria, and meeting space.

As the town grows, shops will be added to the north with a market, bank and additional housing convenient to the Center, and a restaurant that overlooks the trees and park. Near the entrance and Route 2A will be a gas station combined with a town garage and police and fire stations. Building will be done in partnership with private enterprise. Land will be developed available to developers willing to work within the plan. The concept had been unanimously approved by the selectmen and planning commission for inclusion in the Town Comprehensive Plan.

So far it was all on paper. There still remained the problem of getting the new project built on the town's property. It was about this time that Armand Beliveau was appointed to fill out the term of a resigning selectman. A year later, in 1972, he was elected for a three-year term. Beliveau refused to consider going back to the townspeople for the money.

"No more town money involved in the project, that's my criteria. I had told them, 'If you buy the land, I'm not going to come back to the town and ask for more money. None, you understand? None, none, none!' I think it can be done, reasonably. And I think the opposite has no end. If I go back for a dollar, and it comes easy, I'll go back for another two. I don't want any more money. Don't need any."

That utterance in itself, coming as it does from a public official, is unusual. But what follows — when asked how, then, does he intend to build all of the plan? — is even more remarkable. It is here that Beliveau's French Canadian and Yankee horse-trading instincts came into full play.

Beliveau's next move was to approach one of Vermont's leading developers with what sounded at first like a bizarre plan. He proposed that the developer buy a thirty-six-acre parcel adjoining the town property and that he deed it to the town (thereby almost doubling the town's property at the site of the new center). In return, the town would negotiate a contract with the developer to build the first phase of the new town center — on the town's land, and designed to meet the town's design criteria as set forth in the town center plan. The contract would be negotiated in such a way that the developer has reasonable potential of making the same profit by building on town land that he would have realized by building it on his own.

The developer who was approached with this unusual scheme was the president of Green Mountain Meadows, Inc., of Burlington. At the time he was partway through a costly two-year battle with the officials of another town over

What you see in the top photograph on the opposite page is a large portion of the tiny township of St. George, Vermont. The picture was taken from the township's remaining active dairy farm, looking approximately south across the cow pastures toward the site of the new town center, a distance of a little over a quarter mile. The farmer, a Mr. Henry Pillsbury, struggling to stay ahead of rising costs and taxes, is openly skeptical about plans for the town. He complains that it is only a matter of time before he, his wife and two sons will be forced to sell out, like the others who preceeded him.

In the photographs below are the town center's developer, Robert Snyder, and the scheme's principal promoter, Selectman Armand Beliveau. Beliveau wants very much to hang on to the dairy farm and hopes that the methods he and the other townspeople have worked out for controlling growth in the township will prevent just the sale that Pillsbury predicts. The effort that is being made to deal with change in this rural Vermont township is based on the idea that it is not necessary to turn every struggling farm into what amounts to a suburban subdivision.

a proposed development. Beliveau knew this 'and the approach of the St. George town fathers was calculated to catch his attention. It did just that.

"I introduced the idea to him and said, 'Hey, how'd you like to work *with* a town instead of against one?' He recognized it as a huge advantage for him. He kept asking, 'You mean I wouldn't have to get permits? Who would hold the public hearings?' "

Beliveau assured him that he not only would not have to file for permits, he wouldn't even have to attend any public hearings. The town would do all of that for him, because the town was actually functioning as the developer of its own property. Green Mountain Meadows would, in this case, be functioning in the role of a contractor only.

"The negotiation involved some assurance to him that Green Mountain Meadows would make the same amount of profit on our project that it would have on its own, but there were no guarantees. He would be allowed to build so many houses at such and such a price range. Of course we couldn't guarantee he would be able to sell them, but he never knows that anyway. Our deal was much better than he could have done on his own."

There were other advantages as well. The developer would be building on a site on which considerable site-development work was already accomplished. The town, through a grant from the Farmers Home Administration, would provide roads, water, and sewer. Green Mountain Meadows was asked to calculate what the cost of development would ' have been both with and without those site improvements. The difference, which worked to the advantage of Green Mountain Meadows, was to be divided three ways: one-third would be added to the profits of Green Mountain Meadows; one-third would be paid to the town either as a rebate, or as income, to be used for further development; and the remaining third was to be matched by a corresponding reduction in the cost of the finished units to the public. Thus, not only would the developer be assured of municipal cooperation, and not only would it be in the best interest of the town government for him to be successful in the effort, he would be paid a bonus in extra profits in the bargain. It was irresistible. Though the deal was modified somewhat in its final form, and though the negotiations were delicate, the whole arrangement was conducted in a spirit of cooperation, and in February of 1975, the following summary of agreement between the contracting parties was issued:

Green Mountain Meadows Incorporated of Vermont [GMM] and the Town of St. George, Vermont have reached agreement on the first phase development of the St. George New Town Center. This innovative project, scheduled to begin this spring, will include a 10,000 square foot industrial building and a commercial-residential building.

The Agreement being signed today comprises the following points:

1. GMM agrees to deed to the Town 36 acres located adjacent and to the north of the Town-owned land, instead of dividing and developing their land into 2 acre lots.

2. The Town in turn agrees to lease to GMM approximately 3 acres of land for development of Phase I buildings. The lease to GMM is for 45 years with the right to renew for an additional 15 years.

3. *GMM retains the development rights of the land deeded to the Town, that is, the right to construct 18 units of housing at a future date, at which time the Town will convey or lease to GMM sufficient land for this construction. The number of development rights has been determined by the established density of one unit per two acres.*

4. *The Phase I construction will consist of a commercial-residential building and an industrial building to be constructed by GMM, subject to design review and approval by the Town. The Town also has the right to approve the proposed uses and non-residential tenants.*

5. *The Town agrees to provide water, sewer, road and parking facilities for the Phase I buildings through an industrial development grant from the Farmers Home Administration.*

6. *GMM will maintain and repair the buildings during the terms of the lease, and the Town will maintain and repair the road.*

The St. George project is in the forefront of emerging land-use programs and policies that support both the ecology and economy of the community. Both GMM and the Town of St. George hope that the success of this cooperative effort will encourage other communities and development interests to work together.

Beliveau suggested we talk to Robert Snyder, the president of Green Mountain Meadows. He felt it was important to understand the viewpoint of the developer. Too often the developer is portrayed as the bad guy. Beliveau believes this attitude can bring about problems instead of bringing about cooperative, mutually beneficial solutions.

TRIPLOG. *Burlington, Vermont. Burlington is built on a slope of land that reaches down (eventually) to Lake Champlain. The city itself is miniature. A kind of reduced metropolis, a scale model of some larger place. Green Mountain Meadows has an office in a building about a block and a half off the main street of town. We have an appointment to talk with its president, Robert Snyder, a man of thirty who looks eighteen. He has a bush of blond hair combed back, an expensive necktie over a blue shirt, and very erect posture. He used to be a school teacher; he bought into the company during a low ebb in its fortunes, and eventually found himself at the helm after criticizing the previous management. The company's successes since then are proof that he knows what he is about. The firm has a reputation for being one of Vermont's most conscientious and forward-looking, in a business where such characteristics are rare. Snyder is pretty straightforward about the trouble they've had in getting approvals on some of their projects, and describes one eighteen-month siege in which at a single hearing, twenty-three separate agencies were participating! It is clear that working with a town rather than against it has had huge appeal in this case: "When we went in for our Act 250 [environmental review] hearing, it was the selectmen of the town who were doing the work. I attended that hearing when this thing was approved. It lasted about three hours, and I didn't have to get up once! I just sat in the back row of the place while the stuff we had developed was explained by the townspeople and their engineers, and the permit was issued. It was beautiful!*

Easy as pie. There was some opposition. But the [state] commissioners could see that this was a good thing. I'm not convinced that they cared to understand the intricacies of the whole arrangement. But they could see that the town and the developer were working together for a change."

We asked Snyder if his company had ever been involved in any such arrangement before. He said no.

"That was one of the difficulties in reaching an agreement. We called all around: Urban Land Institute; AIA, other groups such as that. We asked if other groups had done such a thing, and is there an agreement that we could copy or at least get some help from? And the answer was no. So our agreement with the town is truly unique. It was hammered out between people who had never done anything like this before. And I think it's pretty good. It's a little complicated, maybe. But everybody had their own interests, and I think we were able to reach an understanding that satisfied everyone."

Snyder's board would not agree to the purchase of the thirty-six acres of adjoining farmland until an agreement was reached, so the company took an option on it during the negotiations. The first phase of construction was to include commercial spaces and a small industrial building. Green Mountain Meadows did not want to obtain financing for the construction of these spaces until they were satisfied that tenants could be found. They also wanted to be sure that after spending months on the agreement, the town would not run out and contract with another developer who would right away build structures that would compete with theirs. The town, on its part, wanted to be sure that to the extent possible, local people would be given jobs that would be made available by the construction, and that they would somehow be given first chance to occupy the finished spaces. These and other accommodations were reached. Snyder seems genuinely enthusiastic and optimistic about the outcome.

"I think this project provides an example of how private enterprise and a public agency can work together for the benefit of both. It's certainly a better alternative for the town of St. George and Green Mountain Meadows to be working together than to be fighting each other. The money that we might spend fighting each other could better be spent in building better buildings.

"I think this kind of set-up could work in any small town. I think it is a perfect solution to a lot of the problems of growth management. Once we've got this thing nailed down, we're in construction, and it's visibly there, I think it would be politically feasible for us to do it, or for other people to do it — at will. You could almost stamp it out. You have to be careful, you realize, because there are certain anomalies in each town, but I think it could be done to the benefit of both parties in almost any town."

THE ST. GEORGE SCHEME ELSEWHERE

In all states, municipalities derive their power (and their limitation) directly from the state constitution. We have not investigated the legal limits on what towns outside the state of Vermont may or may not do concerning the control of their own development. But the issue is a hot one in any growth area, and is becoming increasingly difficult for rural communities to cope with, in all states. Since all municipalities are able to buy and sell property and enter into contracts, we see no reason in principle why the St. George model could not be replicated almost anywhere.

It is important to realize that a basic feature of the St. George plan is that all arrangements are negotiated separately and defined by contract. Nowhere is there legislation that deals directly with this subject. And the writers of the St. George zoning and subdivision ordinances were careful to be sure that nothing in those regulations could be construed to put limits on such contracted arrangements.

The principal advantage of doing business in this manner is that it makes it possible to tailor each arrangement to the specific needs and conditions present in each instance. Were the basic arrangement defined by law, the law would be necessary to anticipate, measure, and deal with every variable. The result would either be a legal nightmare that would discourage all comers, or constraints so great as to limit severely the effectiveness of the partnership.

Strictly speaking, St. George's arrangement with Green Mountain Meadows was not a classic case of transfer of development rights, since in the St. George instance the developer actually deeded his property to the town, retaining the rights to develop eighteen residential units at a later time — a good example of why contracted arrangements, which can accommodate such variations, are probably better than ones defined by law or municipal ordinance. But here is how a classic transfer of development rights would work.

In such a transfer, the developer or owner would come to the town with a scheme to develop property. He or she would be told by the town: "You have the right to do that. (Such rights are defined by law and are intrinsic to the ownership of private property.) But we would prefer that you build a comparable development (or one of equal profit potential) here on town land."

If the developer's or property owner's scheme happens to be out of phase with local zoning, the town obviously has the upper hand. But the threat of a fight is always implicit, regardless of zoning. And if the town can make a counterproposal which is equally attractive financially, it would make no sense to oppose its plan.

Assuming then that the property owner goes along with the idea, a contract is drawn up in which the nature of the development and the responsibilities of each party are defined. At the same time, a covenant is written that describes the resulting limits that the transaction imposes on the owner's property from which development rights are being removed. His potential for realizing a profit on the deal is defined (insofar as it is possible) by the contract.

Let's assume that the applicant is a developer who has just purchased a one hundred-acre farm and wishes to subdivide it. He has purchased it from a farmer whose taxes have made it impossible to continue farming profitably. Once the development rights have been removed from the property, the developer could resell it (nothing in the arrangement prevents it). He might even sell it back to the farmer, who, having made a profit on the sale to the developer, buys it back at a *lower price,* because it now lacks development

65

potential, and could theoretically, go right on farming it. He might now find farming profitable, *since the property could no longer be taxed on its potential as a subdivision.*

There are variations. An example is that the property owner might negotiate with the town to keep some development rights, and transfer others. Assuming that the one hundred-acre farm were in a land-use area zoned for ten-acre minimum lot sizes, the number of development rights on that property can be defined as ten. The property owner (developer) could contract with the town to retain one or more of those rights on land that is marginal for farming, transfer the balance, and then resell the land that is suitable for farming, minus the development rights.

Implicit in this arrangement are legal limits on growth, a topic that is particularly touchy and has been the subject of Supreme Court review recently. Does a town have the legal right to declare itself "full" and then effectively close its doors to additional population? Is this an infringement of an individual's freedom of movement? Those are loaded questions. The Supreme Court has ruled that a town *does* have such rights. But it is a decision that will be tested over and over and will be the cause of much controversy in years to come.

The St. George plan gets at the heart of the matter. If a town's boundaries are fixed, and if, within those boundaries, the town has "used up" all available development rights in a series of legal transactions, then its growth potential is fixed by those transactions, unless, and until, its boundaries are enlarged.

Though there are many methods for insuring that open spaces will be preserved where they are needed or wanted, we have not yet encountered a scheme that seems as practical in achieving that objective as this one. The normal method for preserving open space is to accumulate land and declare it somehow set apart, it is hoped in perpetuity. The problem is always the cost — first of acquiring the land and then of maintaining it. Whether this is accomplished through a land trust, or by dedicating the land to some public agency in the form of a park or some other reserve, there are always such costs involved. But by transferring development rights, the entire question of the costs of acquisition and of maintenance is done away with. Property from which development rights have been transferred will be maintained in an undeveloped state because its potential for development has been legally extracted.

The advantages to all parties are numerous and of considerable importance. To the town which wishes to involve itself in this kind of effort, it suddenly becomes possible to translate dreams and plans into direct, constructive action. Town ownership or control of the land and the existence of a workable plan seem to be prerequisites. The town, in order to be in control must have something to trade for its cooperation and support. It must also have a plan that will be taken seriously by developers who are used to looking at any plan in terms of its commercial viability. Given these conditions, the town can put itself squarely in control of growth, directing it to locations and into formations that best suit its citizens and their needs. There is also the possibility of generating income for the municipal entity that chooses to work in this way.

Of course fundamental to the whole idea is the assumption that those who administer municipal affairs are willing to invest the energy and time that it takes to initiate and operate such an undertaking. One way of looking at it is that in many small communities, these same people will be spending an equal or greater amount of time fighting off unwanted or ill-conceived development and gaining nothing except perhaps a winner's grim satisfaction in the process. And of course, there is never a guarantee of winning.

For the developer, there is the considerable appeal of being a partner (and hero) instead of an opponent (and scoundrel). As is plain in the St. George example, the developer may also benefit directly in the form of considerable cost savings when working with a municipality that can obtain grants and other assistance unavailable to private enterprise. He also has the assurance that the entire community will be behind him rather than in his path. Aside from the possible time and money savings gained by avoiding delays and opposition, there is the considerable psychic advantage of knowing that everyone's interests will be served if the project succeeds.

But perhaps the ones who will benefit most in St. George are the people who live there and who love their small town. Though it is clear there has been an enormous amount of hard work done by Armand Beliveau and a handful of townspeople, it is also clear that the project belongs rightfully to all the citizens of St. George. At every step of the way when decisions were required, whether it was the purchase of land or the approval of an agreement with developers, the issue was put to popular vote. All negotiations with the developer were conducted as open meetings. At no time during the entire process was the public excluded from the proceedings. As a result, the entire town has benefited, not just by the new town center they will have, but because of what they have learned. For them, the advantages can't be measured in time saved or in dollars earned. They have found a way to make positive and constructive use of their status as a community. They see that they have power, and that that power may be used to make real things out of dreams.

From a modest investment of $48,000, this tiny community of 500 people has conjured up a new town center, a workable plan for growth and its control, and the certain knowledge that if their town changes, it will be because they wanted it that way.

Part Two
New Beginnings, Old Dreams

The Art of Sticking Together

The first time it occurred to us that our town was something like a large family was when our youngest daughter graduated from the eighth grade. It was a rite of passage for her and, in a way, for the town as well. The auditorium was stuffed; people stood at the doors with necks craned to hear the names of the youngsters announced and to watch them file slowly, two by two, down the aisle. Surely, we thought, these people aren't all relatives! Most were next of kin but many were family friends, townsfolk who had watched these children grow up. The children were taking a step toward maturity, toward being the next leaders of our town. It seemed important to everyone. After the ceremony, the boys and girls lined up outside the auditorium. The towns-people passed down that line shaking the hand of each child and giving gifts and cards along with their congratulations. Our daughter was a newcomer; she had been in the school only two years. But she, too, received gifts from mothers of friends and from neighbors. It was a touching evening for our family — a kind of initiation for all of us. For the first time, we felt like we belonged here.

One of the things we noticed as we visited the fifteen or so small towns that were our preparation for writing this book, was that at the center of many of them was a sense that people seemed to have of belonging to one another. This sense isn't limited to small towns — you occasionally see it in city neighbor-hoods — but it is more visible in smaller aggregates rather than larger ones. In a way people tend to mind each other's business in these places. This tendency has its good and bad points. Newcomers from cities accustomed to anonymity usually feel put upon by the lack of privacy in small towns. Old-timers are used to it and look upon their interest in other people's affairs as helpful. And their interest can be helpful, especially when a person has a problem that needs community-wide recognition. For example, in one town we heard about a man who was partially crippled and grossly overweight. His entertainment and so-cialization consisted of driving his car around town several hours a day waving at friends and seeing the sights up and down the town's two main streets. When he had to shop for food, he only had to drive up to the store and honk. A clerk would come out, take his order, fill it, and carry it out to the car.

City folks, new to the small town scene, are often dumbfounded by the amount of gossip that circulates around town. A casual trip to town to pick up a quart of milk can take a couple of hours. Everybody in town has a word or two to say. A casual hello won't always do. Encounters usually pull forth comments about the weather, dismay at the news of a marriage on the rocks, the fact that someone saw your teenage daughter speeding through town, a promise to come by and visit, and sighs about the price of meat and coffee. Day after day, year after year, these conversations go on. Slowly you get to know a lot about people.

It is hard to put your finger on this phenomenon of a family feeling — to explain how it comes about, and why it occurs in some places and not others. We have noted that the people in the communities in which it is most evident have these common characteristics: they've been together a long time, generation after generation; they've shared both good and bad times, prosperity and depression and wars; they possess a profound understanding of the needs of other community members: no person is left alone in a time of personal crisis; they share a regard and respect for their countryside and the character of their town; they think their town is the best. While they may squabble among themselves at times, none would trade their community for any other.

In the stories you are about to read, you will meet two towns that have always been like families. Stump Creek and Adrian may be somewhat unique because they are former coal company towns, but they certainly fit the criteria noted above. The situation confronting them now is how to keep that sense of family intact while they master the skills necessary for self determination.

On the other hand, the urban people that have come to Cerro Gordo to build a new town from scratch are fully aware that they have never experienced such a sense of community. You will understand when you read the Cerro Gordo story that building a community from the ground up is hard. A community is an organic form. You can't idealize how it should be. It has a life of its own. Just like a family, you live with the folks, enjoy them, tolerate them, share their miseries and their joys. A good community, like a good family, won't let you down — and that's worth a lot.

Stump Creek
as Kramer as Our Town

STUMP CREEK, PENNSYLVANIA

Ninety-five wood frame houses perched on a hillside. One hundred and forty-two people. Families with kids. Old folks. Stump Creek is near the center of Pennsylvania. It's what is called a "coal patch," a community that sprang up around the entrance to a deep vein bituminous coal mine. The Kramer mine closed in 1959. But the town was apparently more than a place for miners to live, because it is still there. Kramer was originally the name of both mine and town. It became Stump Creek in connection with what appears to be a post office shuffle. Townspeople acknowledge the new name, but don't much like it. We are told they think it sounds too much like "hillbilly" stuff. They still refer to their town as Kramer.

The people! They are something. They remember. Not just old times for the nice feeling it gives. Old times because that's the way they live. Stump Creek is getting famous now because the people are going to buy their town. They are being helped to political and economic "majority" after having been isolated as tenants in a company town for over half a century. There are two questions: What do they have to do to become independent? What do they have to leave behind?

It's kind of like poking around in a fire that looks dead. You do that and, sometimes under the ashes, you find embers that are still alive. The fire isn't out at all. It's just waiting. It's called "laying low."

Stump Creek recently has attracted a lot of journalists — including us. One of the phrases that some of them have used to describe the place is "ghost town." The use of those words to describe a community which is inhabited by 142 flesh-and-blood souls is at least biologically inaccurate. But the fact the term was used tells a lot about what is regarded as the minimum criteria for "life." In objective terms, if you compare Stump Creek with other small towns, there are some conspicuous differences. Among the most prominent is the absence in Stump Creek of any kind of commercial enterprises except for a tavern at the foot of the hill and a tiny candy factory down the road a bit. There are no places to buy things for miles. There are no parks. Most of the streets are unpaved. The buildings show the marks of years of neglect. From almost any criterion that can be measured and is commonly used to determine worth, Stump Creek is without value. Which is to say, dead.

73

But the people, and their beliefs, are another story. Here are 142 people who love where they live, and in the ways of small rural groupings, take care of one another. They share, to a high degree, commonly held belief systems and values. Though they live in what is referred to as an "economically depressed area" and have few of the advantages taken for granted by most middle-class Americans, they choose to stay where they are, and will go to a considerable effort to preserve their way of life.

It is a mark of our time, and its confusion of values, that we are able to assign the phrase "ghost town" to a place as alive as that. The Stump Creek residents know more about "alive" than the rest of us.

FIRST THERE WAS THE MINE

First there was the mine. It was called Kramer, and it was owned by a subsidiary of the Erie Railroad, the Northwest Mining Exchange. While the rest of the mines in Jefferson County, Pennsylvania, were in a decline that would eventually shut them down, on March 4, 1921, the fathers of the Erie Railroad put 10 men to work in the new Kramer mine, digging fuel for steam locomotives. The mine was leased by the Peabody Coal Company who operated it and built the town. By 1935, the 10 men had increased to 1,200; they worked the mine three shifts around the clock.

Stump Creek was intended to be the last word in company towns. Each of the 104 houses had concrete foundations. All of them were single-family residences, which was unusual for the type of town. They were built with two exterior walls — normal siding, and under it, a second sheathing. Each house had running water, also an unusual feature at the time, and the 10 houses built in "Bosstown" for the mine foremen, had indoor toilets as well. The rest had outhouses.

During its ownership by the Northwest Mining Exchange, the town was managed by the mine superintendent who had something approaching complete control. The people in Kramer were fortunate in that during most of that period, the superintendent was a benevolent and caring gentlemen by the name of Clyde Buhite, whose names is still a legend in the town. His interests ranged from personally seeing that lawns were mowed and outhouse paths kept neat and tidy, to organizing the best baseball team in the county, as well as the town's Boy and Girl Scout troops. He attended to any needed repairs immediately. The people took much pride in their town. To live there carried status. There was a long waiting list for workers' housing — and there were few vacancies.

First there was the mine. Then there were the miners. Though the list of residents' surnames contained over half that were clearly of northern European extraction and were American-born, the rest were immigrants from a remarkable variety of countries. An analysis of the population during the period of mine activity shows heavy counts of Poles, Lithuanians, Italians, and Slavs, in that order, with representative Germans, Croatians, Ukranians, Swedes, Dutch, Russians, Austrians, Irish, Greeks, and Hungarians. Many of the residents who were born in this country were first-generation natives.

We weren't there when the picture opposite was taken. It was supplied to us by the town project office after our visit, but it looks to us like a fair representation of the people of Stump Creek, Pennsylvania. By now, these people are probably used to looking at cameras. Their effort to rehabilitate their one-time coal company town has attracted a fair amount of attention. Below the picture is a sketch of the town's layout, also supplied by the project office. As you can see, the town has no business district. Public facilities are pretty much limited to the old school building (which now houses the town's new community library; school age kids are bussed elsewhere), the ball field, and the rod and gun club which, as far as we were able to tell, is a place for the men to gather and play cards — that is when they aren't using the school basement. Square 162 on the left side of the map, labeled "Community House," is where the town project office is located, and it comes as close as anything to being a town hall. Next door is "The Idea House" which was the first house to be renovated, an effort which involved a number of local people and served to show the rest that it really could be done. Empty squares represent houses undergoing renovation or waiting their turn and unoccupied at the time the map was drawn.

VILLAGE OF
STUMP CREEK

Stump Creek was a melting pot. The people in it were working stiffs. They had little and worked much. No one gave them anything. One supposes they had no expectations beyond an opportunity to work at their share of the dream that made America, in the first half of this century, a place of great hope. They brought their ways with them. A former Stump Creek school principal remembers hearing thirteen languages in a classroom of thirty children. The cultural tensions that tore other Pennsylvania coal towns to pieces had subsided by the time Stump Creek reached its steady population of 500. The relatively small size of the community made it possible for all the residents to establish personal relationships with other townsfolk. Under the watchful and paternal eye of Mr. Buhite, social disorder was practically nonexistent.

Imagine or remember those years during the thirties. The depression was on. The total U. S. population was 122 million, 13 million of which were unemployed. In New York City, builders had just finished the Empire State Building and the George Washington Bridge. Pearl Buck's *The Good Earth* was the national bestseller. There were three million radios in the country and Mickey Mouse had just made his debut. Prohibition was over. The New Deal was about to begin. Amelia Earhart was preparing to make her transatlantic flight. The average American's longevity was fifty-nine years.

Here is how it was in Stump Creek, as told by the people who were there. The following remembrances are taken from *Stump Creek as Kramer,* a publication prepared by Stump Creek residents.

THE MINE

Of course, the most important thing in town was the mine. The morning shift got up at 5 A.M. washed, dressed and had a light breakfast. The elevator — or "cage" as everybody called it — took them down the 350 feet to the work site where it took another half-hour to get ready to work. Because miners were paid by what they produced not hours on the job, they frequently took no breaks — not even for lunch. If they could manage it, they ate a sandwich while they worked. Shifts operated from 7 to 3; 3 to 11; and 11 to 7.

The miners carried a 7 to 9 lb. battery on their backs to provide the current for their safety helmets. Earlier, of course, their work was lighted by the carbide lamp on their hats. In the 30's they bought their own pick and shovel, plus rock bits, coal bits, dynamite and caps. They eventually wore safety shoes and knee pads, the latter because the clearances were sometimes only 30 inches. Many men chewed snuff; no smoking was permitted due to mine gas. If they needed to go to the toilet, they went where they were.

During the winter if a wet place was being dug, the miners' clothing froze. If it was zero outside, it ranged between 10 degrees and 30 degrees in the mine. The icicles along the shaft were sometimes as big as a man's leg.

All mining was hard work, but the "butterfly" was one of the worst places to work. It was really low and wet, being under Knarr's swamp.

There were rumors that if you changed your politics from Democrat to Republican, you could get to work outside jobs. It also helped if you were a good baseball player or were in the band. It was thought that a few on the payroll not only didn't load coal — they didn't do anything!

Because the Kramer mine was one of the last to open in this area, nearly all the men they hired had previous experience, coming from Punxy, Elinora, Cascade, Irton and even the hard coal regions. Most of the earliest bosses were Johnny Bulls: English and Welsh. But as more of the Poles, Slavs and Lithuanians studied with the instructors who came from Penn State and took their exams, they, too, were promoted.

If the power went out, as it sometimes did, the miners had to walk up 100 flights of steps — or from the safety shaft up behind Stratiff's near the bony pile. When they reached the top, the miners rushed the two miles to the wash house so they could take a warm shower. The shower room was kept rather clean for the number of men who used it. There was also a block 4 feet high and 3 feet by 3 feet square that they stepped on to prevent athlete's foot.

They checked out at the lamp house, as they had checked in, and started the long walk home. Kids would frequently come to meet the miners — partly because we were glad to see our father return, and partly to get what was left in his lunch bucket.

Supper would be served as soon as dad arrived. Although we had chicken on Sunday, meat was rare on the other nights because you had to buy it. There was always plenty of food, but it was primarily home grown vegetables, potatoes, and homemade bread. (If we ever got store-bought bread, we regarded it as cake.)

When the mines were closed, both fathers and children picked coal. The Company didn't object. Very few people bought coal in those days. What we picked as waste was better than what you can buy today.

Few kids were allowed to play down by the mines because of the great danger from the railroad cars. Sometimes though, we did play in the sandpile, watch the miners descend in the cage, and get water from the spring. We were fascinated by the rock-lorry as it traveled on its cable and tracks from the tipple to the dump. A bony pile was first started close to the mine, when it filled up, they began the one at the west end of town, its present location. Even though it caught fire spontaneously and its sulphurous stench sometimes blanketed the town, the bony pile area was still the lovers' lane. It was the only deserted place around where the neighbors wouldn't see you.

Sadness, too, was part of living in Kramer. Many families were touched by the hazards of working in a mine. The big Whistle that marked the change of shifts went almost unnoticed by us until it sounded when it wasn't time. Then we waited, knowing it was an accident. Was it bad? Would it be your house they would come to? Despite the sadness, we learned the value of friends, of appreciating neighbors who help, and not to give up — not to be overwhelmed even by tragedy.

SCHOOL

The school was built in 1923 for eight grades, 80 kids in each of the four rooms. Among the early teachers were Mamie Buhite for first and second grade, Mrs. Rider for third and fourth, Ira Bailey, Walter Pifer and Mr. Snyder for fifth and sixth; and Vinton Killer for seventh and eighth. Two of the first four lived in town: Mrs. Buhite and Mrs. Lumberg. There were always

77

two grades in the same room — which caused certain problems. Chances were that someone in your own family was also there with you, and if you got into trouble at school your brother or sister came home and tattled. That meant you got it at home, too — and if you slapped the tattle-tale you got another lickin' for hitting.

Was there ever a child who attended our school who didn't love Mr. Bailey? On the first day of 6th grade he would look enormous to most of the kids. He'd rub his prominent stomach and say to the class, "Do you know why my stomach is so big? I eat little boys and girls for lunch!" And we'd believe him — for a while. But we came to find out he was one of the kindest, warmest men we could ever know. At lunch time he stood lifting a never-ending line of children on his shoulders to see an egg-laden nest. He played baseball with us, showed us a beaver dam down on East Branch, and on song days would open the windows and tell us to sing K-R-A-M-E-R and "There Was a Little Hen That Had a Wooden Leg" so loud we would shake the windows at the tavern.

Students would have to carry coal and help make the fires in each of the classrooms. It was sometimes so cold we kept our coats on half the day. Some of the cleverer boys would try to smother the fire so it would smoke and make the teacher send us home.

Kids in Kramer were remarkably healthy — even though it was common in some families to miss 30 or 40 school days a year. This was usually because there weren't enough clothes to go around when some of them were being washed —not because of illness.

A perfect attendance record was of special pride, and those who had several years of perfect attendance were severely tempted to go to school when they shouldn't have. One girl with 8 attendance seals wore extra clothes to hide her chicken pox — thereby infecting the whole school.

The biggest school event of the year was the Christmas play, directed every year by Mamie Buhite. The first four grades would put it on, with crepe-paper costumes for shepherds, wise men, angels, clowns, elves and jack-in-the-boxes. The play usually depicted the Nativity plus a different additional story every year. Kids worked for weeks at memorizing their lines. It is remembered with gratitude that Mrs. Rachel Pudlo made costumes for many children who wouldn't have had them otherwise.

Even the toy band played; if you couldn't make it on the triangle you got demoted to the rhythm sticks. It was an enviable responsiblility to be trusted with the tambourine or cymbals.

There was also an exchange of 10 cent gifts, usually coloring books and crayons.

The daytime performance was for the upper grades, while the one in the evening was for parents, relatives and anyone who wanted to pay 25 or 50 cents to help defray costs. If a kid's parents didn't come he was heartbroken.

After the play many of us went home to decorate for the holiday. The Sunday before, the fathers and kids went to cut the Chirstmas tree, having picked it out months before. Sometimes we had to drag it 3 or 4 miles to get it home, but no matter how big it was, it went in the living room. We didn't have too much to put on it. No electric lights or fancy ornaments although we made paper chains in school and strung popcorn and cranberries at home. The decorations of Santas and wreaths made for the windows at school were brought home and hung in our windows. Down in Bosstown some had wreaths with red electric lights which many of the rest of us went down to stare at and admire.

The family usually gathered at 6:30 or 7 o'clock for our Christmas Eve supper. Its specialties included sauerkraut, pierogies, nut rolls, poppy seed rolls and a variety of fish — primarily smelts and bakala. (For those of you who don't know, bakala is dried fish which has been soaked in water for 4 days, gets thick and is sold primarily in Italian stores.)

Later we went to midnight mass.

SICK

Being hurt or sick was a serious matter. One boy broke his arm when he fell from the diving board over at East Branch. His older brother carried him all the way to Dr. Cooper's office. The boy got fixed up, but he got a beating when he got home because they had to pay the doctor $2.00.

Dr. Cooper — and later Dr. McGinley — was called Sawbones by the people there. The office was upstairs in the building that now houses the post office.

Doctors in those days not only treated patients, but dispensed medicine. Mothers would frequently wash out the cough medicine bottle and send the kids to the doctor's to get a refill.

It was a rare occasion to go to a dentist, partly because it cost money — and partly because you had to get to Sykesville to see him. It wasn't so bad hitchhiking up there, but if he pulled teeth or did anything drastic it wasn't much fun trying to get a ride back. Usually when a tooth was pulled, it was done at home.

Midwives did most of the work in delivering babies, but the doctor was still called. Children were sent to a neighbor's house until the doctor left, but when they saw him coming with two suitcases they knew they were getting a new baby. For a long time the kids thought the baby was in the second satchel!

When the baby was two weeks old the Catholics would have big christening parties with all the relatives invited. And this was whether the child was the first or the 12th in the family. It was held primarily to solicit presents, which were either money or baby clothes. (If the father was often seen in the tavern, the presents would be mostly clothes.) If the family didn't have an heirloom christening dress, the godmother would buy the baby's outfit. But all other garments that the family supplied were either hand-me-downs or homemade — including the diapers.

BIG FAMILY OCCASIONS

In several houses one of the high points of the year was the making of rootbeer. The whole family worked on the project. The kids rewashed all the old ketchup bottles, the mother mixed up the batch, and the boys (and father) did the capping. Everybody borrowed Stankovick's capping machine, it was the only one in town. Our homemade rootbeer seldom had any fizz because we drank it before it ever fermented. It was real sweet — but we loved it.

79

Other kinds of drinks were also made here, especially home-brew and wine. One father made home-brew in a crock. It had to set for a couple of weeks until the yeast worked. The foam would come to the top — which the kids would scoop off and drink. Sometimes it wasn't mixed right or the pressure was too great and the bottles would blow up. The dads were always anxious to get the brew into bottles so they could start to drink it.

A number of people also made wine. A few people would grow their own grapes, but it was never enough. The town sometimes bought as many as 100 crates of grapes from a truck that would come through. The driver would open up the crates for the men's inspection — and give the kids some to taste. Most of the houses that made wine in barrels would have wine clubs in their basements. The men would come there after the tavern closed at midnight — or on paydays — and drink wine while they played brisk and poker or bocci in the daytime. They also sold wine for 40 or 50 cents a quart. Some ladies would pay kids 10 cents to buy them a quart, but if their husbands found out and told the wine owner not to sell any more, the kids would be told to say it was for someone else.

In addition to getting new shoes, we also celebrated Easter by coloring eggs with onion skins, coffee grounds, or food colors. The kids also got marshmallow bunnies; we never saw any chocolate ones. On Easter Saturday the priest came to the community hall to bless a sample of the special food, plus poppy seed rolls, nut rolls and wine. At about that time we made horseradish, too. Everybody grew their own, and when you ground it up and couldn't control your tears anymore, you gratefully were relieved by somebody else.

Duckin' Days were important to the Greeks. They visited each other's houses in long white robes and big orange hats. Easter Monday was men's day and Easter Tuesday was women's.

They threw water at each other, drank and ate traditional Easter foods. This was an adults-only celebration but the kids would sneak around to watch and listen. The kids were fascinated but mostly scared.

KIDS ACTIVITIES

Even though we didn't have a playground or fancy equipment, there was always plenty for the kids to do. When it rained or at night we played cards or jacks; Helen Rokosky could play pinochle, hearts and rummy before she could read. Outside we played Hide and Seek, Hit the Boot, Run Sheep Run, Mother May I, baseball and marbles. And were we good at walking on stilts! Sometimes we had to go up on porch steps to get on, but then we could run and even jump over fences!

The area back of the Felix home, now occupied by Shirley Kelichner, was known to everybody as Woodville. The girls would make play houses there. They swept out a spot between some trees and hung old clothes out on the branches. Their furniture including bed springs was dragged from the dump, and they canned ink berries and milk weeds for pickles. Those woods were a great place to pick your Mother's Day bouquet of wild violets. There used to be a tree there inscribed with "Tom Mix's Horse Died Here". . . and a date. We always wondered if it were true. I wonder if that tree is still there? I wonder if people remember who Tom Mix is?

We don't know quite how this got started, but one thing the girls did a lot was making "graves" in the woods. They would bury a little object — an old piece of jewelry or shiny stone — and then decorate the small mound with colored glass, lucky stones — or even real flowers. Some made them of clay with little clay crosses on top.

Occasionally they didn't bury anything — just spent nearly a whole day finding a good spot and making the "grave" pretty. There might be 6 or 7 graves in one place. On another day they'd go out and try to find somebody else's graves and mess them up. Even boys did this: they didn't make any but they'd go looking for them. When we found some we'd report it at school and when we could tell what it looked like and where it was, the ones who made it would admit it. If it took too long for a grave to be found — and sometimes it was several months — we gave clues. Nobody wanted to have made a grave that remained intact!

We occasionally took what we called "vacations." We'd start at 7 o'clock in the morning with our box lunch and go to Knarr's dam. There would be a wiener roast in the afternoon. Some went swimming but a lot of kids didn't know how to swim. Even so, water accidents were uncommon. It was fun just to play in such a lovely place.

In the winter the big activity was sledding down the miners' path on hunks of cardboard or linoleum. A few kids had toboggans made from tin and turned up in the front. Some had real sleds, but the miners' path was too steep for them and those kids frequently used cardboard and linoleum just like the rest of us.

We can remember that the miners strongly objected to sledding on their path because it became so slippery for them to walk. The miners would ash the hill to keep the kids away but the kids would pick the ashes off and cover the spots with fresh snow. The miners got maddest about it on Saturday nights when some were drunk and would fall down.

We also went ice skating at Knarr's dam, building big fires and having great fun. For those who didn't have skates, a crushed tin can on each foot worked almost as well. Some made skis out of wooden barrels with old leather belts attached to put your feet in.

Up on the hill we also made snow forts out of square blocks and had regular battles. The sides were more or less even, although each side picked the littlest or weakest kids last.

When we were outside playing, we always had to listen with one ear to hear if we were being called home. If our mothers called, we could take it a little easy —but if the old man yelled, then we ran like hell. If they had to come hunting us, look out. Then we really got a licking.

A COMPANY TOWN

The company saw to it that the town was neat and clean. Particularly when Mr. Clyde Buhite was here, Kramer was a model. The houses, toilets, garages, roads and vacant lots were maintained by the company; they even hauled away

81

garbage. In the 30's rent for the bungalows was $6 a month and for the big houses $12 with both water and electricity free. House shingles were stained; foundations and even some tree trunks were whitewashed. The company kept repairmen in town permanently. If something broke you immediately reported it to the carpenter at the shanty and it would be taken care of. Windows were puttied every winter. Once a year there were garden competitions: prizes of $25, $15, and $10 were awarded for the best lawn, the best flowers and the best vegetables. People were so protective of their yards that some erected wire fences — even barbed wire — to keep out the kids.

Families were large. Sometimes there were 4 children in one room, two in each bed, although in the winter they frequently chose to all sleep together just to keep warm. Because the small houses were so crowded there was always a waiting list for the big houses. The Sitosky family waited for 10 years to get out of a bungalow. Many families also kept boarders in the basement. You had to have a good reputation to get a house and it helped if the father was a ball player. But you were carefully screened as to your previous background, especially that you were a hard worker, paid your bills and were clean. People seldom moved out when the mines were really producing; vacancies were caused by death. If you were fortunate enough to get another house, you carried the furniture with you. There wasn't much by today's standards: beds and dressers, icebox, stove, table and chairs, and the dynamite boxes you used as benches, storage chests and tables.

Kramer families bought from the company store across the highway, Marino's where the post office is now, and Fred Torretti's at the top of the hill. All offered credit. The company would deduct what was owed the store from the miner's pay; if he owed more than he made his balance sheet had a wavy line at the bottom which the miners called "getting a snake." Miners were paid every two weeks, and the company store lured them with shoes, furniture, fabrics, stoves, clothing, etc. in addition to food. Your credit was good as long as you had a job. It was the store's loss if somebody stopped work while he owed a big bill. At Marino's many people remember that they could seldom buy bubble gum there: Mr. Marino said it was bad for your teeth. Toretti's sold not only groceries (keeping their records in Italian) but also served as a local finance agency. Mr. Torretti provided loans for cars — at no interest — and also would cash war bonds. (If the owner wanted them later, he would exchange them.) When Fred died, Cuddy and Dorothy took over with a reduced stock and variety — mostly canned goods. They kept the store open until 1968.

A butcher also came through periodically, pedaling poor quality meats and other leftovers from his DuBois store. Used furniture and household goods passed from family to family as newer merchandise was added.

Mr. Buhite wanted the people to be proud of themselves and their town. He decreed that pig pens, chickens, even fences had to be moved. He made the rules and everybody went by them. Some people had already arranged to keep cows at nearby farms, doing all the feeding, bedding and milking themselves. One lady sold her cow to buy a son's graduation suit: he was the first of the 8 children to graduate from high school. Fathers generally didn't approve of

82

education. When you were 16 you went into the mines or the area factories: the silk mill in Reynoldsville, the shirt factory in Sykesville, the Cameron TV tube plant in Reynoldsville, and the Sylvania plant in Emporium. Only the Olsens, Lumbergs and Buhites went to college. It was enough of a problem to walk to Sykesville to high school every day. But back to Mr. Buhite.

Mr. Buhite was not only the company's most important representative in town he was a friend to the people. He mingled with them and cared for the whole family — starting Boy Scouts, Girl Scouts and the baseball team. He saw to it that the ball field was maintained and accompanied the players on trips to Dayton, to Youngstown — even to the big game in Washington, D.C., in 1938 when they won the championship of the J.C. League. It was a good team, winning pennants regularly. Jimmy Forrest was the manager for most of the 30's. If a player hit a home run, he also earned a whole carton of Wheaties. A big parade usually celebrated the team's victories; it was led by the band, and joined by many of the residents.

The Kramer Band was one of the best around. It had about 50 members, men, women, girls and boys — all taught by Mr. Rutherford. Their grey and gold uniforms were a welcome and familiar sight throughout the area.

KOVALCHICK BUYS THE TOWN

In 1949, the buildings and land that constituted the town were sold to a local real-estate corporation operated by the Kovalchick family. The various members of this family, at one time, owned or controlled seventeen such towns in the state of Pennsylvania, collecting rent on the houses and doing very little else. The fate of the town as a physical entity thus passed from the paternalism of Northwest Mining Exchange and Clyde Buhite, to the benign neglect of one Michael Kovalchick.

On May 13, 1959, the Kramer Mine was closed for good. Though there had been a decline in mine activity for years, and in the preceeding three, workers who had not been laid off were put on reduced time, the closing of the mine stunned residents. But even the collapse of their source of livelihood did not set off an exodus. Most stayed. They worked at whatever they could get, and they passed tips to each other about any jobs they heard about. Whatever it was about Stump Creek that made them happy in the best of times, kept them there still.

During the years following, the people who could find jobs more or less nearby — sometimes they were as far as seventy miles away — stayed in Stump Creek and drove to work. Others left the town for distant cities, most of them thinking of Stump Creek as "home." Without the full-time attention and work crews of Northwest Mining Exchange, houses began to go to pieces. Those who could did their own repairs. Some couldn't. The water system began to function intermittently. The town water tank, once a proud landmark, leaked. The pipes were broken and corroded with age. There were days when there was just a trickle of water. There were days when there wasn't *any* water. The Kovalchicks were implacable. The rents were the lowest available. At those prices, they could afford no frills. An occasional can of paint was as far

83

they would go toward capital improvement. By 1972, 142 of Stump Creek's best were still there, and it looked as though they'd stay as long as the town was upright. But Michael Kovalchick had started to think of selling. A group called the Institute on Man and Science was interested in buying the town.

INTERVENTION

The Institute on Man and Science, located in Rensselaerville, New York, is a nonprofit "educational center concerned with new approaches to critical and social problems." One of the things the institute does is conduct demonstration projects. One of the areas of its concern is small communities. In the fall of 1972, the institute was talking to Michael Kovalchick, among others, about buying the town as a first step toward restoring it to its one-time vigor. Michael Kovalchick was listening.

In a subsequent publication, the institute listed the characteristics that made Stump Creek a good place to do its work:

A population sufficiently large to make possible some baseline sense of community, yet sufficiently small to allow for comprehensive effort with very limited resources.

A beautiful and distinct geographical setting and close to a 4-lane highway and within a State-determined growth area.

A proportian of some 50% of the rehabilitable homes presently unoccupied —allowing for community planning and a renewal of population without new construction.

A set of some 100 houses which are structurally sound and basically appealing.

A general similarity (in terms of physical, social, governance, and economic characteristics) to other declining small towns built by companies and/or centered on an industry which has died or left.

A sense by almost all residents of physical decline and a clear desire to do something about it. For some a feeling that there is much to gain — for others a sense that there is little to lose.

A lack of obsolete public works. While Stump Creek lacks many physical support systems (e.g., sewage), it is similarly not burdened with things which are obsolete or outmoded.

The presence of concerned, active and capable residents, some with a capacity and willingness to assume leadership.

A meaningful sense of revitalization, in that there is something to restore. Residents recall with pride the earlier days of mining activity. There are feelings of time and place on which to build.

The institute's scheme was to purchase all the property, deliver to the town sufficient money and expertise for revitalization, work with residents to encourage and train resident leadership that could sustain what was started, then withdraw, selling rehabilitated homes to residents at prices they could afford and common property (streets, undeveloped land, the old school site) to a resident-controlled nonprofit community development corporation. By June of 1973, a deal had been worked out with Michael Kovalchick, with the participation and approval of residents. Kovalchick was to receive $175,000. A regional nonprofit housing corporation was given title to the property — all the houses, inhabited and otherwise, seventy acres of unimproved land, and the water and other "public works." The Institute on Man and Science was in the small town revitalization business.

It is a tricky business. One doesn't just buy a town, nip in, remodel falling-down houses, then nip out. Though there was no question about the need for physical improvement, the extent and nature of the impact on human lives would decide how to proceed. The residents of Stump Creek knew they needed help. And the people from the institute knew they were dealing with a group of people who were a community in the fullest sense of that word — indeed in ways unmatched by the most "normal town" — despite the physical state of their surroundings. How to improve one without wrecking the other?

From the beginning, the institute's project staff conducted three distinct types of work: restoration; socio-political training of residents through encouraging maximum participation in all restoration projects; and beyond this, a continuous effort to learn as much as possible about the people of the town — their values and their special qualities.

As the project sets forth, we recognize that it carries clear and potent risks. Some are associated with project failures: Expectations of Stump Creek residents will have been considerably raised. If they were to be completely unfulfilled, the human costs will be high. The negative effects of holding out desirable things to people while denying them access to the resources needed to reach them are well known. . . . Other risks attend the possibility of success: The Project could start a dynamic, which once in motion, proves difficult to control. Rising values of the properties surrounding Stump Creek, for example, could lead to land-use patterns quite out of keeping with the community, its small scale, and its rural premises. . . .

TRIPLOG. *Leeper, Pennsylvania. Somewhere in the woods in central Pennsylvania. Jane Schautz said on the phone she lives in a forest. She isn't kidding. The house is tucked back almost out of sight of the road. There are weeds and a Volkswagen Ghia in the front yard. Jane comes to the door. She has red hair and blue jean overalls. We talk for about three hours. She tells us about Stump Creek, and about the new institute project she is working on in Dunbar, Pennsylvania, and something about the institute. As she talks it becomes clear that she understands the people in both communities in the way only someone can who has had much contact with the people and has much respect for them. It is in this conversation that we hear Stump Creek described in terms of a "family" for the first time. She tells us that one of the normal patterns, in cases where a single-industry town loses its single industry, is that the strongest members leave — they are the ones who are willing to take the risk of finding new work in an unfamiliar setting. But in Stump Creek it didn't happen that way. She tells us that the Stump Creek people aren't ambitious in the way Americans are supposed to be. They have another idea of how to live. She describes it as wanting to maintain a life in which they are free and unencumbered by the demands of "civilization." They aren't cut off from*

85

contemporary life — all the kids have the trappings of a TV culture, for instance — but these people won't be yanked along by the culture. They like being where they are and are willing to go to considerable trouble to stay. Lots of people left Stump Creek when the mine shut down. But those who remained were resilient and tough. She calls them "gutsy and bushy-tailed folks."

Jane Shautz arrived in Stump Creek to work in June 1973 as assistant project director, shortly after the purchase of the town was completed. Her co-worker, and project on-site director, Steve Pholar, arrived in August. Both were to spend full time in the town. Pholar was to live there during the week, returning to his family near Pittsburgh on weekends. Jane commuted to her house at Leeper. There was a lot of getting acquainted to do. Though it was clear that the people of Stump Creek wanted help, there were inevitable suspicions and there was uneasiness all around. After all, no one from the "outside" had ever exhibited any interest in the place, and certainly no one had ever approached residents to offer the kind of assistance promised by the institute. To some, it sounded too good to be true. There had to be a catch. Also, some were worried that any change in the community would obliterate the very things in Stump Creek that people cherished the most. Though the decision by residents to permit the institute to "intervene" in their behalf was a clear invitation, under the surface, feelings were mixed.

Institute people, aware that the revitalization of the town meant that their presence there had to be a temporary one, began from the start to build in their own obsolescence, a process that continues until the institute's withdrawal, which at the time of this writing, was scheduled for the end of 1977. During that first summer, the institute staff and advisors began an extensive series of house-by-house interviews, and established the Stump Creek Residents' Council.

The interviews were conducted in order to seek out all the residents of the town (not just those who would attend meetings), and learn as much as possible about their ideas and needs. In this initial series of interviews, and in a series conducted the following summer, the special qualities of the town began to make themselves visible in stated preferences and opinions. This material was, and continues to be of enormous importance to institute people in planning and assisting in decision-making.

The Residents' Council was formed as the first in a series of steps that would ultimately place all decision-making about the management of the community in the hands of residents. Such management, such decision-making was a wholly new thing for the citizens of Stump Creek.

The legal status of the community of Stump Creek is nonexistent. Despite the use of the word "town" in this book and elsewhere, the place is technically "an unincorporated portion of a second-class township." One of the assumptions in the revitalization process is that there exists some local apparatus capable of making — and enforcing — decisions. Significantly, the town has no habit or machinery of self-government. From its start, Stump Creek was personal property, and the responsibility for decision-making concerning its operation and future was that of its owners. For the first time, with the completion of the institute's work, the town's residents are to own property and will be required to make plans and decisions for themselves.

For obvious reasons, these responsibilities are not part of the habits of Stump Creek residents. They have never received a bill for property taxes. They are only generally aware of the agencies at the township, county, and state levels of government which have jurisdiction over their affairs as citizens and property owners. They have not attended public meetings for the purpose of conveying their wants and needs to elected officials. In this regard, they are not unlike an enormous number of American citizens who, for one reason or another, have declined to take an active part in the operation of local government and have become estranged and remote from its functioning. For the residents of Stump Creek, however, to make the transition from tenants in a dying company town to residents in a revitalized community, responsible for their own affairs, it was necessary that these new responsibilities be learned and assimilated into the cultural fabric of the town.

In our view, the most important aspect of the partnership of the Institute on Man and Science and the residents of Stump Creek is the creation of a political body that is a product of the unique social character of the place — and a reflection of its values. It is a delicate business for both partners. And it is risky, for there is no turning back. Once the success or failure of the enterprise may be determined (for us, this will be some point in time after the institute has withdrawn and it is clear that the town has been strengthened or diminished by intervention), it will be too late to restore affairs to their original condition.

The first council was elected by the people of Stump Creek in August of 1973. It consisted of seven members, none of whom had ever held public office of any kind before. These seven people, and those who have succeeded them, are also the officers of the nonprofit corporation, Stump Creek Residents, Inc., to which all of the residents belong and which manages the business of the community. This structure is as close as you can get to local government without incorporating as a town.

TRIPLOG. *Carol Long's house. Stump Creek, Pennsylvania. Carol Long is Stump Creek's "press relations" person. Since the institute's intervention, Stump Creek has been under the glass of a lot of reporters, most of them urban, most of whom tend to regard the place as quaint, if not peculiar. Residents, Carol Long included, have come to resent the implicit superiority of "city people with indoor plumbing who treat us like hicks."*

The little town is on a bluff above, and almost entirely out of sight of, the road. Coming at it from the north, there is a sign, "Village of Stump Creek," followed a little farther by what looks like unpaved driveways to the right; and above, a few dark-colored buildings. Farther on is a second — and it turns out, the principal — access to the town and a tiny sign which announces that the Stump Creek project is up the hill to the right. It isn't until one has passed it and looks back from the south, that the town shows itself as a "place." Even then, it doesn't show very much. A handful of dark buildings and a screen of trees. We drive up the hill. Even in its present condition, the town has a solid and peaceful quality about it. The houses are lined up in rows, each building some fifty or sixty feet from its neighbor and twice that from the one behind. And there is an expanse of mowed grass around the lot of them. Inside Carol's house there is a radio going, and someone hammering.

Carol Long gives the impression of someone who has had to learn to be wary, but would prefer not to be. She looks to be about thirty-four, has an open face and dark eyes. She is pleasant and invites us to come into her kitchen, but it is clear that we must convince her we mean well.

She tells us that before the institute bought the town and the idea of owning a house wasn't even a dream, some people in the town spent a lot of money fixing up their houses anyway. Some even went to the expense of putting in bathrooms. She tells us this was because most people didn't think of the houses as belonging to anyone else. They knew otherwise, of course, but they had such a powerful feeling that this was "their place" that on a day-to-day basis, they acted as though they owned the houses. Now many people are fixing up the insides of their houses in anticipation of being able to buy them. The first houses will be sold in another couple of months.

The institute has already put new shingle roofs on all occupied houses in the town, repaired porches, and put $500 worth of winterizing material into each house. Residents who decide to purchase their homes in the first group to be sold will pay an average of $3,200 for house and lot, with monthly mortgages comparable to present rents (about $80 per month).

Carol tells us that in lots of ways living here is like being in one big family. "There are only forty-seven families here, and most of them have lived here all their lives." She says that people come back to visit, "and they don't want to leave. And when they visit, they don't just visit with the ones they come to see, they make the rounds, and visit everybody!"

She tells us that church affairs are important here. Weddings are big social events. She says hers was a quiet affair, mostly family, "There were only 500 people." When her sister got married, "It was really something. We kept running out of paper plates, and had to set up more tables. They just kept coming. The tables took up so much of our dancing space that the band had to move onto the stage. It was a wonderful wedding. We didn't mind the extra people. And no one went hungry, even though we served almost 800. We'd planned on 450 but we figured they'd eat a lot, so we had fixed enough food for 1,000!" Weddings are so important that people who aren't invited go with friends who are. "But no matter what, everybody brings a gift."

Carol has two children of her own, and is deeply involved in the town's library program and homecoming activities as well as being a member of the Residents' Council and on "just about every committee in town." She thinks that the council is important and that it is getting stronger. She tells us that sometimes, when the council asks the institute for help, they get the problem back in their laps with the advice to work it out themselves. She tells us that they are "getting better at doing that."

The changes in Stump Creek are exciting — and they are sometimes wrenching. Weeks later we read in a copy of the **Stump Creek Re-Mined,** *the* *little town paper, something that Carol Long wrote later that month, on the day the old Kramer water tower was pulled down, so it could be replaced by a new water system.*

"I'm sitting here at the window looking up at the old water tank. I know that there are men and equipment ready to pull it over any minute. From the information I have, it will fall at such an angle that it will appear to be coming in my direction.

I remember it as a child, and many memories are coming back to me now as I look up there: playing ball in the field near there with the tank in the background; taking a dare to go up the ladder, and being caught by an adult and sent home to be scolded; playing beneath it in the summer when it was overflowing; sitting for hours watching it being repaired by . . . . There it goes! I heard a dull thud here in the house, and felt a little tightness in my throat. Out with the old and in with the new, can, as in this case, take away a little from childhood memories, but never are they completely erased."

TRANSITION: THE FAMILY THAT STAYS TOGETHER

In March of 1976, the first houses were offered for sale to the town's residents under arrangements developed by the residents themselves. Those who bought at this time became "charter residents." They paid $2.50 per square foot for the building, measured at its outside dimensions, and $.04 per square foot for the land. The cost included the new roofs put on the houses and winterizing, as well as the accrued per household assessment for the new water system ($5.00 per month).

Following the March deadline, available property in the town was to be offered on the open market. However, residents who later decided to purchase their homes, would have opportunities to do so at "charter resident" rates, to be computed on a square foot basis incorporating the investment in improvements up to that point.

Residents who wished to go on renting their homes were permitted to do so. Their new landlord, Stump Creek Residents, Inc., would have until December 1977 to bring all rental homes up to standard for plumbing and electricity. With this new policy, Stump Creek Residents, Inc. hoped to break even on rentals, with the rental price reflecting the cost of any improvements.

There were two aspects of the first sale that were of particular interest to us. The first was that any relative of charter residents who wished to purchase a home in which the relatives would continue to live was permitted to do so at the same rates that were offered to resident households. The second was that any charter resident of eighteen years of age or more was permitted to purchase one additional lot, with or without an empty house, either for their use or that of a relative or friend.

Keeping in mind that all the regulations concerning the sale of these houses and lots were worked out by the residents themselves, it is interesting to us that these special provisions were made to take care of the elderly, young, and non-resident family members in the sale. A total of thirty-six homes were sold by April of 1976.

For many Stump Creek residents the water tower was a symbol of their limits. During the years the town was owned by the Kovalchicks, the water system was a sometimes affair. Sometimes it worked; often it didn't, and there was nothing anyone could do to change it. Or so everyone thought. Finally, when the Institute on Man and Science purchased the town in order to improve and then resell homes to their occupants, the old tower was toppled. In its place is a new system, worked out, owned, and maintained by the citizens of Stump Creek. It is just one of a number of community improvements that will be managed by the homeowners of Stump Creek as they take up the responsibility of running their own town.

In the center of the page is a photograph of Joe Poy. Joe is a kind of legend in Stump Creek. He was, at sixteen years, the youngest community member to be elected to the Residents' Council. The day those photographs were taken, Joe Poy was at work on the renovation of one of the houses, working as a carpenter-trainee under a CETA program. We were told that this young man has also decided to purchase his own house in the town.

Perhaps the most impressive success to come out of the Stump Creek experiment is contained in what is to us an extraordinary document bearing the bland title: *The Revitalization of Stump Creek*. It is, in fact, the "blueprint" assembled by the residents themselves, bit by bit as they made decisions concerning the future of their community, and it incorporates in deceptively simple language the fervent dreams of the people of Stump Creek and much of the apparatus for realizing them. The content is diverse, ranging from a land-use plan and deed covenants to lofty but practical statements describing ethical standards for the community. The language on the first page sets the tone clearly:

In some ways, our plan is rather simple. Using certain straightforward means, we wish to: preserve a sense of small scale and closeness to nature . . . make and carry out many of our own decisions . . . set guidelines for living together that stress the value of human relationships . . . co-operate in civic matters. We could get fancier. But we do not wish to lose sight of these important goals. They are what make our journey toward renewal worth the taking.

Because this "blueprint" is a distillation of the accomplishments of the residents of Stump Creek, and because, in our opinion, it is a model that will have an impact and usefulness far beyond the village limits of Stump Creek, we have decided to include portions of it here.

The plan is divided into seven sections. The first deals with "Governmental Affairs," and consists principally of the by-laws of Stump Creek Residents, Inc., the nonprofit organization that will administer community affairs and holds title to all public property. Article III of the by-laws states:

The primary goal of Stump Creek Residents, Inc. is to manage and direct the public affairs of Stump Creek in such a way that the community best sustains and enriches the lives of its residents. In so doing, the corporation affirms:

the need to treat all residents fairly, avoiding favoritism of any kind;

the need to encourage all persons to participate in the public life of the community, recognizing that some people need special and sensitive encouragment to take part;

the need to affirm a democratic process that is open, honest and responsive to its membership — building a sense of trust between the community and its people;

the need to seek a broad consensus on decisions as greatly preferable to a majority vote determination;

the need, where possible, to stress a direct democracy — in which people represent their own intersts as preferable to a representative democracy, where some people speak for others.

The following article defines the community's membership policy and includes as voting members anyone sixteen years and over.

The second section deals with "Physical Affairs" and contains the land-use plan shown opposite and the "Protective Covenants" which are a part of the deed for each parcel of land sold, and which constitute the only legally binding aspect of the entire blueprint. Generally these covenants state that owners of property in the community must see to it that buildings conform to certain standards, that they are members of Stump Creek Residents, Inc., and are subject to public works assessments; and it defines certain land-use limits such as keeping of livestock, use of temporary structures, signing and so forth.

The third section is titled "Social/Cultural Affairs" and it is here that certain of the town's most cherished values get direct expression in the plan.

The community does not wish to become too large. Our general thought is to grow to a population of some 300-500 persons, inhabiting the original 100 homesites and perhaps a limited number of new dwellings.

We encourage a mix of residents in terms of age, income, religion, education, etc. Further, there is a willingness to accommodate and treat fairly all new residents, regardless of race, creed, or nation of origin.

There is a desire to continue some of the community activities that have been begun during the fix-up project. The library, newspaper, re-cycling project, and the annual homecoming are important ways of involving people. In particular, we will give stress to continuing to fix up the school building as a community center for government, local clubs and groups, recreation, etc. And we will do our best to insure that the school is seen as a place for everyone in Stump Creek. No family or individual should feel unwelcome there.

While certain activities will be created and maintained locally, we do not see, at this time, the need for many formal clubs and groups or for a local church. Indeed, there is value in our going to Sykesville, Punxsutawney, and elsewhere for these needs. It keeps us in touch with these other communities and helps to make sure that Stump Creek does not get too set-aside and set-apart.

While there is a desire to encourage participation and involvement, there is an equally important need to preserve privacy — not only of families but of individuals, too. No one should feel forced to participate, and people should not be made to feel uncomfortable if they are doing something — or not doing something — alone.

No one's affairs should become public gossip in ways that are malicious or harmful. Two cardinal rules for Stump Creek residents: 1) attempt to find out how true a nasty rumor is before spreading it further, and 2) never say negative things about a person behind his or her back that you are unwilling to say to their face. We cannot stop gossip in our town and probably wouldn't want to anyway. But we can make a distinction between gossip that is interesting and gossip that is harmful. We recognize that words can hurt just as much as sticks and stones.

In some ways, Stump Creek hopes to become a more "modern" community. We want to get rid of outhouses, fix roofs and porches, begin a store, start a local government. And, we want all our residents — and young people in particular — to have all of the benefits of life in the United States that are available to anyone else.

But, at the same time, we wish to preserve some aspects of the past of Stump Creek. These include ethnic food, customs, and celebrations and educational values of knowing about Stump Creek's history as a mining community. Perhaps most important, we wish to keep some sense of set-apartness — the sense that this community is quiet, sturdy, friendly, and in some ways, very stable.

The house on the left in the opposite photograph has been completely renovated. This means new foundation, new heating system, new plumbing, new kitchen and bath, new wiring, new roof, siding, and windows, complete insulation and interior finish. In the photograph below, Jessie Fye, the project secretary, is holding a sign which lists the names of the workers responsible, a number of whom were local residents — all were trained on the job.

The drawing shows the land-use plan worked out by Stump Creek residents. The following description accompanied the plan in the Stump Creek Revitalization Blueprint:

Our approach to land-use planning is to divide Stump Creek into 6 major zones, according to the map below. In brief, this plan specified that:

— Any new resident development will be concentrated in Section A, through the extensions of streets 1-6. This section has areas for sewage collection and recreation.

— Sections B and C cover all existing houses and will be limited in the future to this present residential pattern. One exception might be small open-spaces for picnics and play use maintained in the middle of residential areas.

— Section D will be a small game and wildlife conservation area — open to all residents in an undeveloped but managed state.

— Section E will be kept flexible for various uses, with the thought that economic activities be based here.

— Section F, which includes the school and is set aside as a separate parcel, will be maintained for the envisioned uses of the school itself — including community center, offices of the Stump Creek Residents, Inc., library, etc.

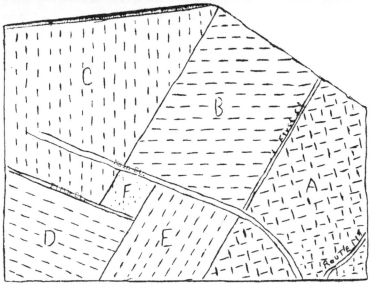

The sense of a large "family" in Stump Creek is important. In particular, young children should feel safe wherever they go in Stump Creek. We know each other and watch out for each other. And we band together when tragedy strikes in our midst or when external forces threaten us. These traits can continue only if new residents are made fully a part of the community.

"Economic Affairs" is the title of the plan's fourth section. In addition to stating that Stump Creek Residents, Inc., will enter the real-estate business by purchasing and operating all rented houses in the community, it describes additional interest in providing employment and services for residents as follows:

Small-scale economic activities are sufficiently desired that the community will consider certain forms of enticement to get new businesses established or old ones re-located. These include long-term availability of land . . . at no or little cost; favorable rates on water and sewage; community help in the construction of needed buildings.

Among the economic activities residents would most welcome are: a small furniture making shop; a greenhouse; a small foundry; a shop making machine parts under contract to a major manufacturer; a processing center for fruits and vegetables, including canning and preserving.

Also, a community store is welcome and will be initiated once the population level rises to some 250 persons. The store will combine sales of selected package goods with the component of a food co-operative, in which certain staples (e.g. sugar, flour) are purchased in bulk to reduce cost. It is anticipated that the store will be operated on a non-profit basis, established with investment shares of ownership sold in the community. This store will serve as the vehicle for other forms of trade which are desired in the community and need a central location. Also, it will attempt to help residents to group or combine their purchase of many major items (appliances, construction materials, etc.) to gain cost savings.

And this paragraph, which is perhaps the most interesting of all:

In general, economic exchange among community residents is not encouraged especially on a profit-making basis. The hiring of young people to mow lawns or baby-sit is considered desirable, but work done among adults should generally be kept on a co-operative basis, with the understanding that if you need help, it will be offered without charge. In Stump Creek, good business is no more important than good friendships.

Section five, "The Transition," describes how the institute will, over a period of more than a year, withdraw from the community, gradually selling out or simply signing over assets it controls in the community to Stump Creek Residents, Inc.

The last two sections deal with a definition of "charter resident" and the special arrangements that were made to enable residents in the town to be guaranteed of their own home at a price they could afford, and a choice of rental or purchase.

When it entered Stump Creek, the institute apparently made a promise to all residents that no one would go without housing for want of ability to pay. A further promise was made: The costs of community improvements of homes and public utilities, to be passed on to residents in the sale price of property, would be determined solely by the amount of loan money invested and which must be returned — but without including interest. Any grant money obtained would be used in full to lower these costs; the savings would be passed on to residents in the form of lower prices for houses.

What these promises meant were (1) that no resident would be forced to purchase a home, or would be forced to leave the community for lack of money; and (2) the institute would agree to walk away from the whole affair without having gained a cent in the operation. (Nothing was said about how much they might lose.)

How these promises were kept and translated into legal and accounting procedures required by various granting agencies and investors, not to mention the residents themselves, is a subject too complex to treat here and is not described, except in the barest outline in the blueprint. The plan concludes with a page for signatures and this parenthetical statement:

. . . When the plan is printed, space will be provided for everyone in Stump Creek to signify general agreement with the plan by actually signing a Charter Copy which could be placed on permanent display in the community. While the plan is not a legal document in any sense, and does not obligate anyone in any sense, it is important in suggesting a co-operate spirit. We would like representatives of all outside groups that have worked with us, including the Institute on Man and Science, Jefferson-Clarion Non-Profit Housing Corporation, and key state and federal agencies to sign also, — as a way of indicating their continuing support of our little town.

AFTERWORD: WITHOUT A GUARDIAN ANGEL

There is no doubt in our minds that what we encountered at Stump Creek is a unique situation. Though there are many depressed rural towns across the land in need of help, there are not enough Institutes on Man and Science to go around. And there are not very many public agencies with the vision and the freedom of movement to accomplish the whole job in any one town. Maybe there aren't any. It is clear as we read the institute's reports on the project that it is a private institution of remarkable vision and sensitivity. We can think of few examples of even change-for-profit where speculators gave any more than passing notice to the intangible qualities of the people and the landscape on whom and which they work change. And we can think of *no* not-for-profit examples. In contrast the Stump Creek experiment is an instance in which the entire operation is based on the pre-eminence of what we have come to call "the quality of life" — that peculiar and delicate product of people and a place rubbing up against each other for years and years. It is a fragile thing. Always changing, never visible except in bits and pieces, it must be *lived* to be understood. The people for the institute not only lived it, but based an entire plan for change around the objective of preserving it. We don't know if they have succeeded, because it's still going on. But they, and the people of Stump Creek, Pennsylvania, are to be commended for trying.

For a long time, we debated among ourselves about whether or not to use this material (it seemed almost too unique). It was something Jane Schautz said, and to which we take exception, that finally decided the issue. Jane told us that she didn't think it is possible for a small town to accomplish, without outside help, the kind of revitalization that Stump Creek is accomplishing with the help of the institute.

She may be right. God knows, when you see how much brainpower and grant money have gone into Stump Creek, it sounds like a modest statement. But if her statement *is* true, it is as gloomy as hell because it means that most small towns are doomed to whatever end unemployment, social dis-ease, political turmoil, and misuse of resources bring around. For those of us without a guardian angel, and no prospect for one, there has got to be a better answer than that!

The careful building of a strategy for change upon an understanding of the ways in which people prefer to live their lives is an enormously significant aspect in the Stump Creek story. The hundreds of hours that went into gathering and analyzing the information about the lives of Stump Creek residents were essential to understanding their motivations and hopes. It would be so in any community. The strategies for involving residents at every step of the way, and the development of a workable mechanism by which they could make binding decisions without having to incorporate as a legal town were both essential parts. Both are possible elsewhere. The need to involve all segments of the population in productive work toward an end is an important aspect. The library, newspaper, and historic commemorations in which children and elderly played such important roles could happen anywhere with the same good results.

There is a long and maybe painful distance that is being covered by the people of Stump Creek on their way from political isolation to becoming active participants in a direct democracy. They are trading a certain measure of rural bliss for the privilege of self-determination. But the distance they will travel, the lessons they will learn, and the price they will pay for the control of their community are no more and no less than the effort required in any community.

In Stump Creek, the past dependence of residents on the whim of some distant power is easy to see in the almost feudal relationship of tenant and landlord. The parallel is less apparent elsewhere. But it is there. Any place a community has put its future in the hands of political professionals, or makes its decisions solely on the advice of technical experts, or believes that democracy can function by periodic appearances of the electorate at the ballot box might just as well deed its physical assets to the highest bidder.

In short, there are valuable lessons to be learned in Stump Creek, and anyone who is concerned about the future of a small town somewhere would do well to pay them heed. It cannot be that the distance Stump Creek has traveled can be done only through the largesse of a guardian angel. For they are traveling to the self-determination, the democracy, that is the center of this country's spirit. And that is where we all want to go.

Hey! Johnny!
You Want to Buy This Town?

ADRIAN, PENNSYLVANIA

Down the road from Kramer is Adrian. Another coal patch town. Another Kovalchick town. The only other one, besides Stump Creek, that has sold. Only the Institute on Man and Science didn't have anything to do with this one. "Oh, terrific," we say to ourselves, "now we can compare one with the other. One where the people help. One where they do it themselves." Well, it didn't turn out to be quite that way. The people *did* buy their own homes in Adrian. And it's true, they didn't have any outside help. But they didn't really need any outside help. They had Johnny Miklos.

It's hard to describe John Miklos and do him justice. What you are about to read may make him sound like some kind of egomaniac. He isn't. The whole time he told us his story, and the story of his town, it was in a very matter-of-fact way. He's not exactly humble, because he is very proud of what has been accomplished in Adrian. And not exactly dead-pan, because he is lively and, in some ways, driven. He has high blood pressure. He's had one stroke, and before that, some mysterious ailment that lasted several days had him unconscious, bleeding from the nose and mouth, and the priest administering last rites. A week later he was out of bed putting up Christmas decorations in the church. "You can't keep him down," his wife Anna says, "something drives him." He says, "I've just gotta be doing things." But it isn't just a matter of keeping busy. It's something else. We don't know what it is. And we don't think John Miklos does either.

TRIPLOG. *Punxsutawney, Pennsylvania. Miklos is going to show us the way from Stump Creek to Adrian. He is of medium height. Close-cropped hair. We're expecting a Greek, but he doesn't look Greek. He has deep-set eyes, high cheekbones, and looks more like an Eastern European. Turns out he's Hungarian. His name is pronounced MICK-LOSH. We follow him home. Adrian sits on a hill. It's more imposing, better looking than Stump Creek. Steeper terrain. Nicer layout. Nice views through the village and around trees. It looks like there might be more money here. But not much more. There are a couple of big company buildings at the foot of the hill, more houses, and a big brick church on the top of the hill. We see no sign of commercial buildings,*

97

but it turns out there is a little store up the hill near the church, and a post office. Miklos's house is part way up the main street. It has been completely overhauled. New siding, new porch, aluminum window frames. The works. Some of the others have had similar treatment. Most of them haven't.

Adrian was built in 1888, just two years after the Adrian mine was started. It was built by the Rochester & Pittsburg Coal & Iron Company (or the R&PC&I). During the life of the mine, which lasted until 1941, a total of 36.5 million tons of coal was removed from the hill under Adrian. When the mine was closed, the town was sold by the R&PC&I to the Kovalchicks. There were 250 homes on the hill then. Some were single-family houses, some were duplexes. As in Stump Creek, the residents didn't know what would happen to the town. Many left to find work. Some of them stayed. John Miklos stayed. He was twenty-one then.

Miklos was then, as he is now, on the town's church committee. The parish priest, Father John Keating, asked John to go with him to Sykesville to see if Nick and Mike Kovalchick, the town's new owners, would be willing to continue the coal company's policy of providing free coal, water, and electricity to the Catholic church.

"So we went up and while we were goin' up the priest told me, he said, 'Why don't you ask him if you can buy your place?' So we went into the office and Mike and Nick said, 'What can we do for you?' So I told 'em that the R&PC&I were givin' us free coal and free water and electric, and would they do the same for us, for our church? And they said they can't see why not, why they couldn't do that, so after we got through, they even gave our priest $50 for his time, for comin' up, see? While we were there, Father said, 'Why don't you ask them, Johnny?' And Nick said, 'Well, if you have anything on your mind, let's get it off.' So I asked him if there was any chance my buyin' my house up here. And this Nick Kovalchick said there was no way for him to sell this house up here because they just bought the town. But he did say this, he said, 'Now, if we ever sell anything in that town, you people'll get the first chance to buy it.' "

That was in 1941. It might have been one of those promises people make to end a conversation. It certainly was hard to imagine in 1941 that anyone in Adrian would ever have enough money to buy very much of anything in the real-estate line. The people who lived there were poor sons and daughters of immigrant mine workers. They had earned $.25 a ton for loading coal down in the mines, or, if they were salaried, $8 a day for running equipment. Now many of them were earning nothing. Rents were $9 a month. There wasn't much spare cash for real-estate speculation. Nick Kovalchick was perfectly safe in making his promise. But Johnny Miklos remembered it.

Years later, in 1973, the water company in the neighboring town of Anita was dickering with Nick Kovalchick to buy the Adrian water system. Miklos got wind of it.

"The guy who was collecting the rent here, and everything, his name was Gabe Simon. I stopped him one day when he came here, and I told Gabe, I said, 'think that's a dirty trick what Kovalchick's doing to us.' He said, 'What d'you mean?' And I said, 'Y'know, he told me in 1941 that if he ever would sell

Most of Adrian is built on a hill. (In Pennsylvania it might be called a mountain.) The surrounding countryside is mostly rural with occasional small towns, the nearest of which is Punxsutawney, nicknamed "Punxy" by local people.

Miklos, who we thought would be Greek, turned out to be Slavic — Hungarian to be precise. His father was a miner at Adrian, and later Miklos followed him for a while until the child labor laws of the thirties forced him to work elsewhere. Miklos wants a better life for his own grandchildren and the town's other youngsters. The ballplayers in the top picture are at least two generations removed from the tunnels that lie empty, dark, and submerged in water under their feet. To them the twelve hour days, six days a week are the stuff of family mythology. It took those two generations for the people of this small place to outgrow their dependence on corporations and landlords and learn how they could have things their way. When Miklos proved they could buy their town and showed them how to go about it, they believed him. And now that they are homeowners, they can consider other improvements such as a playground for the smallest children and a post office in a shiny mobile home. But in any such enterprise, there is inertia to overcome — mountains of it — and in a community such as Adrian, where the people were first immigrants and then virtually indentured workers, resistance to change, any change, runs deep. The change from a company town to an independent community was a wrenching and painful one, and Miklos was cursed as often as he was blessed for his vision. It will take years for the people here to become thoroughly accustomed to their new situation.

At the top of the opposite page is a photograph of part of the Catholic church. Next to it is the parochial school, now unused. The children are bussed to public school in Punxsutawney. The church sits at the crest of the hill, near the center of the village — a position that reflects its importance in the lives of townspeople, if not its present state of activity. Though the place is scrupulously maintained by the town's church committee, the priest comes from another town, and the church is no longer the center of social and political affairs that it was when the town was full of miners' families. Across the street from the church and just a little down the hill is the town's tiny grocery store in the front two rooms of a modest-sized house. (The rest is living quarters for the store's owner and his family.) In front of the church is the community's new playground and around both church and the unoccupied school is an acre or so of grass. It is a commons area used by everyone. Because the town is old and autos are fairly recent here, the streets are narrow, winding; one gets the idea that this is very much a walker's town.

anything up here, we'd get the first chance.' So Gabe says, 'I'll tell you what,' he said, 'Don't do anything, I'll go down and see Nick and mention this to him.' So he went back down there and mentioned it to Nick Kovalchick, he said, 'Johnny's mad up there.' And he wanted to know why, and Gabe said, 'You promised them people that if you were ever selling anything you'd give them first chance.' 'Well,' he said, 'what is it?' He said, 'Johnny said he'd buy this water company.'

"I figured that was a chance, you know, to get in. Then maybe later, we could buy the town. Three or four weeks later this guy came back and said, 'Nick wants to have a meeting with you on the day that you're off.' Friday's my day off, I never work on Friday, so I told him I'd be down.

"I tried to get some men from up here to go down with me. And I couldn't get anybody to go down. Nobody wanted to go down. They figured it wouldn't happen, see? That he wouldn't sell, because that's just the way he operates. He's really rough, he is.

"So I went down to his office and Nick and his wife were there. And Nick says, 'What can I do for you?' And I says, 'I think you know what we're down here for.' He said, 'What're you after?' And I said, 'I'm after the water company you promised Anita. I don't think it was right, you promised us that if there was anything sold we'd get it.' 'Well,' he said, 'I'll tell you, I'm going to do better than that.' He said, 'Instead of selling you just the water company, I'm going to sell you everything. Town and all.' So, I didn't know what to say, then, you know? [Laughs] I said, 'What do you want for it, Nick?' Well, his wife was talkin' about $250,000 plus interest — around $300,000, for everything. Well, I thought, where am I going to get that kind of money? So Nick says, 'Well, I'll tell you what,' he says, 'you go back and see if you can come up with a price for this town.' "

It's to the credit of Nick Kovalchick that he honored his promise to Miklos, whether he remembered it or not. But it should also be kept in mind that in the thirty-two years since 1941, a great deal had happened. By the time the conversation just described took place, the Kovalchicks were talking with the Institute on Man and Science about selling Stump Creek.

John Miklos went home to try to figure out what price to offer Kovalchick, and how to raise the money. He asked the banks to appraise the town. They said that they could not do that. They had never heard of anything like this. Neither had the real-estate people. They wouldn't get involved either. Finally, Miklos appraised the town himself and came up with the figure of $140,000, for the buildings and the 193 acres on which they sit. Several weeks passed. Then Kovalchick sent a message up to Adrian with Gabe Simon.

"He said, 'Hey, you tell Johnny if he isn't here by next Friday to forget about it, we're going to sell it to somebody else. We've got people from Pittsburgh wants to give us $190,000 cash.' "

John Miklos had talked to the people in his town. Some of them wanted to buy. Some of them didn't. They told him to go ahead and see what he could do, that they would be behind him. The next Friday, Miklos took an attorney with him to Kovalchick's office. Nick Kovalchick's wife had died in the meantime, and in her place was his son, Joe. Nick put his cards on the table.

"When we talked to him that night, Nick says, 'Well, the best thing I can do is I'll come down to $160,000 plus interest.' That would be a total of $172,000 or $173,000, and three years to pay for it. So he asks me, 'What figures did you come up with?' I told him the best I could see was $140,000, and I told him all that was wrong with the houses. I told Nick, I said, 'Nick, I came down here with good intentions that you're honest to us, and that's the way we came down here, we want to be honest with you. We don't want to beat you, and I hope you don't want to beat us.' He said, 'Why?' And I said, 'You come up with a figure of $160,000 and I come up with a figure of $140,000,' I said, 'there's $20,000 there, let's split this $20,000. Let's make this $150,000.' Well he was going to go along with it. He was ready, he wrote something down on a piece of paper, but his kid called him on it, he said, 'Let's have a recess, Dad.' They went out. When they came back in the kid says, 'No, there's no way we can drop the price down, because somebody else is going to buy it for more money,' he said, 'but what I'll do, I'll give you four years to pay for it.' "

So they made the deal: $160,000 plus interest for the houses and 193 acres of land; four years to pay; one payment each year; the money to be raised as people purchased their homes. There were some conditions. They were imposed by Nick Kovalchick and are evidence of how well he knew the people he was dealing with. Both were pressure tactics. The first was that they would be given three months to raise the first payment of $46,000, and if they couldn't do so, Miklos would default and Kovalchick would sell to his Pittsburgh customers. The other was more subtle. Kovalchick knew that the people who had spent the most money and effort in repairing and improving their homes would be the first to buy and that the others would be less inclined. So he told John Miklos that if the number of homes sold was insufficient to swing the deal, and he was forced to repossess whatever property did not sell, he would move in all his junk and fill the remaining houses with undesirable people, and turn their dream into a nightmare. Kovalchick is in the salvage business as well as real estate and Miklos knew he could do exactly what he promised. Though the tactic was heavy-handed, to say the least, it worked. And John Miklos is the first to admit that without Kovalchick's threats hanging over the town, the people of Adrian might never have acted.

A nonprofit development corporation was formed to take title to the property, with Miklos as president. He and the other officers of the corporation began hunting for financing. They found friends at nearby Keystone National Bank. The bank was willing to provide mortgages for anyone in Adrian who wished to purchase their home, and even more impressive, it would require no down payment. The money was put into an interest-bearing escrow account and held until the annual payments were required. Prices for the homes were $4,500 for a full house and $2,250 for a half house (duplex unit).

Miklos tells us that they needed fourteen buyers by October of that year (1973) in order to make the first payment. After he got the first fourteen, he says he didn't worry any more. There are a couple of good reasons why he didn't. The first is that all rents were raised from $34 a month to $70. This was done as protection to insure that if houses didn't sell, there would still be enough income to make payments. But it also worked as a prod on reticent buyers who knew that for about the same amount of money, they could be buying their home. It was also announced that eventually, all homes would be put on the market by the corporation, which of course meant that renters might have to move. Two families continued to rent until March of 1974. By April first, everyone had bought their home.

Getting those first fourteen buyers, he says was rough. That was the hardest part. And they were afraid. They thought somehow, they would be cheated. John Miklos says, "Too many times, somebody beat 'em one way or the other, y'know?" Few of them had had any experience buying property. They had no idea what was involved; some had trouble understanding the process and language. More important, many of them had put their own hard-won savings to work installing bathrooms, remodeling kitchens, fixing the roofs on Nick Kovalchick's houses. And now they were being asked to cough up $4,500 or $2,250 for the privilege of staying! In the eyes of many, the thing was outrageous. The houses were *theirs*. Nick Kovalchick's name on a deed meant nothing. He was the man to whom they paid rent. But the houses belonged to them. They *lived* in them, some, all their lives. To have to pay $4,500 to maintain the status quo was like being held up at gunpoint. All the anger that had accumulated against the Kovalchicks' heavy-handed policies was suddenly directed at Johnny Miklos. They'd call him in the middle of the night. Someone put tacks on his driveway. They accused him of being in cahoots with the Kovalchicks. Rumors had it that he was in their employ. That the whole thing was a trick.

TRIPLOG. *Adrian, Pennsylvania. We take the camera and walk around the town. The sun is low and the light on the town is beautiful. We walk up the middle of the street. The afternoon has been warm for this time of year, and people are out. They call to Johnny from their porches. He waves and calls them all by first names. We tell him we'd like to take pictures of the people on their porches. So Johnny takes care of it. He says to them, "These people are from California. They're writing a story about Adrian. They want to take your picture." He doesn't ask them. He tells them. Everyone poses. We get the feeling they love him. Up by the church, there are four kids heaving a football around. Johnny orders them into formation for a picture without explaining our mission. The kids clown around. He shouts at them to quit messing up the picture, then grins at us. The kids go right on with their crazy poses. Everybody laughs.*

He shows us the church. All his life, the church has been important to him. He has tended the grounds around it for years. We stand in front of the door and he tells us a little about his life. His mother died when he was nine years old. He was the oldest of six children. A year later his father remarried a young girl, just eighteen and a year after that he died. Johnny was eleven. When he was fourteen, he went to work on the tipple at the mine, cleaning out cars. But he had to quit because the child labor laws went into effect, so he worked for the church as a janitor for a while. When he was old enough, he went back to the mine as a repairman on the tram. Then they raised the minimum age to

103

eighteen, so he had to quit again. He joined a WPA project and went to work "napping" stone. They give him a twelve-pound sledge and he broke up rock for road beds. In 1937, he went back to work at the mine and earned $3 a day. He worked there until the mine closed, then he moved to another mine, but went on living in Adrian.

He was always a hustler. He set up and ran a poolroom in Adrian for years. He organized dances with live bands and refreshments and somehow commandeered a bus that he drove all over two counties picking up kids who wanted to come to the dances but had no way to get there. All this while he worked regular jobs. For a time, he had three jobs — a shift in a nearby plating plant, the poolroom, and a "country bank" (a midnight coal operation in which off-duty miners dig surface coal for $1.50 a ton). Everything he did seems to have worked, and the people usually came to him for help. When the church needed someone to organize a benefit, the Father would come to Johnny. When the local tavern (owned by the church!) was about to go broke, they came to Johnny to put it in the black, and he did. Later on, he organized residents to protest the quality of the town's water and forced Kovalchick to make repairs and install filters. He convinced the Kovalchicks to deed a right-of-way to a private utility so the people on the hill could have gas. Then he arranged with one of his brothers to provide inexpensive pipe and labor so that each household could afford to connect.

One by one, these facts emerge. But he tells them as stories, speaking the various parts and describing situations with great humor. He takes credit for what he does, but doesn't dwell on it. It amuses him.

By the time we get back to the house, it's dark and a cold wind has come up. Anna Miklos has ham sandwiches, pickles, hot coffee, and shortcake with frozen strawberries on it waiting. We plug the tape back in and sit around the kitchen table talking with our mouths full of deviled ham.

Just as the sun was setting on a Sunday afternoon in November, we walked around Adrian with Johnny Miklos. The people came out on their porches to meet us, mostly because Johnny wanted it that way. The interesting thing about this page of faces is that you can see the future here as clearly as the past. Many of those we spoke to were young people who moved to Adrian (some of them returning after a period of absence) because they had sampled life in a city or suburb and realized they wanted a ramshackle frame house in this old miners' town instead.

For John Miklos, the purchase of Adrian by residents wasn't the final step. They're now building a playground up by the church, so the kids will have a place of their own. They are about to embark on the development of a sewage system to replace existing septic tanks and cesspools. The final two payments for the town are in the bank drawing interest, and the corporation has an operating fund of $7,000 in the bank to cover its expenses. Meetings of residents are called and most important decisions are made by direct vote.

Miklos has been approached by agencies who want to "help" Adrian. Word has gotten around that the town is a good bet. He says, "Why should we take help from them if we can do it ourselves?" Nick Kovalchick has offered him a job. He wants him to go around and help the other fifteen towns that the Kovalchicks own do what the people in Adrian did. Miklos said no. He'll stay at his job at the carbon plant. He doesn't seem ambitious in that way. There is plenty of challenge in Adrian.

Miklos can't really explain why he does all this. We asked him several times and in several different ways. About all he can do is convey that he likes it, and that he doesn't feel right when he's not doing something for the town. Apparently he has been doing it for so long, the reasons are back deep in his

past. Somehow or other, the people of Adrian have chosen him as their leader, and like anybody who wields power, he is both loved and hated for it.

John Miklos is fifty-six years old now. He looks healthy, but he takes shots for his high blood pressure. His wife wants him to cut down on his activities. She tells him he cares more about the town than he does for her. She worries about him. She thinks the people in the town don't appreciate what he's done.

Johnny is philosophic about it. He says, "Just like a guy told me downtown, he said, 'Hey, Johnny!' he said, 'I'll tell you one thing, after you pass away,' he said, 'they'll put a big plaque up here and say, "Hey! There was nobody but him. Look what he did for us." But now that you're livin' they won't say things like that.' "

106

Starting from Scratch

CERRO GORDO, OREGON

In a way, there are two stories here. One is about the town of Cottage Grove, Oregon. That story would deal with what a small, established community does when suddenly confronted with the specter of a new town of 2,000 souls looming on its doorstep, a whole new town of urban ex-patriots — and an advance guard that arrives to set up housekeeping right downtown. At first, we thought about writing that story — and treating the future new town as another, albeit very unusual, development. But like any of these stories Cottage Grove may be looked at in a number of ways. And after months of indecision, it has become clear to us that the other story is more important, for a number of reasons which should become clear as we tell it. This second story is one in which a young man named Chris Canfield decides he will start a new town good enough to be a home for his family — and then proceeds to do just that. An "impossible" story.

We think that there cannot be too much telling of "impossible" stories. It has occurred to us in our roaming about the country working on this book that people are much more convinced of what they cannot do than they are aware of what they are capable of doing. Potential is expressed in terms of the limits on action: what the banks will finance; what one law or another permits; what this regulatory agency or that commission is apt to approve; what the public will accept. It is not thought of in terms of the action demanded by the circumstances, or as in the case of Chris Canfield and those who have joined him, the action demanded by circumstances and the imagination.

It seems that we don't do much soaring any more. One of the themes you often see us turning to in these stories is that of the maverick — the one who refuses to accept matters as they stand and insists on having it some other way, despite the fact that practicality, the Board of Supervisors, and the law of averages are plainly opposed. But it isn't that we are interested just in loners (though eccentrics have their own place and value). Instead, we find ourselves drawn to those who chart a course against the tide, and then enlist others to come aboard. That is something else again. It is the stuff of which learning is made. It is high drama. And it is the kind of action that changes people's lives. Like so many of the other stories we found, this is the kind of story we discovered in Cerro Gordo.

107

It is tempting to use the word "utopia" in connection with Cerro Gordo, but utopia is a tricky word. The impulse behind Cerro Gordo was born out of the decade of the sixties and the moral introspection brought on by an unpopular war, a rising tide of civil and individual rights consciousness, and the clear evidence that we were fouling our nest with whatever pollutants and poisons could be imagined. Somewhere in that decade, the industrial state peaked. And with its zenith came the image of Armageddon. What is commonly thought of as the "back-to-the-land" movement — the withdrawal of middle-class Americans from the mainstream — began then. It was as much a rejection of the consumer economy as it was of the political machinery that seemed intent on sustaining an endless war in Indochina. It was as much a retreat — a rout if you will — as it was a clear articulation of any viable alternative. The communes and "communities" of the late sixties and early seventies were utopian in that they were separatist in motivation. They wanted "out" and attempted to arrange themselves accordingly. Like the utopian colonies of the late nineteenth and early twentieth centuries, they also embraced an ideology — however vague — having essentially humanist characteristics. Some were religious. Most of them, except for the ones with the strongest religious ties and the longest traditions, were short-lived. It is probably unwise to say they failed, since the criteria for success are unknown and permanence may never have been considered important. But their impact was limited to those having direct contact with them, and they have gone leaving very little legacy except that embodied in the lives of participants.

"Utopia" literally means no place — or existing nowhere. The implication, of course, is that to attempt to construct a utopia is to attempt to defy the whole of human nature. If you examine utopian efforts in this country since the Civil War — a fascinating study by the way — you will find several common features among them. All of them were efforts led by a person or persons of charismatic appeal — some men, some women. All were separatists in that they attempted, in one way or another, isolation — either physical or social or both — as well as economic independence and political neutrality. Most of them involved some religious or quasi-religious structure and content. And most of them, even the most substantial, lasted little more than a generation or two past the death of their founders.

One does not come away from this look at history with the conviction that we are doomed to a brutish existence because our higher instincts lead always to an early end. But it is remarkable how consistent the patterns are — and how, despite an incredible variety of examples with great diversity of content, they end with striking similarity.

If a word like "utopia" may be defined by such efforts, then the definition does not fit Cerro Gordo. Chris Canfield's town has attracted people because it promises to live up to its participants' highest ideals for community experience. But it is no enclave. It is very much of the world and in the world. Chris Canfield's dream was to create a perfect community by bringing together a group of people on a piece of land and making it work in the most practical terms. What has come of this is a first class thrash — and the beginning of something the likes of which is to be found nowhere else.

Cottage Grove, Oregon, around 1915, and as it looked when we were there sixty-one years later. It was to this small mill town that Chris Canfield and his new town friends came in 1973. The town, which had changed so little for so long, was suddenly confronted with a migration of new people and a 1,158-acre new town site in its backyard. The hill at the end of the main street, called Cerro Gordo, is near the new town and privided its name. It means, loosely translated, fat hill in Spanish.

COTTAGE GROVE ORE.

TRIPLOG. Cottage Grove, Oregon. We come into town on the old highway to Eugene, past a couple of big mills and the usual welter of roadside stuff: elderly motels, auto parts stores, wrecking yards, and hamburger joints. Just then it is apparent we have been approaching· the town from its back door. The central district is suddenly visible to our left. Some nice older buildings. A little river running through. Some trees. Nice old houses. Not bad. The Cerro Gordo project has just taken offices in the old hotel — evidently also the hangout for local indigents. The place is depressing and the offices are locked. We telephone some numbers and find there will be a wait to see Canfield. We visit the local newspaper office. By chance, the editor is there and willing to talk for a few minutes. He is short, energetic, friendly, and quite frank.

"We've had quite a few California friends up here. Some of 'em are super people. My big hangup is that they haven't got jobs, a lot of them. Some of 'em got little kids. Some of 'em got big kids. And all you gotta do sometime if you want to get to feeling real down is to stand at the supermarket checkout stand and watch the food stamps go by. Sometimes I walk out of there steppin' on my lower lip. I've got two girls I've got to start in college this year and I don't know how in hell I'm going to do it. But I look around and someone is helping those folks. Then I look at my tax bill and I can figure out real quick who it is. You can't really blame 'em . . . BUT. What this community really needs is some high-end people — what I call people with skills that can draw jobs. This is strictly a lunch-bucket town. We need to balance out a little. If those [Cerro Gordo] people can convince me they can bring jobs here, I'd probably be the first one to jump on the bandwagon."

SELLING A TOWN BY MAIL

Chris Canfield doesn't look or act like a charismatic leader. He is pale, quiet, a little diffident. He is reasonably well-dressed and looks respectable. It is almost as hard to imagine thousands of people sending him money in support of his search for a new kind of new town as it is to imagine him as a real-estate developer disguised as a hippie. What he actually looks like is an upper-middle-class graduate student in, say, architecture or medicine at a private university. His manner with us is polite and cordial and almost shy. He speaks to us openly of the problems of the project, but he is the sort of person who, despite candor, discloses little of himself. He is cool and controlled, and it is the superb control that makes us wonder a little. The whole thing is so *unlikely*. What is going on here, anyway? It is truly hard to believe that this young man has caused people to turn over large amounts of money, uproot their families, move them — sometimes great distances — to this little town at the foot of the Willamette Valley, do battle with local authorities — and each other — all for the sake of a dream. And yet it has all happened. Of course, it might just be that Chris Canfield is exactly what he says he is — and no more.

"We got into this because this is what I wanted to do and what my family wanted to do — not just build a new town but the process. We'd thought many times about moving out into the forest, and we'd looked at land several different times, but it was real clear that we didn't want to just go out and live

110

there by ourselves. We wanted community. We couldn't get that in Los
Angeles, and even though Santa Barbara was a pleasant retreat from there for
a few years, it still didn't have what we wanted. So we just started pursuing the
idea that we could do it ourselves. We got a lot of people together and started
analyzing what it would take to meet our fantasies. I'd been involved in
working with alternative community groups in Southern California —
environmental groups, free schools, community action groups, growth centers.
They all seemed to go together in my mind, yet in the city they were all having
a good deal of difficulty surviving on their own. To me, it was just because they
didn't have their complimentary parts. So early in 1971 we came up with the
idea that we should build a whole new community."

During that year and the next one, Canfield, his wife Sherry, and a growing
group of friends talked about what kind of town they should build, where they
should build it, how they would populate it, and how it should be run. Most of
these people were activists of one description or another, involved in the
environmental movement, in the anti-war movement, in civil rights work,
women's liberation, and other efforts. They brought their ideals with them,
and out of such stuff the first fantasies were spun. Canfield made a couple of
trips from Santa Barbara to Northern California looking for land. As the
talking went on, and the whole enterprise seemed more and more plausible,
the circle of friends was organized as the Pahana Town Forum, a nonprofit
educational corporation.

During this time, Canfield maintained his job as a vice president and general manager of a group of three small electronics manufacturing companies in
Santa Barbara. He describes the work as something that came naturally to
him. He was well paid. It was pleasant work. But there was no challenge. He
says he could have done it in his sleep. The new town was something else again.
It occupied most of his interest and more and more of this time.

Finally in 1973, a forty-page *Town Prospectus* was issued by Pahana. In it
the idea for the new town was described. On the front page was a drawing of
an Elizabethan village scene in a courtyard surrounded by half-timbered
buildings with leaded-glass windows. Inside, following the names of all who
had participated (Canfield is listed as "coordinator"), was a discussion of seven
topics: the land, living with the land, building, community systems,
livelihood, education, community —followed by an invitation to join up.
Interspersed with the prospectus proper were commentaries by those (one
assumes) who participated in the original discussions, along with, in most
instances, their pictures. Canfield had decided that if they were to build a
"community" (as opposed to a "town") they would have to start acting like one
from the very start. Individual personal contributions have always been an
integral part of the Cerro Gordo project — sometimes, as you will see, with
painful results.

It is an earnest document, this *Prospectus*. Almost agonizingly so. It borrows
from such figures as Ian McHarg, Ken Kern, Max Ehrmann, the Hopi and
other Native Americans, and states without hesitation, and with little
apparent self-consciousness, just how things should be. There is not a cynical
sentence in it. It is unabashedly idealistic, and looked at from the perspective

111

Town Prospectus

First Edition   Winter Solstice, 1972   First in a Series

We're building a new town
in the forest of Northern California

A presentation of concepts & plans

A beginning for community discussion & involvement

An invitation to join our community

Cluster Housing

There is a reciprocal relationship between the way the members of households in the neighborhood customarily relate and the configuration of the homes and land holdings of the neighborhood — each influences and determines the other. For example, the typical suburban placement of houses in rows facing the street, with yards separated by six-foot concrete block walls, clearly reflects and reinforces the all-too-pervasive lack of exchange and interaction among people who live in such housing tracts.

We propose a new way of grouping homes to encourage and facilitate the interaction between neighbors and the extended family living that many people seek. Houses are grouped around a large open green held in common by all of the households in the cluster. Depending upon the wishes of the group, common facilities could be anything from a picnic area to a stable and farmyard to a common house with kitchen, dining hall and meeting room.

Individual houses are owned by each household, as are the small, semi-private yards in the front of each house which adjoin the common land. Large yards at the back of each house provide the necessary private space for immediate family life.

Ecosystemic Design
An Ecological House & Greenhouse

Designed and under construction by Grahame Caine, a student at the Architectural Association of London. Caine's design exemplifies the alternative technology movement, which aims not only to reduce pollution and resource consumption, but also to replace big, alienating utility technocracies with human-scale techniques that people can run themselves. Material costs for the 1500-square-foot house and garden are $1,500 to $1,750. Washing and drinking water will be collected on the roof. A wind generator and electrical power storage system will supplement solar heating. From the 500-square-foot greenhouse, a maximum yield of about eight pounds of vegetables per square foot is expected. Warm air will collect in the central dome to make a hothouse for growing tropical fruit.

14

Recycling & Composting

A Recycling Center

There are much better ways of dealing with solid waste than filling up canyons with "sanitary landfills." Of course the best way is preventing waste. A lot can be done on the community level. For example, we can eliminate the greater portion of disposable food packaging by purchasing food in bulk, and using and re-using containers delivered and picked up when empty by the community delivery service.

There are existing markets for most solid wastes. Separate pickup will be required for newsprint, aluminum, steel, glass and other recyclables. A recycling center with large bins will keep the materials segregated. When a truckload of some material is accumulated it will be loaded onto a truck by skiploader and shipped off to a buyer. Funds generated thereby will defray costs of collection.

Organic wastes can be composted or treated so that they can be converted into methane gas and fertilizer by the sewage plant. Perhaps the community can develop uses for some of the waste materials which are not now commercially recyclable. For example, a simple process might press non-recyclable papers into a surrogate firewood for home use. Maybe we should reserve a bin at the recycling center for stubbornly non-recyclable materials such as plastics; each accumulated truckload could be shipped off to some large producer of such materials as a reminder that the ecosystem does not have a means of re-assimilating and re-using such materials.

20

An Underground Conveyor

Retailers need a constant supply of products; production companies need to receive raw materials and ship out finished products. In order to eliminate delivery vans and trucks from the townsite, we propose a conveyor transport from roadside to village center. At the roadside will be a loading dock and small warehouse supervised by a shipping clerk. At the village end of the conveyor will be an attractive small dock where shipments can be delivered and picked up by handcart. Essentially a large airport baggage conveyor, it could handle packages as large as four feet on a side. For aesthetics we may choose to place the conveyor underground in a large cement conduit.

Conveyor Dock in the Village

Roadside Loading Dock

19

4. Community Systems

Transportation

A transportation system designed to eliminate automobiles from the townsite is an important means of realizing the tempo and lifestyle we desire for the new community. A comprehensive system of trails for horseback, bicycles and walking will be supplemented by quiet minibuses on their own narrow roads. Radio dispatching the minibus in response to telephone calls will improve service by reducing response time. A community delivery service will make it easier to ride into the village to do marketing.

The roads that will become minibus and delivery service roads will be open to automobiles during the first year or two, when the population is too small to support these community services. As soon as the services are set up, however, access will be limited to emergency vehicles and the occasional moving van. Parking areas on the perimeter of the townsite will be serviced by the minibus. People who feel the need to park their car next to their home should locate their home on the edge of the townsite.

Minibus Waystation

18

customers; or perhaps their sales are handled through regional sales representatives. Possible types of businesses include: (1) light manufacturing and assembly, such as electronics, and (2) remote services, such as design and development or mail order retail. Some other likely industries are woodworking, ceramics, clothing, toys, publishing and printing, furniture, and scientific research.

Experimental College & Growth Center

A small experimental college has often been suggested as an important aspect of the community. Common to several proposals is the concept of a university without walls, which emphasizes self-directed study, a strong personal relationship between student and teacher, and the reduction of academic study to allow for direct involvement with meaningful projects. Another common theme is for the college to provide a living situation emphasizing self-discovery and interpersonal relationships along the lines of a growth center. Other related proposals are for a growth center and a state-funded residence for children who are wards of the state.

25

of five years' worth of hindsight, simplistic. In a sense, it is not even a prospectus, since the document makes no specific offering beyond a pitch to join the Pahana Town Forum, enter the "dialogue," and subscribe to the series of publications that were to follow.

Aside from some criteria for the land to be sought, and a general description of how that land ought to be used (no vehicles, low-impact site development and architecture, a commitment to energy conservation), there is very little in it that would give one any specific notion of what the town would be like to live in. Most of the descriptive matter is vague; an expression of the kind of common sense consensus that might be the product of a year's worth of talking among intelligent, if inexperienced, people. Which is just exactly what it was. The most revealing parts of it are the personal comments of participants. They convey a kind of intense yearning for what can only be described as "rightness." It is as though most of what they were dealing with on a daily basis was unacceptable, and they were reaching out to each other for confirmation that there must be a better way to live. There is real hunger in their words.

Mostly, there is magic in the whole, unexpressed in the parts. There is no other way to explain the effect of the document on those who received it. Ten thousand copies were printed of which 7,500 were mailed to people whose names were on a number of environmental mailing lists Canfield had accumulated during his community work in Southern California. The response was staggering. Almost overnight, the Pahana Town Forum was in the publishing business.

Canfield had solicited written responses to the idea of the new community and had promised to publish those in a second document called *First Feedback*. One has only to read some of those published responses to see what an impact the idea of this new town, based on human brotherhood and sisterhood, and a loving respect for the earth, had on the environmentally aware of the early seventies.

There are sixty published responses in *First Feedback*, representing eighteen states. Many have photos. The faces look various. Some young. Some old. Some freaks. Many middle-class (if appearances mean anything). From the comments, some have businesses they are willing to move. Many are looking for a direction. Many for a job. But in the words of all respondents there is the same yearning, the same hunger. Here are six of the most radiant letters.

At last! Received gorgeous Prospectus *yesterday in mailbox; dropped parcels all over ground; yelled with delight; neighbors' children came running; I hugged 'em all and ran up the 22 stone stairs to read, read, read!*

Six floor plans, one more review of Prospectus, *seven hours of phoning and one detailed financial statement later, I'm ready for you, if you're ready for me!*
— *Anne B. Soule*
Cottage Grove, Oregon

Cindy: Our family is most interested in the possibility of becoming a part of the actualization of your plans. This whole concept has been in our dreams for years, and to see it within reach is, well, breathtaking. My own motivations for wanting to become a part of something like Pahana are easy to express. I feel that life is a great adventure, and I want to be where I can be me to the fullest. I also feel that unless we shape up on this planet, our days here are numbered.

It seems to me that to be a part of Pahana is to be an immediate part of the reshaping of this world — in active involvement in change — at a very personal, tangible, concrete level. I have had stirrings within me that cannot find expression here or anywhere where people are not consciously and willingly working together. I did have a desire to combine the nitty-gritty with the spiritual, sort of a condensed soup of heaven and earth and clouds and dirt and deer eating your garden and your baby holding a fawn.

I'd like to change willingly, with joy rather than under pressure, as will surely happen as time passes. I see about me a need for change greater than any city will ever be willing to make, and I see a need for people who see the need to do something. We have whole communities of friends — creative, thinking people — who are progressing in life as if life were always going to continue to offer the things that are available today. I see that people who can must make a change to a simpler, more giving way of life.

> — *Cindy & Nick Cutting*
> *Oakland, California*

First of all, yes, God yes. Before any of the negatives, YES! My wife, my children, myself will rip up whatever scraggly roots we have imbedded in this goddamned rock and join you today. Where are you? How do we get there? What can we do to help? I am so full of enthusiasm, so full of questions and things I want to say that I don't know if my fingers will work fast enough to put everything down as it comes to me.

I am forty years old. I have lived in New York City, in Manhattan, for twenty years, as has my wife. My children, ages 15, 11, 8, were all born here. We have lived here because, until now, there never seemed to be a viable alternative.

We live along in our apartment with 45 other tenants where we have lived for ten years. I don't know the people next door who have lived here longer than we. Sometimes I say "Hi" to them. Things go wrong here, I call the super; he'll fix it. The bathroom ceiling leaks; so it leaks. Outside, black smoke billows from the building across the way; the air stinks; so it stinks. The subway system is intolerable; the fares go up; so they go up. I live here. This is my city. But I am no way a part of it.

The children go to school in a system that is nothing more than an eventual pension for their teachers if they stick it out. The teachers don't care about the kids. My oldest son is 15 and in high school, a brand new building, a factory. He jumped at a new chance and is now with a day-care center. He loves it, and the kids love him. He will get "credit" for doing this; but what about next semester when he will have to return to the factory? So now you come along and tell me that there can be a place where helping and working within the community is not an "alternative decision" but the decision. And I say, yes.

> — *Dane Knell*
> *New York, New York*

We've lived through and participated in the movements of the Sixties and have been torn apart by the escalating violence and dehumanization caused by confrontation politics.

We are not content with creating the good life for ourselves only, by isolating ourselves from the struggle, buying our space with our affluence. Withdrawing back to the land, to nostalgia for a simpler era, is a dead end. Part of our growing up, our coming-of-age, includes the desire to be a participant in the events that shape our lives and our world, to share in the decision-making, to make a difference. This is the powerlessness and alienation we feel in the dominant culture.

We do seek a life without distractions from the things we cherish most — the search for truth and meaning in life, the opportunity to share our gifts with one another through warm, honest touchings.

> *— Carol Strode & Bob Kanetake*
> *Honolulu, Hawaii*

After reading the Town Prospectus, *I haven't felt closer to anything since the womb.*

The Prospectus *has articulated my own thoughts and dreams so clearly and empathetically that I feel already a part of the Pahana Brotherhood/Sisterhood. I sincerely want to become an active and supportive member in genuine mutuality.*

> *— Norman A. Baldwin*
> *Santa Barbara, California*

I feel a new release of energy at just the prospect of getting to actualize some of the ideas and values I would like to live by. Moving a whole society in the direction of more humane treatment of people is almost insurmountable. But to build one small town without some of the rasping discontents of our civilization seems like a possibility.

> *— Polly Ash*
> *Springville, California*

Many of the responses were less ecstatic and asked more probing questions. Nick Cutting wanted to know what the financial and legal structure of the organization was and where the money would come from. He asked the question: Would the organization have financial control over the land? Paul Chapin regarded a commitment to the town as the end of his profession in linguistics and asked whether or not it would be possible to consider part-time participation. He was concerned about the "encounter group" tone in the prospectus and wanted assurance that those who do not wish to participate in such community activity would not be discriminated against.

There may also have been responses that were outright negative. But they did not appear in *First Feedback*.

In the interval between the appearance of the *Prospectus* in 1973, and the publication of *First Feedback* in 1974, considerable organizational work had been done. *First Feedback* for example, listed the addresses of eight "area   115 coordinators" in towns up the Pacific Coast from San Diego to Seattle. Later there would be groups out of state as well. The purpose of these local contacts was to help organize local participation through small round-table discussions, and particularly to assure good turnouts at a series of area meetings that were held during the initial stages of the project to acquaint those members outside Santa Barbara with the people and the plan on a firsthand basis.

Further, of the several thousand who, on the basis of the *Prospectus,* subscribed to the Forum and asked to receive all publications, a hundred households joined something called the "Special Program." These were the people who were ready to take immediate action — become directly involved in planning the town, who would visit the site once it was selected, and were prepared to put their money where their mouths were. They were the first pilgrims — and the vanguard of what was to become the Cerro Gordo Community Association.

Most important, the organization that evolved among the various levels of participants was masterfully put together, in light of the fact that none of the organizers had ever done anything remotely like it before. Canfield had spent his first year and a half well. In essence, the structure for the new town effort was conceived in that period and has endured in basically the same form ever since, despite radical setbacks and severe tests.

It consists of three parts. The first is the Town Forum itself — essentially regarded as having an educational function. It is nonprofit, solicits members, reaches as many readers as possible in order to find those relative few who are willing to go to work. The second part is the Community Association, which is the group of people who will live in the town, own their own property privately and the balance of the land in common. Community Association affairs are administered by an elected council of seven members serving eighteen-month terms each. The third part is Canfield Associates — a limited partnership in which Canfield would be the general partner and the investors the limited partners; and this entity would function as the developer of the site.

This three-part structure encouraged and facilitated an enormous amount of exchange between members, but it also reveals a canny recognition of the fact that authority must be placed in the hands of those who were willing to make full commitment to the project. It permitted the organizers of the project to solicit and encourage full participation of any who wished to contribute, but gave those with the responsibility for making it happen the authority and flexibility they needed to get the job done. So while the largest number of Town Forum members were idling along with their fantasies, considerable business was being done. Later, this very structure was to come under heavy attack by some members who suddenly realized the full implications of the organization of the group and balked. But in the early stages, it permitted remarkable progress to be made — progress that was essential if the dream was to seem realizable to people who were being asked to lay out hard cash.

And it worked. By the time *First Feedback* went to press, the editors could announce that a land planner had been retained and that negotiations were underway for a site. Though it was not spelled out in *First Feedback,* the site

was to be a ranch of 1,158 acres on a south-facing slope above Dorena
Reservoir, five miles east of the town of Cottage Grove, Oregon, at the foot of
the Willamette Valley.

TRIPLOG. *Dorena Lake near Cottage Grove. The road winds out of town to the
east, along a creek and through a kind of rural suburb. There are houses out
here with an acre or more, and many of them appear to be equipped with the
trappings of little farms — a barn here and there, a chicken coop, a horse
corral. It is gentle country, and once there were probably real farms here.
Most of the people who live here now work in town. The road climbs up the
north side of the lake (past the Cerro Gordo site). We are going to visit Lucy
Eckstein. She is the most outspoken opponent of the new town on the hill
above the lake. We want to hear what she has to say.*

*Lucy Eckstein is little. She is one of those people who pack great energy in a
small body. Her voice is small and high, but it carries. She gives the impression
that she is hard to intimidate. Her husband sits off to one side and occasionally
offers comments. But it is Lucy Eckstein who has organized opposition to this
new town, and it is Lucy Eckstein who does most of the talking. We have our
tape recorder. And she has hers. It is clear she won't leave anything to memory, chance, or our good intentions. And why should she?*

*She and her husband and children live on a hill overlooking the lake. There
are a few other homes out here. Some of the people have been here a long
time. Others, like the Ecksteins, are more recent arrivals. But everyone who
lives here likes the fact that they are* not *living in Cottage Grove. They like the
lake. And they like the quiet. It is not surprising that they do not like the idea
of the new town. There is no doubt that Cerro Gordo will alter life on Dorena
Lake. And though their opposition is translated into specific terms about the
nature of the development and its impact on the environment, and though
much of the opposition may be justified on objective grounds, it is the fact of
the change — any change — that is really at issue.*

HIPPIE GO HOME

Early in 1973, residents of the Dorena Lake area were invited to hear about
the plans for the new town. The meeting was unofficial, called, no doubt, by
Canfield in an effort to be open and straightforward with the new neighbors
about his intentions for the 1,158-acre site above the lake. Though the land
planner had been retained, and work had been started, there was very little
information to present except the general kind of specifications that had been
discussed all along within the Town Forum itself. To the residents around the
lake, the idealism of the Cerro Gordo people was commendable but hardly
redeeming. The worthy objective of the group was a little like discussing the
parking arrangements for a public execution — nice, but hardly central.

Additionally, there were problems with the site and with its proposed use
that Lucy Eckstein and her supporters came to believe were being ignored or
glossed over by the new town advocates. During our visit, she mentioned several of these: traffic; the disposal of sewage and the possibility of contaminating

117

the reservoir; the presence on or near the site of a slide area, which was not mentioned in the geological analysis by the town planners; periodic problems in the area with water contamination by natural arsenic; the long-range effects of multiple-family dwellings in a predominantly rural district.

Though the Dorena Lake residents number only a few, the area is a valued recreational resource for the town of Cottage Grove and neighboring communities. Lucy Eckstein and her neighbors were to find others who would join them in opposing the new town. The opposition wasn't always well-informed and reasoned. Some of it was based on the theory that these high-minded new neighbors were a front for some kind of mastermind-developer who would get his foot in the door at Dorena Lake, then run amuck in the county. Others were sure that all the Cerro Gordo people were hippies, dopers, and welfare artists who would sit on their hillside above the lake, smoke pot, and run up the public assistance share of the tax bill.

Not quite so easy to deal with, or to dismiss, was the fear that these citywise folk from out of state would come to Cottage Grove and displace residents from their jobs. Cottage Grove is not a depressed community, but its unemployment rate hovers at the high end of the scale, and white-collar jobs are at a premium. Even mill workers talked about the impact of the new town on their chance for keeping themselves employed. It is a subject that is still discussed and will be an issue until the new town demonstrates its ability to attract new jobs to the area.

Rumors start quickly and in great profusion in small towns, and Cottage Grove is as fertile a bed for such stuff as any other community. While stories were flying around about who these people were and what they would do, Canfield and his friends were getting ready to establish themselves in the community in the only way possible — by living there. By the end of 1973, the first "settlers" had arrived and taken up residence in rented houses in Cottage Grove. And on January 17, 1974, the 1,158-acre Cerro Gordo site above Lake Dorena was purchased as the site of the new town.

Organized opposition to the project by area residents would continue for months, but such opposition was not the only cause of major delays or setbacks in the project. Some of those have been brought about by the process behind the whole scheme — the complexity of dealing with a constituency of members and would-be residents scattered over the entire country, the steady work of relating daily to those who have come to help make it all happen, the scores of agencies and individuals that must be served and satisfied if the dream is to become built, and finding a safe path through the labyrinth. Actually, there is no safe path through the labyrinth. And that is the root of the trouble that Canfield and his friends have had to deal with from the start.

THREADING THE NEEDLE

The year 1974 was a turbulent one in the history of the Cerro Gordo community. It was the year that the idea-machinery, which Canfield and his friends had set into motion in 1971 and 1972, suddenly took on physical form and its own momentum in the real world. By the end of that year, almost 5,000 persons had joined the Town Forum. The site had already been

Opposite: The new town site with Lake Dorena in the background, and Chris Canfield, the man who dreamed of starting a new town from scratch.

purchased, the initial plans developed. The warm ideals for human relationships that came so easily in the responses to the *Town Prospectus* were being tested harshly in one confrontation after another.

Some of the disputed issues were inevitable: Should automobiles be permitted on the site at all? Some were amusing: Should dogs and cats be admitted? More significantly, attempts to organize the Cerro Gordo Community Association and write its by-laws were proving unsuccessful. There were also budget troubles as the costs of maintaining, for the first time, a staff and office consultants, and a full-time developmental effort turned out to be greater than the income from publications and memberships. And continually, there was a massive amount of input from members.

In practice, the most active participants in this whole company of players fall into two groups: those who had either moved to Cottage Grove at the end of 1973 or early in 1974 to set up and run the organization as the new community was planned and built, and those who lived elsewhere but had committed themselves to move sooner or later and had invested money in the operation. But the organization of the whole enterprise encouraged input from all, wherever they might be. And ideas and plans came, reams of them. Canfield and his fellow organizers were serious about wanting the new town to reflect, as much as possible, the thinking of all who might someday wish to live there. The area coordinators were active, and regular gatherings were held at which those involved on a daily basis made presentations to their distant community members and listened carefully to their responses.

We depart at this point from our more-or-less organized narrative in order to plunge our readers directly into a small but representative portion of the hundreds of pages of published dialogue issued by the Town Forum during the years 1974 and 1975.

There is nothing orderly about what you are going to read now. That is because there is very little that is orderly about the process of a group of several thousand individuals scattered across the landscape, each with his or her own ideas, attempting to reach some kind of consensus about what a perfect community should be. You have the further disadvantage of having entered the conversation in the middle. On the other hand, many of the Cerro Gordo participants who joined either the Town Forum or the Community Association itself (those who had committed themselves to residence status) during the same period found themselves in just the same situation.

In a Town Forum publication called *Gathering of the Townsfolk,* Dorothy Walker chronicles the year 1974, and a sense of its density and frenetic pace comes through clearly. We reprint here selections from the first and last three months.

JANUARY *begins in Cottage Grove, Oregon, with a handful settled in — Barbara Kelley and Alan Katz out at the farm, in town, Anne Soule, Dan Berg, Lew & Marilyn McFarland with Laura. Rain comes down, establishing a new record. The first issue of the Community Association monthly* Newsletter *appears, with a temporary mailing address of 704 Whiteaker, the mustard-colored house that will be our nerve center. The* Newsletter *has 24 pages, the final 3 with ⅓ of the summary responses to a November questionnaire on community lifestyle preferences. Christopher Canfield, leader of the project, says that the* Newsletter *marks the transforming of the Special Program into the Community Association, one of the 3 entities of the Project; the other, the Town Forum (incorporated in December 1973) and the "land purchase partnership" to begin this month. Area meetings will continue, he says; also large community gatherings such as last Thanksgiving's at Santa Barbara, with one on-site this summer. Chris calls for assumption of leadership, responsibility and commitment to form the Community Residents Association.*

First the energy systems meeting reported, as well as issues of transportation, economic development, the possibility of organic farming for outside cash. Patrick Stevens of San Francisco proposes that the time-tested Quaker method of reaching decision by consensus be considered.

The major event of the month occurs on Jan. 17 when the 1,158-acre Cerro Gordo site is purchased as a townsite on Dorena Lake. The reaction at the Los Angeles Area meeting, Jan. 20: "Shouts of joy and sort of like New Year's Eve! We broke into groups of 4-6 and just talked about hopes, fears, needs, skills." Same day, Chris and landplanner Chuck DeDeurwaerder talk with Lane Co. Planning Dept. official who expresses doubt about the choice of the site.

FEBRUARY. *Offices are set up at 704 Whiteaker with Leas Averill and Mark Lowenstine driving the files (loaded by Santa Barbara volunteers) north from Santa Barbara. Mark goes north to Corvallis to meet with Oregon State University profs assembled by Chuck DeDeurwaerder, for their expertise on alternate energy systems. Visitors to Oregon are offered emergency gasoline by Al Stout in Medford and Lew McFarland in Cottage Grove. Doug Still (one of the original signers with Al and Lew) reports on filing Limited Partnership papers, hopes for early filing of share-offering prospectus with Oregon Securities Division so we can begin the internal capitalization, and possibly by next year, translate partnership shares into homesite equities. Responses to the rental cluster proposal published, plus comments, which focus on the size of the parking lot — too big? Should it be temporary? Why let cars in at all? Patrick Stevens critiques the townsite: BLM road there, an area to be logged, non-control over Dorena area growth, the acoustical funnel of the lake, high visibility from the road. Dan Berg advises prospective newcomers to be prepared to withstand weeks or months of job-searching. . . .*

MARCH. *Dorena Lake Community Meeting of Feb. 17 (Dan Berg, Moderator) reports procedures spelled out. Architectural taste-test prepared by Chuck DeDeurwaerder experienced in Seattle, San Francisco, Santa Barbara and Los Angeles. . . . San Diego hears a report from Linda and Steve Carlson, recently returned from trip to Oregon. Chris spotlights a need for $2,000 monthly to cover office and planning expenses. Chuck makes first of monthly reports on planning: 424 hours in January go to specifics of application to Lane County. Patrick Stevens summarizes impressions of his inspection of architectural forms, advances seven points including: "Do not design from the outside in." Progress report, in advance of intended quarterly statement shows community*

121

Association took in $1,950 in subscriptions, spent $1,243. Chris says Community Association must have 4,500 member households by fall to meet capital construction needs. Violet Orr proposes setting up an encompassing co-op to conduct all business including selling or leasing of homesites. Personal statement from Cindy Cutting of San Francisco, including, "I don't care so much what the buildings look like as I care about where we go as a whole. I want to be part of a community that is a living example of a new kind of life." Doug Still articulates basic positions and ramifications for our town in terms of people with common interest in the goal, capital for the base plan and economic enterprises, leadership willing to assume risks and inspire participation. Document on Limited Partnership sent out.

OCTOBER. *Chris reports 70% (121 persons) approve a contract between the Communtiy Association and Limited Partnership; no's from 27, abstentions 25 or 14%. He calls for a return to relationships of trust, love and acceptance to "restore the easy-flowing joy and excitement we shared a year ago but (which) has been too rare in recent months.*

Council meets Oct. 11-13 at Tori's home in Cottage Grove, hears of disagreement on approach to Town Forum financing and program, and Chris's plan for an interim board and program for 6 months to restore credibility and regain enough momentum to allow transfer from Pahana, Inc., to Town Forum of assets and liabilities. Dan Berg and Lew McFarland resign. New Board: Chuck DeDeurwaerder, Becky Jones, John Mowat, Mike Howell, Eleanor Weider. Chris will serve as interim manager with Mike assisting; the goal for '75 will be to stabilize the debt, increase subscriptions to 7,500 so the Town Forum can be self-supporting. Tori Moore and Patrick Stevens (newly elected to Council) accept Community Association job for membership recruitment and relations. Council decides to hire Chuck Missar to work on economic development, commissions sending of package on by-laws, develops plans for Thanksgiving Gathering.

With an imaginative assist from Hanna Still, Jan Tuininga and Don Nordin stage a treasure hunt for young Cerro Gordians complete with gold rock and other treasures. Cottage Grove Area meeting discusses trust — can Council members be trusted as Community Association employees? Bill Courtney: "We need less judgment here than in everyday society." "Goodbye" said to Jim and Fran Edwards, headed back to San Diego. A concluding campfire circle sings, "He's got the Limited Partnership, Community Association and Town Forum in His Hands." At next Area meeting, feeling is voiced, "Don't think we understand what is going on."

Los Angeles Area meeting decides it spent the first 6 months discussing financial issues. Chris materializes and is greeted as The Source. Sept. 6, Sun Dance Schools incorporated: Tori, president; Midge Shore, principal; pre-school and elementary sessions begin (the latter with Kim Cutting as first and only student). Two cars of Cerro Gordians visit a Quaker-based farm, Alpha, near Deadwood, and are impressed with their processes of interpersonal dynamics. Sara Chambers suggest need for cats and dogs but not for their progeny. Zero Population Growth! Barbara Kelly sharpens the

122

focus on agricultural development. Two pages of background info on domestic
animals, food and shelter costs, purchase prices.

NOVEMBER. *Los Angeles Area meeting discusses by-laws with Rene, decides to check with Paul Chapin on progress in finding Native American name to replace Cerro Gordo. San Diego meets with Chris: "Many fears and objections were laid to rest, but some of us feel that the situation is still critical." Dale Van Metre, Utah, thinks the Council member/employee issue involves not present persons (who are admirable) but need to avoid future possibility of a self-serving Council. He disapproves idea of a single wage rate. Dog trainer Sheila Cordray offers her services in the new town to "educate dogs to their duties and responsibilities." Alpha Farm leaders, by invitation, visit Cottage Grove, observe "our usual hostile patterns" (Cindy). Gordians thereafter decide to try small groups for improved interaction and to clarify their goals. In the area of the Summer Gathering barbecue, intrepid Gordians have an overnight camp-out, relate on the first cold weather of the season; Barbara Kelley serves elderberry pancakes the morning after, followed by volleyball.*

Council meets Nov. 8-10, accepts Kay Smothers's resignation as Newsletter *editor. By-laws, corrected by 3 small lawyer's revisions, approved and sent to printer. Reviewing promotional efforts, Tori points out that the community is 90% communication. Norm Baldwin's (Santa Barbara)idea of a Proposal Log is adopted, to take effect next month. Elements of the Base Plan are articulated.*

Cottage Grove Area meeting hears reports on its Growth Center in Washington St. house of Kay Smothers, Becky and Steve Jones, Doug Edwards, Midge Shore, Fred Ure. They open the Center with a lecture on proposed new U. S. Constitution by Al Stout followed by a work party to install library shelves for Fred's gift of over 2,000 books to the community. Sun Dance Schools begins to meet there.

Santa Barbara meets to prepare the 4,000-copy mailing of the finally-ready Land Planning Package, *formally named* The Cerro Gordo Experiment. *Los Angeles proposes by-laws changes. Writing to Midwest Area, Chris explains his need for future compensation to offset his present take of $3.50 per hour. Franz Dolp, uncomfortable with the Limited Partnership device, thinks it precludes access to the "Diversity, practicality and strength of the broad group of people associated with this project." Brian Lighthart, involved in the architectural planning, observes, "The idyllic community you were invited to is on the other side of a lot of work and sacrifice, give-and-take, and pride-swallowing and frustration." Responses to 59 agricultural questionnaires show 42 "agin" any pesticides. Principal Midge Shore reports on Sun Dance Schools, with a staff of herself, Hanna Still, Bonnie Lorentsen, Steve Carlson for primary, with Kim Cutting (and Heather Lorentsen added) as students. Sharon Courtney heads pre-school with 5-7 students. All faculty are volunteer.*

DECEMBER. *The newly-formed Ash Resorce Center (ARC) describes its work/goods swap system. Thanksgiving Gathering at St. Dorothy's on the Russian River in No. Calif. brings 42. Says Patrick Stevens, "The whole weekend was filled with what was for me a beautiful balance of spontaneity*

123

and structure." Back at the Grove, 50 Gordians assemble at the Presbyterian Church for a feast. Council meets Nov. 29 at St. Dorothy's, reviews defeat of the by-laws, revises presentation in a new ballot.

Glimpses of the month-long Media Tour begun Nov. 15: 25 radio and TV appearances. In Santa Cruz, thanks to Doug and Sharon Davis, a first meeting for 70 people. Figures: Los Angeles 240, San Francisco 160, Santa Barbara 125. Everywhere, Patrick's slide show is a great hit. The final weekend (Dec. 14) a follow-up to the general meetings.

Gordians meet and hear (Dec. 21) the implications of the Cease & Desist order served on Chris and the Limited Partnership on Dec. 16 by the Corporation Commissioner of Oregon. Nick reports to Area meeting Chris's view that the situation is not unusual, he's not discouraged, intends to enjoy Christmas and hopes others will, too. He'll appeal, hopes to be able to make an offering by April.

Jock says it took him 2 months to recover from the Summer Gathering! Asks how can we avoid draining the energies from our most dedicated, most recently involved Rene, who worked so skillfully long and hard on the by-laws?

In the preceding chronology, approximately equal emphasis is given to trivia and disaster. Several things happened during 1974 that might, with the clarity of hindsight, be classified as "disaster." One was the Lane County Planning Commission's denial of a development permit for the first cluster phase of construction. Another was a mounting crisis of confidence among some members of the limited partnership who began to think that residents would not have sufficient control over the development of the site. A third was the cease and desist order served on Canfield and the limited partnership by the Oregon Corporation Commissioner who claimed that an offering of shares was being made illegally. All in all, it was a grueling twelve months, and a severe test of the dream. We'll look at these tests in some detail.

Chris Canfield's association with planner Chuck DeDeurwaerder goes back to late 1971 when the two met in Corvallis, Oregon. DeDeurwaerder was a professor of landscape architecture at Oregon State University there, and Canfield was testing his idea for a new town by looking for land. When the option on the Cerro Gordo site was taken in 1973, DeDeurwaerder's land-planning firm was chosen for the job of advising the new community concerning how to build the new town with a minimum of damage or disturbance to the site's natural equilibrium. Chuck DeDeurwaerder had been working out the techniques of site analysis and planning for some time. That part was relatively easy (though the techniques he used are not common in most commercial development). But working for a "client" which consists in effect of several hundred individuals, each of whom has a set of preferences and prejudices, was something else again. Brian Lighthart comments on the problem in a presentation of the project's Phase I Cluster Proposal to the Lane County Planning Commission in the spring of 1974:

With several hundred people involved in pursuing this new community, the architecture of the buildings and the specifics of community utilities and lifestyle became issues in need of resolution, and we experimented with various methods of learning people's personal preferences. We found we had a community of several hundred people in a design process. But the real uniqueness of this problem lay in the geographic dispersal of our population. This was eased somewhat by the organization of most of the active participants into "area groups" which met twice a month. Nevertheless, the problem was, and is, monumental.

Basic alternatives open to us for first construction were (1) begin with dispersed development which would have minimal impact, be easier to gain approval for, but might incur high costs for utilities and access and violate our village orientation, or (2) begin with the village center as a cluster of housing and light commercial spaces in one of the areas suited to relatively intense use and near to the existing access. We chose a path closer to the second alternative, with a site at the edge of one area suited to intense use, with the idea of testing our land-use studies with this first cluster.

Early in 1974, two questionnaires specifically aimed at architectural issues were circulated among those involved. Several sets of drawings, sketches, plans and proposals were circulated to the area groups. . . . Ongoing task forces dealing with issues such as energy use and production, education, and construction have had and will have things to say about building designs.

Meanwhile the professionals have been struggling to try and deal with all the input — which varies widely in form, specificity and clarity as well as content — all the while injecting their expertise in the elusive way designers do.

The plans that were submitted to the County Planning Commission were not for the design of buildings, but rather for the use of the land. Spaces were alloted for buildings of a certain size and density, but the actual design of structures had not taken place. DeDeurwaerder's efforts had been confined to a painstakingly detailed analysis of the carrying capacity of the 1,158-acre site and to producing a site or land-use plan for the first phase of development. It had been decided that the first construction should be a cluster of buildings that would be used initially as temporary housing for the first on-site residents (while they designed and built their own homes on their own sites) and ultimately as rental and overnight accommodations for people who wished to "try out" the new community before making a purchase commitment. What Canfield and his friends were asking for was approval by the Lane County Planning Commission for a *site development permit* or permission to proceed with the design, and ultimately the construction of the first buildings. They were turned down. Here is the story as Canfield tells it:

"Early in 1974 we began the process of presenting our plans to the Lane County planning authorities for approvals. We knew that properties in the Dorena Lake region were as yet unzoned, and would remain so for some time pending completion of the regional plan for that area. The Planning Department staff [professional planners who advise the Planning Commission] discouraged us from presenting our plans for the entire proposed community, since the unfinished regional plan would be needed to judge the impact of so large a development. Instead, they encouraged us to apply for an unzoned area development permit for the first phase cluster only. This we did, but when the staff report by the Planning Department was issued a few days before the first Planning Commission hearing in April, we were dismayed to see a negative report treating the concept of a whole new town for 2,000 people rather than the first cluster for 150 to 200 people specified on the application.

"At the hearing Chuck DeDeurwaerder presented our ecological studies of the site and the region, and we then asked the commission to continue the hearing to another date and have the planning staff do a report on the first cluster only. This they did, and when the report was issued late in May it was positive on all criteria except two: the proximity of the proposed cluster to the Bureau of Land Management road, which they felt could be remedied simply by increasing the distance, and the lack of a public agency to assume responsibility for maintenance of the proposed sewage treatment facility. The planners did not forsee any technical difficulties with regard to sewage treatment; rather, their concern was based upon a history of poor maintenance of such facilities by private entities, and so as a matter of policy they required a public district to assume maintenance responsibility.

"We were, of course, willing to set up such a district, but we soon found ourselves caught in a bureaucratic Catch 22: You can build as soon as you set up a district, they told us, and you can set up a district as soon as you have a hundred residents. We ran around that circle several times before we learned that that wasn't our real problem. [The unzoned area development permit made provisions for specific guarantees of performance which were more than adequate for the interim period prior to establishment of a public district.]

"The problem, we learned, was the fact that there was an organized opposition to our proposal. Some of our neighbors were convinced that we were a hippie commune moving in on them. Some of the most fantastic rumors were circulated. Letters were written to the Planning Commission, and a door-to-door petition drive was organized. When it came time for a decision, the commissioners responded to the political reality that a lot of people were opposed to our plans, in spite of their awareness that many of the fears that motivated the opposition [hippies, pollution, welfare, inadequate schools] had no basis in fact.

"We appealed the decision of the county commissioners, but we allowed the appeal to die without a hearing because it was clear that we had a lot of people to meet, fears to quiet, and support to muster before we could expect official endorsement and approvals. We have elected to proceed with construction on a more modest basis in order to demonstrate our concepts and our capabilities while we enlist the local support we need for our long-range plans."

While Chris Canfield — who by this time had moved to Cottage Grove with the other Cerro Gordo staffers and first residents — was doing the two-step with Lane County officials and beginning to realize that in their haste to break ground they had overlooked the need to make friends with their neighbors, the Community Association and Town Forum members, in and out of Cottage Grove, were busy working on other parts of the project. Various area groups who had responded to the initial questionnaire about building design were working on their own architectural ideas. Aspects of the community "base plan" were under consideration by other groups. One was at work investigating various low-technology methods for moving people about the site. Having

When the first families move to the new town, they will move into houses that will look something like these. At the top of the opposite page is the architect's sketch for the first solar duplex, a prototype which will eventually be followed by twenty similar units. These structures are modular in design, permitting residences of 500 to 2,500 square feet, their component units arranged in a number of configurations. They will be built by the community's own construction company, using resident labor as much as possible. The buildings have been designed to reduce normal residential heating demand by as much as 75 per cent. The design incorporates six inch walls, ten inches of fibreglass in roofs and first level floors, double windows, air lock entries, and a number of other features. This initial residential construction, constitutes the phase one plan — roughly 10 per cent of the community — or a total of sixty homes to be built over the initial three years of construction at the rate of twenty homes per year. At the same time, planning and engineering studies will go on covering the remaining 90 per cent of the new town with particular attention to the new community's governance, health care, educational facilities, and other amenities. Planning will be done by residents.

The other drawing shows the first industrial duplex, also based on a wood-frame modular design. The first unit will be built to accommodate project offices upstairs and the community's Sundance School downstairs.

Participants in one of the annual summer gatherings share a meadow on the site with one of the resident horses. These gatherings helped to keep the dream alive for many who lived too far away to take part in the day-to-day activities of the project but had invested (fiscally and otherwise) in the effort.

As we ready final pictures and captions for the publisher, it appears this story has a happy ending. Happy insofar as what started as a gleam in Chris Canfield's eye is now, five years later, taking the form you see opposite on an Oregon hillside. The first solar duplex is under construction. Somewhere on the tortuous way from dream to the very first building, a new towner spoke at one of the many gatherings to the hopeful but discouraged participants. He said, "The idyllic community you were invited to is on the other side of a lot of work and sacrifice, give-and-take, pride-swallowing and frustration." He was right.

made a commitment to abandon the automobile at the front gate, it was felt some alternative was in order. Bicycles, minibuses, automated "peoplemovers" (moving walkways) were given study and compared for effectiveness, cost, and impact on the site. A piece called "The Zen Art of Waste Management" was published as part of the ongoing discussion about what to do about that subject. It is such a good statement of "recycling philosophy" and so aptly put, that we have included it at the end of this chapter in its entirety. Its author is unnamed, but is to be congratulated for the piece has relevance to any small community faced with the need (or opportunity) to take a fresh look at this old subject.

Others were at work on the ticklish task of trying to arrive at a reasonable criterion for residency — in other words, how to choose who would be admitted to the community, assuming that there were more takers than spaces. Still others had assumed responsibility for the investigation of the agricultural potential of the site and/or nearby land that might be leased for farming. Meanwhile, a group of first residents in Cerro Gordo were attempting to direct their attention and some effort to scaring up going businesses that could be relocated in the new town in order to provide badly needed employment. An enormous amount of written material was being generated by all these groups, and most of it was circulated to the various memberships of the organization either through a family of publications (including the Community Association *Newsletter* and the Town Forum *Feedback* series) or directly as reports presented at group gatherings: area meetings held monthly; Community Association Council meetings held monthly (often out of the Cottage Grove area in order to accommodate nonresident members); and general community gatherings held usually in the spring, summer, and at Thanksgiving.

It was at the spring (Easter) 1974 gathering in Cottage Grove that the first indication of serious dissent surfaced. An area group leader, Doug Still, arrived in Cottage Grove for that meeting with a mission. He came from his home in Washington, D. C., having organized, with his wife Hanna, an East Coast area group of some twenty plus members. His people were suspicious. It sounded too good to be true. They needed reassurance, and for that purpose dispatched Doug and a second member to the community gathering in Oregon. Specifically, they were to ascertain, if possible, Canfield's true motives, and to bring back assurances that the Community Association (then being organized) would have real independence from the limited partnership, which had taken on the role of site developer. They needed to be sure that the group to which they had pinned their hopes, would in fact have control of the land and its development.

Doug Still had more than hopes pinned on the Community Association. He was a member of its council. He and his wife had invested $5,000 in the project and were among the first members to have become part of the Special Program (the people willing to contribute money and themselves to realizing the objectives of the Town Forum). They were, in fact, limited partners in the limited partnership. They then realized that their status as such gave them virtually no control over the development of the site, and they now wanted to be sure that the Community Association, as it was formed, would have the control that they, as limited partners did not and could not have. It was not, all things considered, an unreasonable position. Few of the members of the group could afford to risk their savings in a venture which gave them no control and little recourse. Furthermore, the ideals of the community from the start had been forged in the language of shared responsibility and democratic process. As the dream began to take real form, the fears that lay dormant, or were subdued by visions of brotherly and sisterly love, began to gnaw.

It must have been painful gnawing. Born as the project was in the spirit of fair play and hunger for a lifestyle governed by reason and compassion, the project asked for the best that each participant could offer. To doubt, to ask for guarantees of safe conduct, to demand control, considering the climate of the group, must have seemed like treachery. But given the structure of the group, with Canfield firmly in legal control, the rift was inevitable.

At the Easter gathering, Doug Still gained the assurance that the residents, through the Community Association, would have independence from the limited partnership and control (though what kind was never made clear to us) and he returned to Washington satisfied. But the dissention was structural, and it would surface once again. Meanwhile, the Stills prepared to move to Cottage Grove.

TRIPLOG. *A visit to the home of Doug and Hanna Still. Cottage Grove, Oregon. Doug and Hanna Still live out on the edge of Cottage Grove, on the way to the new town site. Their house is set back from the road, behind a big meadow, in a grove of pine trees. As we bump down the drive, we see that there are a number of cars. As usual, we wonder what is in store for us. Lunch is ready. The house is warm and so are the people in it. Hanna and Doug Still are there, their sons Dean and Gregory, and Steve Carlson. The defectors. Or more accurately, a delegation of defectors. Hanna is one of those women who was born to be a mother, grandmother, spiritual advisor, and guide. She has an apron, a limp, and one of those soft, expressive faces that takes care of people. She also speaks her mind without hesitation. We sit down to eat, and while we eat, we prop the tape recorder up on the table alongside the bread plate. Doug does most of the talking. Hanna nods in agreement.*

Doug Still is a Presbyterian minister with a history of involvement in human rights and environmental politics. He presently works as a coordinator of environmental education in the state of Oregon for the National Council of Churches. He is fighting the development of nuclear power plants. He works part-time. The rest of his time he has devoted to the development of Cerro Gordo. That is no longer the case. He and a group of other Community Association members are about to announce their withdrawal from the Community Association because they no longer feel that the group can realize the goals as set forth in the Town Prospectus. *He hands us a mimeographed eight-page statement dated August 25, 1975, in which they list their reasons. Doug Still explains what happened.*

"After that Easter gathering at which the independence [of the Community Association from the limited partnership] was declared, the Community

Association Council met monthly four or five times. . . . And we succeeded in formulating a statement of objectives for the Community Association that I thought was very fine. We also tried to find a basis on which the council could negotiate the terms for acquiring the site. Part of the independence was that the council would not commit itself to any site until the cost of acquiring the site from Canfield was determined. . . . But by June of 1974, the majority of the members of the council felt that the independent negotiating stance was not going to work, that the three organizations of the project — the Community Association, the Town Forum, and the limited partnership, Canfield Associates, had, in effect, to be one body in three parts, and it was clear that Chris Canfield was *the* major person. His wishes about the Community Association Council and how it operated needed to be dominant. At that point both Linda Carlson and I resigned from the council itself, feeling that the position was invalid, and we wrote, through the *Newsletter,* our perspective about that. The council, since then, has become more and more instrumental to the limited partnership. I withdrew from the limited partnership in July."

Withdrawal from the limited partnership meant forfeiting their investment. That was a financial "disaster" according to Doug Still. But it seems not to have come close to the emotional costs involved. There is a current of bitterness in this rift that is present only when the deepest intimacies are breached. The Stills and the Carlsons wish the people in the project well — and mean it. But there is a hurt down deep that shows in the exaggerated care with which emotional equilibrium is preserved.

At the summer gathering in 1974, the issue of control had been raised once again — both by Doug Still and Linda Carlson, who had already resigned from the council in protest, and by others who agreed with their position: that the council and the Community Association should have independence from Canfield, and control over the property if the ideals of the new town were to be realized. Though Still believes that a majority of those present agreed in principle, the vote went by an overwhelming majority to Canfield, who had put the issue to them rather bluntly.

Canfield told his fellow community members that they had three choices. One was that he would go bankrupt for lack of a base from which to work, and they would lose everything. The second was that they could buy him out: a year's salary plus his personal investment in the land. Or, third, they could allow him to proceed in the manner in which he had planned the project, and he would prove to them that it could be done. Faced with the prospect of losing everything on the one hand, or their leadership on the other, the choice was, apparently, easy. As Canfield put it later, "The people voted to give me the tools I needed to do the job."

Following the August 1974 vote of confidence for Canfield, the Stills and other dissenters remained members of the Community Association. As Doug Still put it, "We didn't wish to abandon the project altogether. We still hoped that events would prove us wrong and that we could again participate fully." But the statement given us during our interview was their declaration to withdraw from the Community Association. The breach was complete.

131

The personal statement of two of the signers of the statement begins:

We regretfully resign from the Community Association because it seems to us that our Council members have abdicated their responsibility to represent the interests of the members in securing conditions for building a community based on the original statement of community goals which begins:

"As members of the Community Association, we seek more meaningful and fulfilling ways of living. We desire to achieve a mode of life which promotes a deeper appreciation of people and recognizes our mutual interdependence. Our ethic is one of self-determination, freedom, cooperation and personal growth."

Months later, after dealing with this crisis, as well as continued criticism from members that he had surrounded himself with a power circle and was oblivious to the needs and wishes of anyone outside it, Canfield wrote:

The most immediate and perhaps the most important community issue is the community discussion and decision-making process. . . . We've encountered a lot of difficulties in our first year. The problem that has worried me manifests itself in several ways: the polarization we've experienced on issues; the either/or mentality that demands one option win and the others be rejected; the quickness to respond defensively or aggressively; voting no without proposing an alternative, thereby voting to stop the whole effort; blasting those who take initiative, responsibility and leadership with criticism, neglect and sometimes abuse, leaving them with little energy left to work creatively for the community. What I'm worried about is the fact that we have not demonstrated that we care much about each other.

We have a very special opportunity in this endeavor we share. We have a beautiful piece of land and we have great ecological plans — but they are only the setting for a very special promise that we can only achieve together. . . . If we are working together to help each other to realize our dreams, then working together on a new town large and diverse enough to include most all of the basics of our everyday lives can provide the realization of many of our dreams. If we are not working together to help each other, with so many dreams at stake, we can exhaust, dishearten and disillusion one another.

I think that the troubles we have experienced in our first year together are indicative of the depth of our emotional involvement with the community. Too often our emotions have worked against us as we have reacted out of fear, trying to protect our dreams from each other. If our emotional involvement is going to work for us, somehow we have got to evolve an ethic and a process that will ease our anxieties and our defensiveness and replace them with an acceptance of one another and a caring and consideration for each other's dreams.

Now I'm not saying that we are all going to love each other and I am not saying we need a touchie-feelie encounter group community. I hope we build a community with a wide diversity of philosophies and lifestyles. What I am saying is that in order to achieve our diverse and separate dreams, we need mutual acceptance of our diversity and mutual commitment to aiding and supporting one another in achieving our various individual and community goals. And we need to question ourselves and each other as to where we have been and where we want to go in a fashion that will enable us to maintain and foster mutual acceptance and support.

It ain't going to be easy. Maybe a few new assumptions will help:

1) We have to make room for each other and a diversity of dreams, lifestyles and viewpoints. Instead of either/or, let's assume that options are compatible if not interdependent.

2) If you vote No on an option before the community, don't leave us without options. Give us an option you can support.

3) Take care of those who take on community responsibilities and give of their time, their energy and themselves. We will have a higher survival rate and more people will dare to take initiative and responsibility.

4) We are not enemies. There are no winners and there are no losers. We either win together as a community or we all lose.

I have a lot of faith in our dream and I have a lot of faith in us all. I believe that last year's problem can become this year's joy.

TRIPLOG. *Cottage Grove, Oregon. (A year later.) Canfield is more relaxed than we remembered him. It may be that he knows us a little better now. More likely, it is because his spirits are buoyed by the promise of actual construction on the site in the next few weeks. After almost five years of dreaming and discussing and negotiating, there promises to be tangible evidence of the new town on the hill above the lake.*

Sherry Canfield brings us a cup of coffee. Chris tells us during the interview that the project has been hard on their marriage. It has drained both of them — kept them from enjoying their family. But he now has more time. The project has changed in the last year. It has developed to the point that he no longer feels that if he walked away from it, it would collapse. He talks about "key" people. How they show up, take real responsibility. Some stay on, others burn out. But the numbers increase steadily and that signifies real progress. This year he took two months off — the first vacation from project work in years.

He talks about the beating that 1974 gave to the dream. The Planning Commission denial. The battle for control of the project. The Securities Commission flap at the end of the year.

FROM THE BOTTOM UP

"The business with the Securities Commission at the end of that year and early in 1975 was our lowest point, just because it was the last of the three crises to hit us. It was just one, two, three, and it was beating us down very, very low. I was very worried at that time. . . . When we came in to respond, to find out what the heck was going on here, we were treated for a few weeks like criminals. Or I certainly was. That was a very difficult time. We not only had the financial worries, but we also had this personal attack on me. [Canfield and the limited partnership had been accused of fraud and misallocation of funds by the Oregon Corporation Commissioner who had issues the cease and desist order.] For a while there, I thought the great bureaucratic machine was going

133

to chew me up. It was a tremendous relief a few weeks later, when we had given them financial information, and they cooled off. But they didn't withdraw the cease and desist order because technically they were right. Technically I wasn't supposed to accept money and give any evidence of indebtedness to more than ten people. I was supposed to be registered to make a public offering first."

Canfield had consulted an attorney before the move to Oregon to be sure that California law permitted him to accept funds from would-be residents who wished to invest in the project. He was told that as long as the number was under one hundred, the law did not consider it a public offering. After the move to Oregon, he again consulted an authority — this time the office of the Securities Commission — where he found that Oregon law considered an offering to more than ten persons to be a public one. By this time, considerably more than that number were involved. The project was not yet in a position to qualify for registration, but Canfield came away with the impression that as long as investments were solicited on a personal basis and the Securities Commission was not forced to intervene as a result of a complaint, there would be no problem. It was a risk, but a temporary one and certainly not the only one involved in the enterprise.

As it turned out a Cerro Gordo staff member, disgruntled over the way in which Canfield was managing thing, blew the whistle with the Securities Commission and very nearly shut the whole project down. Forced by the cease and desist order to refrain from seeking investments, mounting bills and mortgage payments would have driven the limited partnership into bankruptcy.

After weeks of negotiation with authorities in Salem, Oregon, Canfield managed to convince them that he was not, in fact, guilty of fraud or misallocation of funds, and the criminal charges were dropped. The cease and desist order remained in effect, however, since it was technically appropriate, but the project was permitted to continue to solicit investment through a loophole in the law.

During the same period, from mid-1974 through the spring of the next year, membership in the Community Association fell by about a third — from 150 to about 100 families. It was a time for the most committed to dig in and hold tight. Little promotion was done. Instead, efforts were concentrated on a new first phase development plan for the site, under which a group of three small residential clusters and the first commercial complex would be built.

In May 1976, an organizational change took place. Ironically, it is one that might have satisfied the Stills and others who abandoned the project over the issue of control in 1974. Under the new arrangement, a fourth project entity was created, called the Cerro Gordo Cooperative, Inc. It consists of ten families who will be the first homebuilders, residents, and business people on the site. This group has purchased the entire ranch from Canfield Associates (the limited partnership) and will be registered with state and federal securities authorities for the purpose of selling shares. The cooperative will thus assume the responsibility for raising the capital that will be required to develop the site — a role formerly held by the limited partnership. Canfield retains exclusive

Some of the first new towners. Most of the first to arrive settled into small houses in Cottage Grove — some as early as 1973. As the dream of a new town was tested by months of wrangling, hearings, and red tape, some settled in Cottage Grove to stay. Others adopted a wait-and-see attitude. Dorothy Walker on the porch of "Chestnut Spread"; Chuck Missar, who at the time this picture was taken was remodeling an old house in town for his family; Bill Courtney, the owner of one of the community's first businesses, a company that makes and sells model railroad supplies; and Nick and Cindy Cutting and their children John and Kim.

development rights to the site, however, and thereby retains a measure of actual control. The relation between Cerro Gordo Cooperative and Canfield Associates is that of mutual authority. Neither can act without the approval of the other. Membership in the cooperative is limited to those members of the Community Association who are either residents of the town (once built) or those who have filed an intent to reside within one year and have been accepted by the cooperative. As homesites are developed, shares in the cooperative may be converted into land and building purchase. Profits from sales will either be returned to the cooperative members in the form of dividends, or will be put to work as further development capital, depending on the vote of the membership.

Membership in the Community Association has increased again to about 120 families. Canfield is optimistic. He admits that there is a great deal of hard work ahead of the group — raising the capital necessary for construction will not be easy. But in the years since the project's inception, about a hundred families have generated over $300,000. Chris Canfield believes that having survived 1974, there is very little that could stop the project now. It isn't just that public opposition has faded as the Cerro Gordo folk have become assimilated into the Cottage Grove landscape. And it isn't because they have managed to thread their way through the array of bureaus and agencies that control or regulate land-development projects and money-raising endeavors. That process seems to have no end. It is because in the struggle to get a town built this odd collection of people who assembled themselves, sight unseen, by mail, have made themselves into a community. And though the dreams of living gently on the land in a village in the forest still kindle them — it is the discovery that they must and can work together to make it happen that has made the whole thing alive. And it is alive with or without the village in the forest.

Canfield states without a blink — and we believe him — that if the site were lost tomorrow, the people would assemble somewhere and someone would ask, "Well, what should we do now?" And the operative word would be "we."

By the time you read this, there may be the beginning of a town on the hill above Dorena Lake. We don't know what kind of a town it will be. It probably will be auto-less. Its residents may have worked out a system for converting sewage and other solid waste into energy-producing fuel. It will probably include a number of small businesses, either services or light manufacturing, or both. It will surely include a school. The homes will be mostly private, though some may be occupied on a communal basis. Eventually there will be wild areas that are preserved for nonhuman inhabitants. There will be recreational facilities owned in common by the residents and, of course, gardens, both private and communal. There may be farm-scale agricultural efforts as well. The people who live there will probably be struggling for an economic self-sufficiency that will be a long time coming. They will almost surely have attained some measure of fame as a town. For as far as we know, they will be the only new town in the United States to be built from scratch since the nineteenth century by the people who live in it, and governed on a cooperative basis.

When we want it, we get it; when we're through with it, we get rid of it. When we're through with it, it immediately becomes a nuisance, bothersome, hazardous, repulsive, demoralizing and a danger to health. Thus the "good life," the life of material riches, the life to which we claim birth-right, requires immediate disposal of the unpacked, the used, the out-moded, the un-eaten, the excreted. In the city even leaves and grass clippings are considered waste.

What we have lost is the knowledge that the materials which nourish, clothe, and shelter us are made from the same materials we have just discarded. Everything we need for next years's food, clothing, and shelter is in last year's garbage pile. All we need to find is a means for transforming the garbage pile and the energy to do it with.

The model is near at hand, indeed, underfoot. The obvious model is the natural "pyramid of life." All natural life is based on cycles rather than one-way streets. Everything dies and decays in the soil by the action of bacteria and fungi with the release of carbon dioxide and water and the nutrients potassium, nitrogen, phosphorous, sulfur, etc., into the soil, water, and atmosphere. Plants utilize the sun's energy to reassemble the building blocks, and the whole system cycles again through plant eaters and the eaters of plant eaters — each individual giving up its wastes and then its body to nourish another individual or to return to the beginning of the cycle.

We are a part of all that, too, only we are mostly oblivious to our part. The main result of our obliviousness is that we lay enormous waste to the cycles, each individual using raw materials all out of proportion to the value of his return. True, the raw materials laid waste do get returned to the cycle — eventually. But, in our attempt to "dispose" of the "wastes" we bury them so deeply or disperse them so widely that the natural cycles take too long, and a dangerous break in time appears between use and reuse. Thus, two seemingly unconnected environmental problems get connected: (1) the land gets poorer and (2) the streams and lakes get more polluted. What's polluting the stream and that lake is the very stuff we need to fertilize the land.

The solution to this is no stranger to the naturalist, the organic farmer, the eco-freak, and the recycler. Knowing we are in the cycle and not apart from it leads us to support the cycle, rather than confuse, delay, or break the cycle. We encourage the environment that encourages decomposers. We welcome worms, insects, and birds. We return the nutrients we have taken in the harvest, and as more nutrients are released from the decaying rocks below, their concentrations increase, the cycle thus becomes richer, more varied and the harvest more nourishing, more health sustaining.

So what does all this have to do with "waste management" in our town? Simply this; we didn't create cycles, but we are forced to live by them. If we choose to survive indefinitely, we "choose" to live by the laws of the cycles, live in the cycles, love the cycles. That is, we choose what's already so. This creates some priorities for planning. (1) Reduce materials used temporarily or only once (e. g. packaging) to a minimum. (2) If it can be re-used as is, re-use it. (3) If it can't be re-used as is, recycle it, and love the process.

137

"Waste management" usually means planning how to get rid of what someone else has produced. It doesn't deal with the input. In our developing consciousness, we will want to deal with material at the source rather than allow it to become a problem and react to the effect.

The average American discards 3 pounds of waste — apart from garbage — a day. This is paper bags, cardboard boxes, milk cartons, plastic bags, cans, bottles, etc. Nearly all is used once and discarded. We can surely reduce this to one third or less, one pound per person a day. Sometimes we can avoid packaging altogether ("Do you want a bag for your new books?" "No. Save the trees."), but usually some kind of container is required — for the milk or the alfalfa seeds, for example. Here the re-use bags can be re-used indefinitely until ripped; thick paper bags can make a few trips to the grocery before becoming garbage bags or lunch bags. Cans and bottles may be re-used indefinitely if you give them the same courtesy your dishes get. The proper use of plastics is in well-constructed containers, not in throw-a-ways. They last virtually forever until stressed to breaking. An organic food co-op in Corrales, N. M., provides no containers for anything; you bring your own and weigh the beans, honey, fruit, etc., as you fill up.

Getting a new refrigerator or bicycle? Sell your old one to the folks in the cluster, the commune, or the homestead at a price they can't refuse — or give it to them and take it off your taxes. The scrap lumber left over from your new room is not scrap to another — advertise. If it really is scrap, saw it up and carry it down to old Mrs. Jones's woodpile. Pull and straighten old nails. If an old house or barn is going to get demolished somewhere, buy the right to recycle it — very cheap lumber of very good quality. Look through your junk mail for paper used on only one side and use the other side for scrap, notes, even letters to friends. Ask your neighbor if you can sort your garbage for his goats.

"IF IT CAN'T BE RE-USED AS IS, RECYCLE IT."

What you saw in the previous section is our human-activity equivalent of nature's using one individual's body to nourish another. What follows is the equivalent of returning the body to the beginning of the cycle. Re-cycling. Nearly all of our "waste" can be recycled naturally; garbage, plant cuttings, paper products, sewage, "waste" water, sawdust. Some can't; glass, metals, plastic. Let's talk about the latter.

The nearer we can re-use something in its present form, the less the energy cost of re-use. When cans and bottles cannot be re-used as cans and bottles, they can be melted down to make new metal or glass products. This takes more energy than simply cleaning them up for re-use, but less than producing new metal or glass from raw materials. We probably won't be able to support the entire cycle within our town — steel and aluminum cans, glass bottles, and certain plastics may have to be returned to centers where remelting is done on a large scale.

Paper is a good example of a material that can be re-used or recycled at any level. Examples, the re-use of bags, writing on the back of sheets, sharing a *magazine subscription (re-used $$, too), re-using mailing envelopes. When no longer useful in its "suchness," it goes back to the paper manufacturer where it is re-pulped, cleaned, and rolled. More energy is required, but fewer trees are cut. (One Sunday's edition of the Los Angeles Times requires 60 acres of trees.) If all this is not possible, it may be composted, or burned for heat and the ashes composted. Even though its value as paper is gone, all the nutrients are still there.*

Collection and sorting is a problem in most communities — not for any fundamental reason, but because we are accustomed to plunking everything into two fifty-five gallon containers and hauling them to the curb on Thursday morning. Sorting need not be a problem if we deal with it at the source. For example, we may set up local collection centers within easy carrying distance, say for a cluster of houses. The center has a line of containers on a cart. Each container is clearly marked: "Steel," "Aluminum," "Glass," "Plastic," "Re-cyclable Paper," "Compostables." A citizen is not likely to dump his garbage in the aluminum container, but to sort it first; later he (she) will probably use separate containers in his own house to save him(her)self the trouble of sorting.

RECYCLING ORGANICS

Everything that's left, can be treated in natural cycles, cycles which we can give our attention and support. The materials include organic left-overs, e.g. wood cuttings, grass, leaves, garbage, paper, and waste water and sewage. Nature decomposes either with plenty of air, or without it; the results are very different. In aerobic decomposition (with air), organic material is reduced to carbon dioxide, water, "humus," and nutritious minerals. In anaerobic decomposition (without air) some carbon dioxide is formed (as well as humus and minerals), but most of the organic matter is converted into methane, a powerful energy source. Thus both energy and nutrients are recovered if anaerobic decomposition is employed.

One option open to us is to use standard sewage systems and collect everything in one pipe — the 5 gallon flush toilet, the bath, the kitchen sink, and the washing machine. This is what we do now in the city; what we will do with the septic tank system. It has the advantages that all elements of the system are available, installation is standard, and health approvals are routine. It has the disadvantage that everything that goes down the pipe is gone. Recovery of any part, water or solids, is expensive, and difficult once they are mixed. The water dissolves much of the excreta and the effort required to clean it up again is enormous. Meanwhile the excreta are so dispersed in the large volume of water that any collecting of the solids requires a similar effort.

Let us consider a second option, namely, keeping the "waste" water separate from "sewage." If we never mix the soapy, dirty water that comes from the kitchen sink, bathtub, lavatory, and washing machine with the booty from the toilet (and garbage disposal if you must have one) then the product is still relatively clean water. Several advantages accrue. It is easier to get water down a pipe than sewage, so a smaller diameter, less expensive collection system can be built. What is collected also requires a minimum of treatment before it is ready for return to the food cycle. After aeration in a trickling filter (a

139

trickling filter is a bed of rocks over which the water is trickled in open air — flora grow on the rock surfaces and decompose some of the organic matter, releasing dissolved nutrients) the water is ready for algae growth, aquaculture tanks, hydroponic agriculture of animal feeds and aerial food crops, and the orchard. Any run off from these is certainly cleaner than the Row River, but we will want a catch pond just in case something goes haywire, and then the dammed runoff can be pumped up and sprayed into the forest.

If we back up now to where the water was kept separate from the sewage, we find both advantages and disadvantages accruing on the sewage side. The biggest gain is in the resource. Manure of any form is very rich in body nutrients, and still has a lot of its organic potential energy left, too. Human feces is particularly righ in nitrogen (exceeded only by chicken shit) and when mixed with straw, leaves, garbage, paper, or other organic leftovers, is the best possible feedstock for the anaerobic methane digestor. About half of the organic weight is converted into methane (50-60%) and carbon dioxide (40-50%) in a few days time, a most valuable resource if care is taken to keep the capital cost down.

Besides the energy rich methane resource, the liquor from the digestor is rich in dissolved nutrients. A portion of the liquor will probably be returned to wet the feedstock and help keep the environment right for anaerobe growth, but the remainder, may then join the "waste" water after thorough aeration and trickle filtering to assure the death of any pathogens, to help nourish the hydroponic gardens. What is left is solids, organic and inorganic minerals, sludge from the bottom and scum from the top of the liquid, which are solid concentrated nutrition. In Goleta, Calif., these solids are de-watered, dried, and sold for garden compost. We may wish to treat them one step further, a step which absolutely stamps out disease and makes them even more ready for return to the food chain — more later.

The disadvantage: the solids won't go down a sewage pipe by themselves. If we flush them with 5 gallons of water they will, but then they're too dilute for the methane digestor. So we may have to collect our sewage in a holding tank, pump it into a tank-trailer, and carry it to the central plant.

But hallelujah! In the process we have eliminated the 5 gallon flush toilet, that Victorian symbol of body repression, and cut our water demand by 30-40%! A number of reasonable alternatives are available. The 2-quart flush is an ideal replacement if you require the same standards for an odor-free and sanitary existence. This employs a small bowl with a flap valve in the bottom. The small amount of water in the bowl goes down into the holding tank with the solids and a small amount of clean water is run in after the valve closes. If we decide against a central methane plant, several aerobic composting toilets become candidates. The best know is the Swedish Clivus Multrum which passively accepts all body wastes, toilet paper, and kitchen garbage, yielding dry, odorless compost after a couple of years. If electricity power is no problem, the new Biu-let provides similar service at lower front end cost but consumes 250 watts continuously. I hear that a group of creative, independent people in Mendocino Co., Calif., have constructed a variety of composting privys and gotten the county health approvals, too! All these alternatives to the 5 gallon flush suffer the disadvantage that approvals for creative approaches may not be easily obtained in Oregon.

We are left with the largest volume of renewable resources — the paper, food wastes, bones, leaves, garden cuttings, rakings, hoeings, and shovelings, animal droppings, sawdust, wood chips, etc., — the organic "waste." Compost it. In the winter we may arrange to pass much of it through the methane digester to boost our gas resource for heating, but mostly we will just compost it, and carry the clean compost to our gardens and fields. Into the compost rows will go, in addition, ashes from the stoves and fireplaces and the solids from the methane digestor. (Remember the solids from the digestor?) Mechanical composters, huge slowly rotating drums, may compost a given mass faster than piles or rows and take much of the labor out of the process. A well constructed drum could be turned twice a day by hand and the product hand sieved, the coarsest material being returned for another cycle. However, if we can't afford that, we can always compost in rows or piles and turn, aerate, and wet the material by hand.

Now these aren't all the possibilities, obviously. I don't even know all the possibilities....Please complain about the good ones I've missed. Everyone is an expert at this point — which implies that none of us are, even the professionals. Remember, we are building a new town with new ideas (or ancient ones) for a new era in which many of the accepted ideas are failing.

Part Three
Home Ground

Home Ground

This part isn't going to be easy. It's one thing to breeze into a place you've read about in letters, spend a few days, talk to people, and observe their situation with that clarity of vision that distance makes possible. It's another thing to try to pull the same stunt on your home ground, where you know all the back roads. And of course it's impossible here to muster any objectivity at all. We care far too much. For the longest time, we thought of not talking about home. We wrestled with our consciences — torn between wanting to make the book the best possible (and knowing that some of the best stories are right here) and wanting to spare our neighbors the exposure. The people here are jealous of their privacy (why else would they choose to live in so remote a place?) and are properly suspicious of change. In this time, both characteristics have a high index for survival and stability. We don't care to tamper with either.

Sometime after our return home from visiting the other towns we've discussed in this book, a friend came by and the conversation turned, as it often does, to local problems. Michael is a sensitive and intelligent man who has made the study of problems his specialty. Sometimes we think he has a morbid fascination for trouble. God knows he's had his own personal share and then some; you'd think that such a person would take up something cheerful. But Michael has turned his gaze on the problems of the world and has found much to occupy him. The marvelous thing about him is that he is not morose. He manages to immerse himself in trauma and can still see the human condition as a story with funny edges. His sense of humor is as lively as his interest in adversity.

Michael claims to be a farmer. We think he would like to be a farmer. But one doesn't drop a professional career at the age of thirty-five and just "be" a farmer. You have to grow to it. Michael is trained as an economic analyst and planner. And he brings his skills with him wherever he goes. Even to the country. While he's growing to farming, he looks at data and reads in it the future. He compares two sets of figures and finds therein a story that no one else perceives. He understands economic and social problems like few others because he is so passionate about life and because he is as moral a person as you'd find. Michael is one of the few technicians we know who can translate their profession into direct human experience. He looks at the times in which we live, and he sees both disaster and huge opportunity.

In official circles, he is regarded as a kind of pariah. We suppose the excuse might be that he is too "radical." Or that his ideas are impractical. But when you don't know or won't admit that the ship is sinking, the advice to swim for your life always sounds a little far out. We think Michael is a kind of modern day prophet and prophets have never been very popular in local circles. People always sense somewhere in the viscera when they are hearing truth. And often, when it is not good news, they hate both news and bearer.

On this particular occasion, Michael was talking about our county. He was talking about great plunges in production of goods (in this case agricultural products and timber) and a corresponding increase in government employment. He was talking about huge instability. And he was talking about depression. Together we talked about the growth of government, its increasing influence over all aspects of life, and we talked about that deadening of the spirit that seems to overtake people when they sense themselves impotent — incapable of control of their own economic or political destiny. We talked about the traditional California antidote for economic doldrums that always includes a promise of full-employment — the development of agricultural and timber lands into shopping centers, parking lots, vacation "estates" and the ensuing suburbanization of the countryside. The ultimate cheat.

The more we talked, the more we began to realize that what Michael was telling us applied to small towns everywhere. It didn't take long after that for us to decide that, like it or not, we had to talk about our own territory because it was the only way we could deal with the problems Michael was describing, and we couldn't omit them from this book. They are too important. And we simply don't know enough about any other place to show how they work.

Not that we know enough about this place either. I don't think there is any such thing as enough. But because we live here, we can see how the pressures work on people, forcing them into corners. And the hints of some of the answers are to be found scattered about — hardly noticeable and without credibility. They need looking at.

Hard Times Coming

It is real — a kind of spirit that is drawing people here. Take that as you will, but it is somehow at the center of things. The spirit we mean has a great deal to do with the land, and as many variations as there are people to experience it. But it is there, unmistakably. And though we will have to answer to our Los Angeles cousins for this, we have to tell you that in order to describe the spirit, it is necessary to talk first about Northern California.

California is a state that runs north and south. Its principal geographic feature (the ones of scale) run in that direction: the coastline, the Coast Range, the principal valleys, and the magnificent mountains called Sierra Nevada. It is a huge state. To drive from Oregon to the Mexican border could easily occupy two days. Since the principal highways also run north and south one would probably make such a trip on old Route 99 (now Interstate 5) which carves its way down through the enormous and fertile great Central Valley. Once an arid grassland, this huge trough in the center of the state is the source of most of California's land-based wealth. Irrigated by the rivers which drain the Sierra Nevada and cross the Central Valley on their way to the Pacific, it is farmland supreme, and the home of agribusiness. Farming by self-propelled machine was invented in California. The tracklayer tractor was conceived by a man who got stuck in the bogland of the Sacramento River Delta. The first combine was used here. The list is a long one.

The Central Valley ends its northern stretch in the mountains near the Oregon border. Its southern boundary is at the foot of the Tehachapi mountain range just south of Bakersfield. Below that lies the Los Angeles basin, desert, and more mountains.

Somewhere along its length, lying across the state from west to east, is an imaginary line that divides north from south, as real as any political boundary, though unofficial. Any Californian will tell you that it is there — though probably no two of them would draw it in precisely the same place. Though the distinction is apt to be lost on any easterner (most of whom regard *all* Californians as slightly nuts), local observers are quick to point out their own distinctions between those who choose voluntarily to live in Los Angeles and those who wouldn't be caught dead in the place (even though many of us started there).

Climate and the influences originally experienced across the Mexican border once made the two ends of the state very different, but the culture of
147

this century has blurred those distinctions. Los Angeles is the archetypal city of the automobile, that great equalizer, and the tentacles of flash and fast food that accompany the progress of the family car in and out of any concentration of people are now to be found all over the state. The cities of the north (and elsewhere) look more and more like Los Angeles every day.

But underneath the common asphalt, the differences between north and south are still there, and in the countryside they are visible to anyone whose eyes are accustomed to the light. California is still a transition zone from the deserts of the south and Mexico, to the pine and fir forests of Oregon and Washington. The ends of the state reflect those differences and those differences work on the people who live on the land.

Originally, those whites who peopled the north end of the state were woodsmen and homesteaders — folk to whom any group of more than ten was an anathema. Their grandchildren are still here. A few have never been out of the valley in which they were born — except maybe when dragged out by a World War. Some live back in the woods and mountains still — scattered like seeds across the landscape, living entirely alone and by their own hands — the memories of their pioneer ways dying quietly one by one, their cabins quickly recovered by the woods.

Many of *their* children live in the little towns of the northern counties — somehow straddling the past and present. It is an awkward pose: one foot in some kind of imported rural suburb, complete with air conditioning and patio barbeque, and the other on a horse. For the most part, these are people who have tasted the city's exports and liked the flavor, but who are not won over. Their ties with the land — and the past — are too strong. And they have that kind of fierce independence that resists any change and resents any interference. These are the Memory People. They own ranches that they no longer ranch. They work as woodspeople — when they can find work. They work at farming, but sell real estate or insurance to earn a living. Their recollections are large — taking in those sinewy ties with the land that go back generations. The spirit of the land works on them — if no longer through them.

And now they have neighbors. Fleeing the cities, north and south, all manner and descriptions of neighbors. At the start — somewhere back in the sixties — they were long-hairs. Dropouts. The disenchanted — the disenfranchised. Seeking the spirit, they sought the land. In the cities they saw demons at work, so they ran for cover. They hid in the bushes and trees of the north. Their children played in the streams. They scratched in the hillsides to grow food. They experimented with drugs, with religions of the East and the trappings of the Native American. They colonized themselves and lived as huge families, scuffling in the dust for a living and tangling with the law at intervals. They were the brats of a rich culture which could afford to dump its offspring naked in the woods and take its chances — or they were the new pioneers come back to teach us all how to live.

Mostly they were disliked. "Hippietypes!" The words run together as one. It is a pejorative. It is a cry of rage. They sell dope. They practice strange rituals. They use food stamps. To the Memory People these interlopers were the dregs — the very worst that the city had to offer, and they had set up housekeeping in the front yard! It was an outrage. And it still is, for mostly the newcomers have stayed on, gradually blending into the landscape as they became accustomed to it, and as the sight of long hair and beards became commonplace. As they stayed on, many cut their hair, switched from acid to Old Crow, and found work. The assimilation has started. But make no mistake — in the bars and lodge halls, the rage simmers. It will die slowly.

The immigrants still come. Some with long hair, rhetoric, and rucksacks. Many more with vans full of belongings and college degrees. Professors from Los Angeles. Plumbers from Los Altos. Architects and lawyers from San Francisco and San Diego.

Storekeepers. Teachers. Artists. They are moving to the country and to the woods drawn by the dream of independence — stories of a new kind of life — a spiritual quest. The quest centers in the north counties of this state — and has as much to do with what's being left behind as it does with what is ahead. But its effect is unmistakable. The little communities: the coastal fishing towns, the ranch or farm towns, the timber towns will never be the same.

Mendocino is a big county. Two and a quarter million acres or 3,500 square miles — three quarters the size of the entire state of Connecticut. It is the third county north of San Francisco, and to drive to its southern boundary from the Bay Area takes about two hours. It runs from the coastline on the west to the top of the watershed of the Coast Range to the east, on the edge of the slope that drops into the great Central Valley. It is principally mountainous. Timber country, over half of it. On the coast and covering most of the western slope up to elevations of about 3,000 feet are the redwood forests. To the east and in the north are the fir and cedar forests. In between there are forests of hardwood: oak and madrone, at the lower elevations, and on the south slopes where the trees don't do so well, or where the timber has been cut or burned, the chaparral.

Threaded through this mountainous land, for the most part following the watercourses, are the county's valleys. The two largest are the Ukiah Valley (containing the city of Ukiah, the county seat) and the Anderson Valley. There is more flat land at Hopland, in Potter Valley, and in the northeast corner of the county, Round Valley.

Until recently, these valleys were farming lands. Orchards of pears, prunes, apples, and walnuts were common. Toward the coast where the moisture made it possible to maintain year-round pastures without irrigation, dairy ranches were successful. Inland, cattle were raised on the mountain ranges. In the valleys near towns, there was some truck farming. In vestigial form, these things still exist.

But since the twenties, the county's principal economic strength came from the harvest of its timber. And except for the depression years, the harvest rate in the county averaged a little under 200 million board feet per year. The giant redwood and fir of the county were toppled by crews who spent their lives in the woods, working the huge buck saws by hand. All over the county there were small mills which, during the logging season, accumulated timber on their decks and in the winter cut it into the lumber that built San Francisco, Oakland, and Berkeley.

149

Immediately after World War II, two events occurred simultaneously that were to change this timber country forever. One was the perfection of the chain saw, powered by a clamoring gasoline motor. The other was the postwar housing boom. In just four years between 1946 and 1950, the timber harvest in Mendocino County shot from just under 200 million board feet to just over 400 million. But it didn't stop there. In the fifties it climbed again, this time more than doubling, until in 1957, it reached the all-time high of almost 1 *billion* board feet!

During those years, fortunes were made here. The demand for timber and the corresponding leap in local production drew the attention of outsiders. In corporate offices in the East and the Pacific Northwest, cool and appraising scrutiny was directed at this county. Field men were dispatched to roam the woods and talk to mill owners. Plans were made. Eventually, tracts of land were quietly purchased. The people of Mendocino County didn't take notice. If they had, they would not have paid attention. There was plenty of timber for everyone. And the boom was going to last forever.

It didn't. Almost as fast as it had come, the boom collapsed. By 1962, production had fallen to 500 million board feet — exactly one half of the peak year. To be sure, it was still more than twice the rate of harvest of the prewar years, but the boom was over. The harvest rate has remained more or less at that level until recently.

The years during the decline of the timber market immediately following the housing bonanza were years of consolidation. It was probably during that period that the people of Mendocino County lost control over their principal industry. During that time, the many small locally-owned mills that had sprung up as the timber market soared, struggled to keep going. Some of them folded for lack of markets or due to poor management. But many others were forced out of business by the corporate mills that had moved in. The pattern was simple. The large mills simply dumped lumber on the market sufficient to drive the price down. They sat back and took their losses for a year or so while the small operators began to strangle in the glut. In this manner, many of the smallest mills simply folded up altogether. Others welcomed an offer to be purchased by their big competition. Gradually the timber industry in the county became big business, and the people became employees.

It is that way to this day. The timber industry in this county is dominated by four large companies, only one of which (the smallest) is locally owned. Of the other three, two are controlled from the state of Oregon and one from Chicago. Virtually the county's entire timber resources and over one quarter of its work force are dependent upon decisions made out of the county and out of the state of California.

But this is not the end of the story. The timber resource that at one time seemed endless, now appears to be running out. And the big corporations are beginning to have to scramble in order to maintain profitability.

In 1968, the United States Forest Service issued a report in which two important facts were made public. The first was that in order for the timber industry to continue cutting without gradually eliminating the resource on which it depends, the rate of harvest in this region would have to be reduced by about a third — from a little over 500 million board feet a year to about 340. The figure of 340 million board feet per year is called the *sustained yield harvest rate* — the rate at which the cutting of timber is roughly equivalent to the rate at which it grows. The second fact which came to light in the 1968 report was a prediction, and was based on the first fact. It stated that at the then-current rate of harvest (510 million board feet per year) the timber resource on privately owned (timber company) lands would be exhausted by 1978.

As far as we are able to tell, the report was ignored. Certainly there is no sign that the corporations controlling both the privately owned timber and most of the mills which process it, voluntarily scaled down their operations in order to insure that this region would continue to have a timber industry. In fact, the opposite appears to be the case. And the Forest Service prediction now appears to have been quite accurate. As this is written, only a fraction of the first-growth timber on company lands is left, and the second-growth is not yet considered commercially harvestable. Corporate interest has now turned to the timber on *public* lands — those controlled by the Forest Service and the Bureau of Land Management.

What does this mean for Mendocino County? On the one hand, if the timber companies are successful in changing the regulations that alter the present sustained yield policies of these agencies, the corporations will continue to be able to harvest timber on public lands at the present rate and sustain operations at their present scale for a few years more. If that happens, cutting will continue to exceed the growth rate and, eventually, the resource in the county will be totally exhausted. On the other hand, if the sustained yield policies of the Forest Service and BLM remain unchanged, a reduction in the harvest rate, with its corresponding loss of jobs and general depressing effect on the local economy is inevitable. Either way, the people of Mendocino County will lose. And in either case, there is now every sign that when the timber resource has been reduced to the point at which it is no longer profitable to operate in Mendocino County, the large companies will go elsewhere.

In 1975, the harvest rate dropped by about 55 million board feet, or 11 per cent — a figure far short of the one third reduction necessary to bring harvest in line with growth. The reasons for the drop have partly to do with a sluggish housing market (caused in part by high interest rates and little federal encouragement), partly due to rising costs, and partly due to dwindling timber reserves. Whatever the reasons, the effects in the county were unmistakable. During February of 1975, unemployment in the county — traditionally highest during the winter months when loggers are unable to work in the woods — reached an all-time high of 20.9 per cent. The effect of this loss of personal income was felt throughout the entire county and was magnified as it passed through the economy. Though the decrease in the value of timber production in the county for that year was $18.7 million, the total economic impact was a loss of almost $53 million throughout all sectors of the economy, or a net loss of $1.81 for every dollar drop in value of the timber harvest.

It is clear that in a county already feeling the pinch of a chronically high unemployment rate and soaring welfare costs, such a drop in its principal industry, which is bound to come sooner or later, will have disastrous effects.

Those who look in the county's economy for large-scale employment alternatives to the ailing timber industry, are apt to be disappointed.

Agriculture in the county, since World War II, has undergone a complete change. Once a mainstay in the economy, producing a wide variety of field crops and fruit, it is now tending toward monoculture and employs only 5 per cent of the work-force. Crops that used to be grown for local consumption have been replaced by those that can be marketed outside the area. Over half of the county's entire output is in grapes and pears — two export crops that both depend on a maze of middlemen and a distribution system in which the grower receives a fraction of the value of the crop he produces. The result is that, though food prices continue to rise, farmers, faced with rising costs of production (fuel, seed, equipment, and so forth), make less. And local stores must import to the area food products that used to be grown locally.

As the pressure mounts, farmers and ranchers sell out and prime agricultural land is given over to shopping malls and motels. And as the trend continues, the rural county, once a self-sufficient economic unit, becomes transformed into a rural suburb — a satellite economy dependent on the same tenuous lines of supply, sustained by fossil fuels, that feed any city.

The people of Mendocino County have very little economic independence. Their jobs are at the mercy of corporate decision makers far away who put profit ahead of local community welfare. Goods and services come to residents of the county through a similar corporate system over which they have little, if any, control. Prices and quality standards are established elsewhere. Complaints may be directed to the head office. No one is in charge. Everyone is just a cog in the system. No one is responsible. But all are vulnerable.

Into this climate, the city and suburban refugees are coming. Until the last five years, the patterns of movement have been from the cities toward the suburbs. In California, the counties of Marin and Sonoma, directly north of San Francisco have experienced huge growth since World War II. The same patterns are visible in the counties immediately surrounding the Los Angeles area: Riverside, San Bernadino, and Orange Counties have all but filled up with bedroom communities.

Those pattern are no longer so evident. Movement now seems to be leap-frogging the suburbs, headed for rural areas. And many of those moving to the country are moving from the suburbs as well as from cities.

The mountains, redwood forests, and coastline of Mendocino County have always been attractive to visitors. But until lately, the visitors came during the summer and on weekends. The rest of the time, the woods, the little valley towns and coastal villages were left to the handful of people who inhabited them. All that is changing. The tourists still come. But now they look for real estate.

In a setting of economic instability (if not depression) and political uncertainty, any influx of population creates further imbalance. In this county, it is potential disaster. Though the signs are visible in all the county's communities, they are indelibly marked in the coastal village of Mendocino.

152

The Town of Last Resort

MENDOCINO, CALIFORNIA

NOTE TO THE READER: *Elsewhere in this book, you will find the names of real people used in connections with their stories. There was no reason not to use the real names, and one very good reason for doing so: nothing is quite so convincing as fact. In the story that follows, however, we decided to alter our policy. As we write this, Mendocino is a town torn by dissension, and struggling with a number of serious problems, any one of which could change its face and alter its character for years to come. The people with whom we talked were glad to have us do so and recognized the good that could come from an exposure of their problems to those in other rural communities and to those who might be thinking of living in one. But they were not eager to add to their own burden — either as individuals deeply embroiled in controversy, which often takes personal and unpleasant turns, or as a community with enough pressure from outside already. After some discussion, we decided that it would be best to give our respondents what little protection we could by omitting their names from this book. We, and the people of Mendocino with whom we talked, apologize to you for the need to do this.*

Perched on a bluff above the rocks and surf — at the very edge of the Pacific — is a scatter of weatherbeaten frame buildings; old houses, water towers, barns, and chicken coops. One of the most attractive little towns on the north coast of California plunked down amid some of its most spectacular countryside. In the little back alleys and in the empty lots are tangles of berries, flowering weeds, and nasturtiums gone wild. In spots, the old buildings lean on each other for support; the buildings show the effects of poverty and neglect, and the elements have created gardens and secret places. Everywhere you look there is something beautiful — the more so because it was never intended to be that way. It just happened.

There are few places in California more attractive. And there is probably no place that is more distressed. The town, for over a hundred years a home for children, ponies, and dogs, is now being invaded by outsiders. It is too expensive for people with families and modest incomes to live there anymore.

Taxes have soared. And the people are in a long debate over the town's future. Some want the town to cash in on its present popularity — tourists are big business. Some see commercialization of the town as its end and are desperate to preserve it as a place for their children to grow up in. Some say there is nothing we can do anyway. It is an old California story.

The shop was closed. Outside, the tourists were going by. A lady with big cheeks and pink curlers under a bandana pressed her face to the glass on the front door. She vanished and was immediately replaced (at a lower pane) by the scowling face of a chubby kid with glasses — brows knit together in a glare. He stared at us for an instant — and was gone.

"Sometimes when we're up at the house, they open the gate, come up the steps, and right into the living room. 'Oh!' they say, 'We thought this was a shop.' They come right up even though the yard is full of my son's toys."

"How does that make you feel?" A pause.

"Like shit."

C is a newcomer. In 1974, he and his wife moved to the little town, bought a house, and a local business. Apparently, the house they bought and subsequently restored — looks to some of the thousands of tourists who pass through the village each year, a lot like one of the town's little shops, many of which are in converted bungalows, or old stables. Some of the shops are galleries, or sell gifts. Some of them are operated by local craftspeople who sell pottery, leather goods, jewelry, or wood products.

Ironically, it was partly this kind of integration — shops in the same block as residences — that attracted C and his wife to the town in the first place. But the tourists have changed all that. There is no place to get away from them. Once a summer-and-weekend-only feature of the village and a boon to its economy, the tourists are now a part of what is generally considered to be a problem — one of the sets of forces that is seen to be damaging the town as a place to live — and is causing dissension and debate.

Mendocino has been "discovered." Once the not-so-secret haven for artists and beachcombers from the Bay Area who came to get salty faces and drink beer in the local saloon, the town is now considered by holiday-seekers as "a quaint New England-style village on the shore of the Pacific Ocean, right alongside California's scenic Highway 1, an easy day's drive from the Bay Area." C tells us, "This year we got tour busses for the very first time. It used to be we just got people who came here for the same reasons people came here to live. They loved the ocean, and they liked to walk in the open meadows, or in the woods around town. Or they combed the beaches. Maybe they brought paints and took a class at the Art Center — or just read a book. They were more like the rest of us.

"Now we're getting a different kind of tourist. I call them polyesters and double-knits. They come in motor homes. Or on Greyhound tour busses, and they don't seem to be satisfied with the town as it is. They are rewarding people who offer them a kind of entertainment or shopping that we've never had here and have no real use for. They need to be titillated. They don't take walks along the beach. They walk in my front yard. And they don't just come in the summertime anymore. They're coming all year long."

Mendocino often impresses visitors as looking remarkably like a Maine coastal village. The comparison is apt and not surprising when you examine the history of the place and discover that some of its earliest settlers came from Maine. The town was used as a setting for the filming of "The Russians Are Coming! The Russians Are Coming!" — a wonderful story of an encounter between the inhabitants of a small town on Cape Cod and a stray Russian submarine. After comparing this California village with its eastern counterparts, visitors often go on to remark that "they must not have known it doesn't snow in California, otherwise they wouldn't have built such steep roofs." A local craftsman, who has made a study of local history, sniffs at this lack of respect for the intelligence of his predecessors. They knew precisely about California weather, he points out. In fact they knew so much that they made steep roofs to drain moisture brought by the almost daily fog so that their shingles wouldn't rot.

But the tourists are only part of the problem. There is the sewer problem and the tax problem. And both relate to the tourist problem, which is connected to the matter of private property.

WHAT THE SEWER STARTED

Like most of the little north country towns, Mendocino once had its privacy. Some of the long-time residents remember hearing of the days when the town could be reached only by horseback over the mountains, a trip of some six or seven days from the nearest town, or by boat. In those days, it was a timber town. Since the absence of roads made it impossible to consider cutting the timber on the inland slopes, the lumberjacks came in by sea and up the rivers. They cut the trees, skidded them to the water, and floated them down to the sea. The mills were on the headlands at the ocean's edge. And where there was no harbor, the timber people loaded the boats by cable, sending huge loads of cut lumber by wire over the thrashing surf to ships at anchor.

The people who settled in Mendocino were New Englanders, Finns, and Portuguese, with a mix of others thrown in. The town thrived, and a ring of merchants and farmers grew up around the mill to make the town whole and for years it was this way. When the mill closed, the town fell asleep. Many of the families stayed, and their descendants are still there. Many of the New Englanders have moved on or died out. But the Portuguese and some of the others had more children and deeper roots. Their names are still to be found in the town.

In 1959, an artist from San Francisco visited Mendocino and decided it was a perfect place to work. He bought an old, boarded up house for $2,000 and started the Mendocino Art Center. That was not all he started. Others were beginning to explore the north coast country. As the artists came to town to work, some of the big old houses sprouted signs: Rooms to Let; and widows on pensions found they could supplement their incomes by renting beds. Some of the artists liked the town well enough to stay year-round. A colony began to form. A new restaurant and bar opened. The tourists came. First a trickle, then a stream. An artists' colony always fascinates non-artists.

Later, during the sixties, as the pressure on coastal lands in California mounted and more and more of the virgin coastline was sold and developed, a new state law brought into existence the California Coastal Zone Commission — an agency charged with the task of screening development while preparing legislation to protect the public interest in the state's remaining coastal resource. All coastal communities were subject to rulings by the commission, including Mendocino.

To protect the picturesque town and its unobstructed views of the ocean, in 1975 the state of California purchased the headlands — the open meadowland which surrounds the town on two sides — making the area a state park day-use area.

About the same time, quite apart from a serious local controversy we shall come to shortly, the state of California, acknowledging Mendocino's unique contribution to California history and its value as a landmark, made the main part of the town a historic district under the prevailing laws. A Historic Review Board was appointed to examine and make recommendations on new development within the town as a means of insuring that its historic character would be preserved. This board would prove to be the bulwark of the town's anti-development forces.

Finally, the state of California also enacted legislation making it necessary for all counties to file new general land-use plans. The law specified that all rural and unincorporated areas would have to be zoned. The existing general multi-use rural zoning designations were no longer acceptable. The law further required that all counties were to seek their residents' views and opinions in the formation of their general plans. And it gave deadlines by which this was to be accomplished.

During all this time, Mendocino, along with the other little towns all up and down the coast, grew. The empty houses were filled and fixed up. Real-estate offices opened, and "prestige" homes were offered with private beaches and views of the ocean. The gift shops opened, and a delicatessen. The tourists told their friends and relatives and more restaurants were started. In 1970, the town had its first summer water scare. The water table had dropped. There were too many new wells. Around the town, the hills and canyons were full of young homesteaders, couples and families who came to live in a beautiful place, but couldn't find anything they could afford in town, or who chose to live up on the ridges in the trees away from the tourists.

Then in 1972, the federal Environmental Protection Agency sent letters to town residents announcing that they were to stop polluting the ocean with untreated sewage, or be fined $1,400 per week. The town would have to build a sewer plant. The capacity of the new sewer would determine how much growth could be accommodated by the town.

B is one of the "appeals ladies." It isn't a name she has given herself, but she would, I am sure, answer to it. Since 1972, she and a group of her Mendocino town neighbors (both women and men) have scratched and fought for any chance to oppose what they regard as the destruction of their town by its transformation from a rural family town into a commercial resort and tourist facility. Their method has been to use existing laws and ordinances as the basis for one petition or appeal after another — in order to buy time while the zoning regulations called for by the state of California are painstakingly assembled by the local citizens' advisory committee and county planners.

B came to Mendocino in 1969 with her husband and six children in a Winnebago (now the family car — they couldn't afford to sell it — and a source of huge embarrassment). After a seven-month odyssey, her family selected Mendocino as the town in which they wanted to live. Her reasons for leaving the city they had lived in were plain:

"I had lived in the inner city in the East, and I left there when I noticed that there were very few boys over the age of sixteen who were 'making it' — were not getting into enough trouble to end up in reform school. Three youngsters were killed on my street — they were teenage boys, they were shot. I came home one day from downtown and found my oldest son, who was four and a half at the time, on the street in the middle of a gun battle. Guys were on the

157

street shooting at the roof, and there was another guy up above with a rifle. I grabbed up my son. Later on I thought, my God, my kids are never going to have a chance to grow up!

"I really do hold with some of the ideas they have about primate behavior. They have found that baboons that are protected in the inner circle develop leadership skills and feelings of responsibility. The ones on the fringes — the ones that have no security really, who have to defend themselves, do not. I think kids are just like that. I finally decided that my two sons were more important to me than everything else. So we left."

They bought a house on the edge of Mendocino and settled into small town life. Everyone in the family loved it. But it wasn't long before they began to get the idea that they might not love it forever. About this time, a handful of residents — most of them like B, recent immigrants from big cities — began to think that the little weatherbeaten hometown they had adopted, and had brought their children to, was in danger of becoming a commercial bonanza at their expense. In the debate over the town's new sewer, the first lines of contention between the advocates of development and their opponents were drawn.

Lest we be too quick to separate the good guys from the villains, we should point out that it is not always possible to tell one from the other. Like any other place, Mendocino does not fall into two easily discernible camps: those who play the real-estate market and promote tourism on the one hand, and those who raise kids and circulate petitions on the other. The town, like any place one examines closely, is full of surprises. Some of the oldest residents in Mendocino hate what is happening to it, but steadfastly refuse to support those opposing the town's commercial development because they believe that any man should have the right to do whatever he damn pleases with his property. It is a difficult point to argue. Some of the other residents who have long waited for the town's revival, and remember the leaner days, think the more the better. Some of the merchants that one would expect to have the most to gain by a brisk tourist trade oppose the trend most vocally.

It is difficult to predict anyone's actions. Your opponent in one instance is apt to be your supporter in another — if you let him. And of course any property owner who bought more than two years ago stands to profit enormously by a sale now. Some of the town's most articulate defenders have given up, sold out, and departed. There is a little speculator in all of us.

The chain of events that were set into motion by the EPA's warning to the town are now a tangle of actions and reactions — charges and countercharges. At the risk of being unfair to both the town's promoters and its defenders, we will try to state what happened as simply as possible.

Those who had property that would appreciate in value as a result of the sewer, or simply thought that the town should expect growth (by now the trend was unmistakable), wanted a sewer with a capacity beyond the town's size at the time. Those who were opposed to further commercial development of the town didn't. Along with the debate that raged in the town on that subject, the nucleus of a group of citizens was formed who have ever since been at work and see as their mission the preservation of Mendocino's "hometown" character.

But they lost their first fight. Those members of the town's original Sewer Board who were responsible for planning the new facility and wanted it bigger rather than just big enough got their way. The new sewer would wrap around the empty lots north of town, cross the highway and include land up Little Lake Road. Mendocino, it seems, would grow some more.

Apparently the State Water Resources Board, which was the local agency through which federal funds for the sewer were being administrated, wrote a letter to the Sewer Board of the town of Mendocino in which it was made clear that a condition of the federal grant was that the expanded sewer facility not be a stimulant to uncontrolled development in the town, and that no new hookups to the sewer lines were to be permitted on undeveloped lands until there was a new protective land-use plan for the town. One of the reasons for this letter was a part of the environmental impact report on the sewer which had stated that an adverse effect of the enlarged facility was its potential for encouraging further development in the town — something that its citizens had evidently made clear to investigators that they did not want.

About the same time, the Mendocino Historic Review Board was set up. Under a county ordinance it would have the power to approve or reject any proposed development within the town and the criteria upon which new development was to be judged included its scale and economic impact on the community.

The town's Sewer Board sent the State Water Resources Board a copy of the Historic Review ordinance as an effective protective measure and in effect freed the Sewer Board from responsibility for encouraging development in the town, and withdrew the moratorium on new hookups. Because the anti-development group assumed the town had protection, there was no mapping of undeveloped lands.

Within six months, in an initially unrelated action, a local couple announced their plan to build a new ninety-unit motel and convention center on five acres behind the Catholic Cemetery. The Historic Review Board rejected the plan as out of scale with the community and regarded the potential economic impact on the town as undesirable. The decision was appealed by the developers, and on appeal, those two criteria — scale and economic impact, the principal "teeth" in the protective ordinance — were summarily extracted by the Board of Supervisors. The reason the supervisors gave for their actions was that the ordinance, in its unabridged form was an infringement on personal property rights, and therefore illegal. At the time, no one on the Sewer Board, deeply embroiled as they were in building the new plant, thought or chose to send the State Water Resources Board a copy of the amended ordinance. Meanwhile, the original letter which stated the federal requirement for protective land-use measures was nowhere to be found.

Months later, in the midst of a squabble over yet another hunk of undeveloped land, someone sent the hometown defenders a copy of the contract between the state of California and the federal government in which the requirement that there be protective land-use measures was spelled out as a condition. No one knows where it came from. It was mailed anonymously. The defenders promptly submitted a copy of the amended Historic Review

159

Board's ordinance to the State Water Resources Board, which in turn notified the town's Sewer Board that there would have to be a moratorium on new development until the federal requirements could be met.

Needless to say, the news didn't sit well with the Sewer Board, and a public meeting was held during which, according to B, a number of people who didn't live in the Community Services District yelled at the lawyer that the state had sent to represent them. But the lawyer held firm and the moratorium was imposed. The lawyer also announced that it would be necessary to map all undeveloped lands affected by the moratorium. After asking the assembled citizenry who wished to do so and finding no takers, she proceeded to do so herself. As of this writing, the state-imposed moratorium, in effect until a new county general plan with its zoning of Mendocino is completed, is all the protection against uncontrolled development the town has.

BIG MONEY IN TOWN

In 1974, rumors began to circulate in the town that someone was about to buy the old Mendocino Hotel on Main Street. The hotel is one of the town's landmarks and had been operating for years under various ownerships in a semi-dilapidated state. But it had a view of the ocean, the rooms had old-fashioned furniture, it was clean, the food was pretty good, and no one much minded walking to the john. The rumors proved accurate. The hotel was indeed bought, along with nearby property including one of the town's historic houses. P, a Southern Californian who had made a lot of money with a fast-food franchise operation, had fallen in love with Mendocino. He was going to work a little magic in town and money was no obstacle.

Since his purchase of the hotel and the Kelley House lands (and several subsequent acquisitions), P is a Force in the town. Or perhaps we should say, by virtue of his real-estate purchases, he has become a Force. He doesn't live in the town. He lives in Southern California and comes up occasionally when his other business permits. Based on P's actions — at least those that are visible — it is very difficult to suggest that he has ever meant the town any harm. In fact, there is substantial evidence to suggest the contrary. One of his first public acts was to make the Kelley House and part of the property on which it sits a gift to the town. It is subsequently being restored by Mendocino Historic Research, Inc., a local nonprofit group, and will be preserved, along with part of its original grounds and duck pond (when there is water enough).

Those who make skepticism their first line of investigation suggest that P did well by doing good. By giving the Kelley House to the town, he protected his flank and gained an additional source of water for the hotel — a serious matter each fall before the rains come and restore the water table on the headlands. In his purchase he had picked up one of the town's most important corners, at Lansing and Main (the town's two principal streets) and a sagging barnlike structure affectionately named the Ex-Lax Building because it once housed (among other things) the town's drug store. P divided his property, giving the Kelley House and keeping the corner with the Ex-Lax Building. He then proceeded to pour an incredible amount of money into remodeling the

The top photograph opposite is the Kelley House, built in 1861, bought by the new owner of the Mendocino Hotel, and lovingly restored by local residents. The community has attracted many craftspeople who have steeped themselves in the methods and tastes of the town's earlier days so that a project such as this one presents no problem when it comes to authentic reproduction of nineteenth-century architectural details. There is, in fact, a small carpentry shop in town that specializes in nothing else.

The Mendocino Hotel, now refurbished, is located on Main Street facing south. The balcony overlooks the mouth of the Little River.

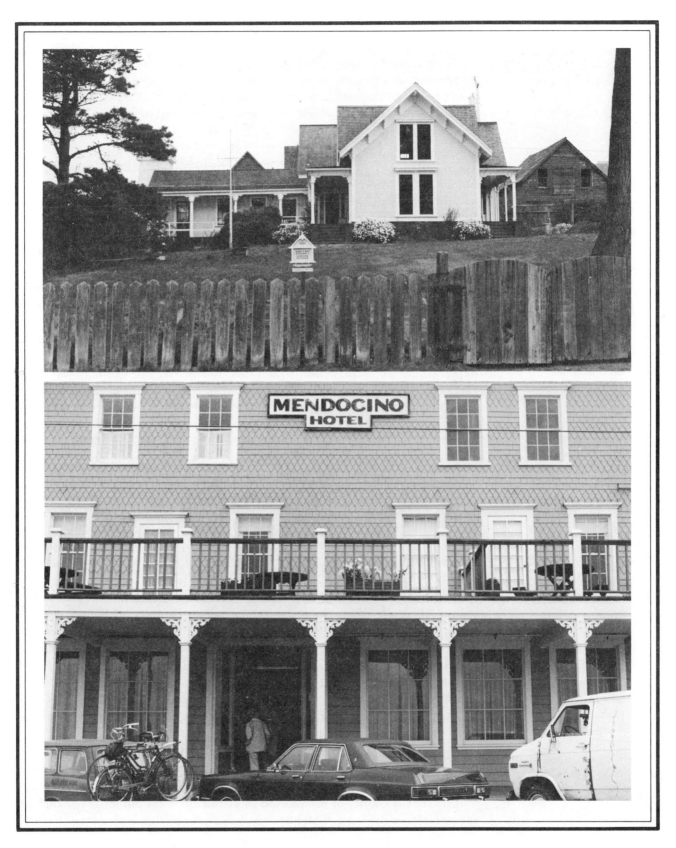

old hotel. He did so with style and taste. The exterior is unchanged. But the interior is all new. It is a period remodeling, to be sure, and in keeping with the town's and the hotel's own history, but much more elegant than the timber wolves who used to come to town on a Saturday night, or the traveling salesmen who needed a bed and a draft would ever have felt at home in. Except for the walk to the john, which was preserved intact, the place is high-style California Victorian.

Since his purchase of the old hotel, P has quietly bought up a considerable amount of other real estate in and around the town. There is talk that he plans to build a big resort across the river from Mendocino on a flat bluff overlooking the Pacific. And recently he has proposed to tear down the Ex-Lax Building. His plan is to raze that building, and then to rebuild it again in its own image as a background for shops, galleries, and boutiques. There would be courtyards and gardens. And tourists, the hometown defenders are quick to add.

At a hearing before the Coastal Commission (whose jurisdiction includes review on the removal of any historic building from California's coastline), P's engineer stated that the building's underpinnings had been damaged in the 1906 earthquake and that the building would have to be torn down because it is unsafe. In preparing the building's defense, someone came across a newspaper article from the period which mentioned that the building had been given a new foundation in 1908. When confronted with this piece of information, the engineer retired in confusion and the commission decided to retain its own engineer in order to try to ascertain the building's true condition.

It is difficult to determine how the people of Mendocino feel about this man P. He is held in respect due to his good works and power. Most fair-minded people would admit that his gift of the Kelley House and his new old hotel have enhanced the town. But he does not live there. He and his wealth come from outside. He is a mystery to the people, and he is changing their town. Our own feeling is that he is feared — not so much because he deserves to be, but because he operates without the constraints, economic or social, that limit the actions of hometown people of modest means who must live with their neighbors.

P is not the only outside entrepreneur in the town. He is only the most visible. There are others. Some live in nearby Fort Bragg, or down the coast at Little River, Albion, or Elk. Most come from farther away in Los Angeles or San Francisco. They come and go. They see in Mendocino a good investment and they buy — paying prices that to those with city incomes and accumulated wealth may seem reasonable, but which bear no relation to the means of those who live in the country. It is the impact of this invasion of outside wealth which has had the most dramatic and potentially the most destructive effect on the little community.

In California, taxes are levied by each county, and are determined on the value of real property. Some counties have sales taxes in addition, but the bulk of the public revenue is raised out of the pockets of those who own real estate.

In 1975, the county of Mendocino re-assessed coastal properties, including the property in the town of Mendocino. It is a process that is supposed to occur every five years. The assessment of the value of property is based on two principal factors: improvements that may have been made, and the value of comparable property in the vicinity as expressed in any recent real-estate sales. The people from the assessor's office came to Mendocino and did their work. Shortly after, property owners in the county were sent, as they are each year, a notification by mail of the county's opinion of the worth of their property. And when the mail arrived, all hell broke loose.

THE TAX STRIKE

No one had ever seen anything like it before. The horror stories circulating in the aftermath were so stunning, one had trouble translating the numbers into some sense of reality. Property values had escalated to such an extent on the coast that taxes would increase by four, six, and in many cases as much as ten times. It was a staggering blow. And for a while, the news was passed by word of mouth around the county. Property owners in the town of Mendocino were hardest hit. Elsewhere, the news was talked about quietly. The tone was apt to be pity for those poor people "over there," relief that it wasn't anything like that "here," and a detectable current of uneasiness that next time it might be. In the town of Mendocino, the tones were not hushed. They were damned angry.

The county sends its notices of assessment in July. Not the bill. Property owners have until sometime early in August to appeal the assessment of value. If the county has said that your Victorian house is worth $75,000 (because others like it down the street have sold for that), but you only paid $13,000 for it and know it needs new wiring and plumbing, you may drive to the County Tax Assessor's office in Ukiah (an hour and a half over the Coast Range from the town of Mendocino), obtain an application to have a hearing, fill it out, and mail it in. Later, the County Board of Supervisors, sitting as a Board of Equalization, will hear your appeal, along with others, and either agree with you or not.

The procedure is time consuming and little understood, since technically it is the assessment of value one appeals not the amount of tax, and the deadline for submitting the application for a hearing comes months before the tax bills are mailed. Though the instructions for appeal are printed on the notice of assessment, the print is small, the language is oblique bureaucratese, and by the time most ordinary citizens realized they could do anything at all, the deadline had passed.

When the tax bills came out in October of 1975, there was open talk of civil disobedience. Some people simply couldn't afford to pay their tax bills. Others were furious because they saw the trend of rising property values and knew that sooner or later they would be forced to leave town. One of these was a middle-aged artist we will call R.

R had come to Mendocino a few years before because it was beautiful and inexpensive. He and his wife could afford to live there, and with occasional teaching jobs, they could get by comfortably enough. R had never been involved in politics before. He is a quiet man, not exactly shy, though his gentle manner suggests shyness. But like most of the rest of his neighbors, the tax situation had changed his temperament — for the time being at least.

"I inquired around town and asked people, 'How do you like your tax bill?' And the answer was the same everywhere. People were terribly upset, but didn't seem to know what to do. Well, I just kept talking around town, and discovered enough people of a common mind to do *something*, and found that some of them had had experience with citizens' organizations of one kind or another, so we just kind of put it together. We thought that from this little pocket chances were we weren't going to change the state law, but we could sure put up a hell of a holler, and that's just what we did."

R and his neighbors called a public meeting and circulated mimeographed sheets. The sheet declared that its writers felt it wrong for government to have arbitrary power such as that evident in the tax increases and asked those who felt likewise to return their copy signed, declaring their intent to withhold taxes. By-laws and articles of association were drawn up, and shortly after the public meeting, the Coast Residents' Forum was announced.

"It was near the tenth of December (the date by which the first installment of the tax bill had to be paid), and we had to work like anything to get the word around. We circulated more of the sheets, and they began to come back. The numbers mounted up. There were a lot of angry people around here. . . . We had decided that a tax strike was the most effective means that a small number of people could use to make their voices heard, and it seemed a lot of people were willing. Then someone, I forget who, got the idea about the teabags. We decided that instead of money, we'd send teabags instead. That seemed to do it. As soon as that hit the local radio station, the wire services picked it up. And for the next week, we were getting calls from all over."

The attention of the national media on Mendocino's teabag tax protest seemed to give the effort added momentum at home.

"That kind of reinforced the home folks. People were looking at us and could see we were trying to accomplish something serious. It helped us gain local support. Well, come the tenth of December, we had to find out as quickly as possible how effective we had been. So we just called up over there [Ukiah] and asked the tax collector what's come in. I don't know if they were *happy* to tell us, but they told us — they had to — and as it turned out, a little over half a million dollars in taxes were withheld — it pretty much wiped out the county's contingency fund. So we could see we had some effectiveness."

Though the county had many tax procedures worthy of the serious scrutiny of taxpayers, those organizing the Mendocino tax strike knew from the start that their real target would have to be Sacramento and the state legislature. The county is only the tax collector for the state. The tax laws of the state of California were blamed for the problems in Mendocino.

To those who draw paychecks for studying such matters — the technicians who follow the camps of elected officials, supplying them with reports on this or that aspect of government — it has been known for years that tax reform was overdue. It is a favorite subject of those seeking office, but one that is seldom discussed with equal fervor by incumbents. But by the time the tax

collector in Mendocino County was wondering what to do with all the teabags she had received, taxpayers all over the state were beginning to feel the pinch and it was clear in Sacramento that the natives were restless.

Of late, connections have begun to be made between exploitative development of land — once thought to be the direct route to plenty and so recently fallen from grace — and the tax laws that encourage this development by using market value as the basis for assessing worth. It began to be seen that communities — old ones in which family roots go back a century or more — could be turned upside down and emptied of long-time residents almost overnight. And some people began to think that a town full of families with a history in one place might be worth more than tracts of "prestige" homes with landscaped streets, a putting green, and neighbors who couldn't tell you when the steelhead run, or how to find wild lettuce in the woods, or why the houses in town all have such steep roofs.

In the months after the Coast Residents' Forum launched their teabag strike, legislators in Sacramento fell all over themselves to introduce reform bills intended to deal with the problem. Members of the forum steering committee made many trips to Ukiah and Sacramento, at their own expense, to give testimony and to assist in any other way possible. At least ten bills were introduced into the 1975 legislature. All but one was killed or shelved for what is euphemistically known as "interim study."

Despite the turmoil on the coast by May of 1975, the Board of Supervisors of the county of Mendocino had taken no action on their own initiative to put pressure on Sacramento in support of one reform bill or another. The Coast Residents' Forum knew that any messages on the subject from officials in county government would carry special weight with their colleagues at the state level. Finally, after repeated requests for a resolution from the Board of Supervisors, with no response whatever, the Coast Residents' Forum called a public meeting and invited the supervisor from their district to come and tell the people why he should not be recalled. It was an angry meeting, and there was no doubt whatever that the forum could make good its threat.

Within three days, the board unanimously passed a resolution in favor of the reform of state property tax laws and went on record in support of legislation proposed by State Senator Peter Behr.

As of this writing, the Behr Bill is shelved, property tax bills are about to be issued in Mendocino County again, and the Coast Residents' Forum is still at work to move the state legislature to act. There are indications that they will in the current session. The tax strike can be considered a success.

But taxation is one thing, development is another.

THE CHAMBER OF ANTI-COMMERCE

The town of Mendocino has two main streets. They run at right angles and meet at the old Ex-Lax Building. One of them is the street called Main Street, which runs east and west along the water at the mouth of Big River. On it is the Mendocino Hotel, Kelley House, a deli, a dry goods shop, the local dentist, and a large number of galleries and gift shops, as well as the local branch of Bank of America. The other main street is called Lansing Street. It runs

MacCALLUM HOUSE

Dear Mendocino,
    Stop where you are!
    Take, perhaps, two very
    thoughtful steps
        Back.
    Please
        do not
        pass
        GO.

Perfection
    as known to man
is very nearly
back.
your friend   Albion Street, Mendocino, California 95460 (707) 937-0289
your friend
    within reach.   Sam Rock 8/26/76

Here is the Ex-Lax Building — local eyesore and beloved of all residents, especially the indigent ones. The building is often decorated with slogans (Tourist Go Home; Save Our Economy — Waste Everything), sometimes outdoor art shows, and weather permitting, soakers-up of Mendocino's ration of sunlight. Like all unused downtown property in the village, the old commercial building lies under a shadow because it is now far too valuable to simply be left in slow decline.

The note was left by a tourist who apparently was touched by the plight of the town and the gentle admonition from residents to tread lightly. It may be that perfection is almost always perceived to be behind us — since it most often seems visible only in that direction. If that is true, it may be that the residents of this village who agonize over its conversion to tourist boom town will simply have to wait until the boom is over — providing of course they can pay their property taxes in the meantime.

north and south, and on it is the town garage, a tiny courtroom, a music shop, real-estate offices, and the town's two markets. One of these has been there for years, selling everything from meat to television sets — a typical rural general store. The other is in rented quarters across the street. It sells food in bulk, health food items, and specializes in locally-grown produce and eggs. It is called Corners of the Mouth.

In September of 1976, the woman who owns the building in which Corners of the Mouth rents its space, announced to the operator of the store that he would have to vacate the premises. The owner of the building had plans to remodel it and use it as the location for an enlarged gift and antique shop. The woman already had one gift shop in town. It wasn't clear whether the new location would replace the existing one, or would be an addition.

Corners of the Mouth is a popular place. It offers quality merchandise at reasonable prices and is the only place in the area to get many of the food items it carries. More important, it is a social center. When the news got out that it was being evicted, many regarded it as one more blow to the hometown and another victory for tourism. One thing the town didn't need was another gift shop, they thought. But they didn't just think it. The threatened loss of their market was enough to turn resentment against tourism into action. It was about this time that SCAT was formed.

SCAT is an acronym for Sensible Citizens Against Tourism. The idea was borrowed from the town of Carmel, California, 300 miles down the coast, and a place that long ago succumbed to the siren song of clean tourist dollars. The people in Mendocino borrowed their idea and rubbed it in by making their slogan: "Don't Carmel-ize Mendocino."

On the weekend after Labor Day, shortly after Corners of the Mouth had been notified that it would have to vacate, the SCAT people were out on the streets of Mendocino. They had planned to park in as many parking spaces as possible with their own vehicles — thereby using the spaces normally used by tourists — put posters on the cars explaining why, and pass out mimeographed sheets and questionnaires to tourists. One of them wrote about it later in the local paper, *The Big River News:*

By 1:30 in the afternoon, we had parked enough local cars for all our posters, and six of us were back on Main Street in front of the hotel passing out letters to strangers, improvising on a general approach:

This is a letter written to you by some Mendocino residents. Will you read it when you have time? On the back is a questionnaire; you can help us by filling it out. There is a myth shared by our Board of Supervisors that visitors to Mendocino want new overnight accommodations (motels) and shops for their convenience built in town; we don't think it's true, but you have to tell them that in your own words. Primarily, you can help us today by being very careful of how you spend your money in Mendocino — that you do not provide financial incentive that encourages developers to tear down our old buildings and fill up our vacant fields. If you do purchase a gift item here, please be sure it is the authentic work of local craftspeople. Shops carrying gift items, both classy and junk, imported from outside our area are one by one replacing the stores that service local residents, eroding the essence of our town. . . .

I spoke frankly about my feelings about the displacement of Corners of the Mouth by a larger gift shop. And standing on Main Street, it struck me why the Corners eviction had made me so angry,˙more angry than any other proposed change in the town. . . . There were very few — for long stretches of time — no locals walking or shopping on Main Street. It is as if we have relinquished the street.

The writer went on to speak of territory — how in one's hometown, it is not so much defined by who owns what but by who uses what. Territory is a visceral matter. If one is pushed too far, one fights back. And some of the residents of Mendocino felt pushed to the limit. Here is what their mimeographed letter to visitors said:

AN OPEN LETTER TO VISITORS

First be assured that it is not you, personally, we are questioning. Person-to-person, had we a quiet context, we would probably become friends; certainly not enemies.

Our problem is that the flood of tourists recently has passed beyond what a small town can handle and still function as a community. Noise of automobiles drowns out sounds of the ocean, even late at night. We now smell exhaust instead of salt air. Streets are littered. Townspeople cannot find places to park. Many young, creative people have had their rents increased and must now move. Taxes are rising and many oldtimers now must sell. The quiet, creative ambience of the town is dissolving, replaced by a growing number of antique stores and other tourist-oriented businesses.

We realize growth is inevitable; most of us moved here realizing Mendocino had an active tourist industry already. We accept that visitors have a legal right to come here and that property owners have a legal right to develop their land as they see fit.

But we also profoundly cherish the fact that Mendocino is a living community; this is our home; families live here. This is still a creative center where artists, poets, actors and students come to live and work and experiment.

We do not mind a reasonable number of visitors, especially visitors who will pause long enough to get to know the town, the people — will trouble themselves to feel the real Mendocino beneath the commercial veneer. We mind the innundation of the town by hordes flashing through for a few minutes or hours. We mind the rapid and sudden investment in Mendocino-as-commercial-enterprise, especially by those who live elsewhere.

So we urge you to come here infrequently, sensitive to the fact that you are entering a fragile community of real people. If you do come back, we urge you to consider staying for more than a night or two — long enough to realize that basic functions of communities are deep and personal... and that window dressing is not the real product. Look for the authentic work of local people. Question what you buy, whether it is locally made, or just shipped here for the tourist industry.

Please do not encourage others to come here. Present facilities — and basic services — are overloaded. We do not want more facilities to further destroy the fragile fabric of community that still exists here. Consider — and we say this respectfully — your own backyard. If you spent the time and energy there that you are spending here, wouldn't you, your family, your neighborhood, and the planet, be better off? Then, perhaps we could someday visit you and have something to gain from it.

Community in America is getting to be a lost art. Commercial, phoney tourist traps are increasingly prevalent. Help us protect, maintain, and develop the former.

  —The Mendocino SCAT Committee (Sensible Citizens Against Tourism)

On the other side of the mimeographed sheet was a list of questions that visitors were asked to answer:

 1.How long do you plan to stay in Mendocino? If staying overnight, where?

 2. What brought you to Mendocino? (How did you hear about the town, what attracted you to come, etc.?)

 3. What specifically, have you most enjoyed here?

 4. What, specifically, have you least enjoyed?

 5. Do you plan to return? If so when? If not, why not?

Suggestions, comments.

The response to all this from visitors was mostly sympathetic. One woman was irate about the fact of and conditions in the chemical toilets provided in the town as a means of conserving precious water. But no one else took afront. And many in answer to question number four stated that what they least enjoyed in the town were all the other tourists.

One woman, reading the mimeographed letter over lunch in one of the town's restaurants, was moved to leave the following message scribbled on a piece of notepaper. The waiter found it and passed it along to the *Big River News:* "Dear Mendocino, Stop where you are! Take, perhaps, two very thoughtful steps back. Please do not pass Go. Perfection as known to man is very nearly back behind your reach." The lady might be right.

THE TOWN OF LAST RESORT

Planning, as it is conventionally regarded by most of its practitioners, is seen as a thing that one *does to* a place and a people. It is an act, or a chain of acts, by which assumptions about the ways in which people do things get translated in physical forms — presumably, ones that are improved. Land uses are regulated. Traffic is routed. Water is brought in, and waste is carried away. In our traditional preoccupation with the tangibles of life, we inventory, measure, hypothesize, and execute.

Sometimes — and increasingly it happens — there is an attempt to evaluate the invisible parts of the environment in an effort to align decision-making with attitudes and values. There is recognition that such things have some relationship to how people function in an environment. But efforts to get at these less tangible relationships are tentative. In the end, since we live in an age that places maximum value upon that which can be bought and sold, decisions are dominated by the marketplace. We are a nation of merchants.

Sometimes, we are asked, as the public to which planning is being directed, to participate in the process. That is as it should be. We live in a democracy. But let no one be misled into thinking that public participation in the process will alter by very much the nature of the outcome. We are still a nation of merchants. We are invited to a gathering in which it is to be determined how we shall live. For the most part, we do not leave our culture, and its values, at the doorstep. Though the decision is one in which we have had a voice (and that is of considerable importance), the decision is still one that is shaped by our peculiar mix of idealist and entrepreneur. And if by chance our decisions in public affairs should not be colored by the mix, our actions most certainly are. The contrast makes us seem paradoxical indeed.

Our culture has attached a price to the earth itself, and has said that it may be bought and sold. We may own a piece of the earth and by doing so, may prevent you access to it, or to its fruits. Though we have no intention of making a case here for the abolition of private ownership of land (we are as much products of our culture as you), we do think it is necessary to acknowledge that fundamental belief systems — those things so ingrained we assume them as God given — place limits on our vision and in subtle ways, shape our actions. It would always be so, regardless of the ideas.

In this instance, one of the fundamental givens has very dramatic effects on the landscape. It results in fences and roads and buildings and businesses — all built on an interlocking system of ideas which have as their base the private ownership of land. The environment, on the other hand, is not so easily marked off with boundaries, consisting as it does of much more than the land and what sits upon it.

A town is only partly real estate. It is also a network of interactions — enormously complex, even in a small community — and constantly in motion. This network is a live thing — and to us — it is the thing that makes towns live. To be sure, the character of the network is shaped in part by the physical environment. But it is a thing apart, a product of collective history — shared experience — and of the most deeply personal elements in the makeup of its constituent individuals. It exists always in a state of changing relationship to what is around it — affected by the environment and constantly working on it in return. To ignore its existence when one is at work in the machinery of public affairs, is to invoke chaos.

It is because we have studied this living network so superficially, and have largely ignored its inconsistencies, that we have evolved a planning process that accounts for only a fragment of the stuff of our lives. It is because we insist on dealing only with the tangible parts of communities, the things we can count and measure in the making of decisions, that we live in a system that accounts for only a part of what we are. The rest is left to chance.

Some of the people in and around Mendocino do not agree with SCAT. They believe it is morally wrong to move to a small community and then tell others to keep away — no matter how polite the language. One of them writes:

Don't get mean with a tourist who has come here to find some beauty. How many of us have done the same, leaving behind the sad city? All we can do is grow, deal with knowledge, using life to determine what is valuable.

Two of Mendocino's trademarks: the gray of salt-weathered wood and the figures on top of the Masonic Hall. When we told our Mendocino friends that we wanted to include their town in this book, they agreed (reluctantly) but pleaded with us not to take photographs that would show off the town's picturesque qualities, thereby adding our readers to the list of potential tourists. We guess we are guilty of ignoring that request, though the matter is perhaps as much a question of the taste of the beholder as it is our intent. It is surely not our wish to stir up more trouble for this beleaguered town — but we do want you to know what it looks like because that has much to do with both its problems and the efforts to save it.

The people in Mendocino who believe they are fighting for their homes, and an opportunity for their children to grow up in a place in which they will learn to be strong, well-adjusted adults, do not agree. At their backs is the Pacific Ocean. At their doors, the promoters of tourism and land speculators. To them Mendocino is a town of last resort. There isn't anywhere else to go.

Any small town is a fragile affair. The less of it there is, the easier it is to unbalance. But who will say how many gift shops are enough? Who will sell for half of what they know they can get? Who will be satisfied with the outhouse when the federal government will pay for a new sewer? A town is also an organic whole — no matter what its condition. It is a living thing, and its condition is a reflection of the truth as understood by those who constitute the town. The village of Mendocino is a product of the people who have come there — to live or visit. We have brought our ways to Mendocino with us. And if it is also a battleground, it is because of the conflict within us.

A Small Farm Revival

COVELO, CALIFORNIA

It takes two hours and eighty miles on the odometer to drive from the town of Mendocino to the town of Covelo. In these parts, that is not a great distance, but in another sense, it might as well be a journey of ten years. You can move your body from one to the other, but it is another thing for the mind to catch up.

Covelo is at the end of a paved road that doesn't appear to go anywhere else. To get there, it is necessary to leave the main highway north of Willits and follow a state road for a thirty-mile trip that takes about an hour as it threads its way through some of Northern California's most rugged, and geologically youngest, mountain country along the middle fork of the Eel River. The trip along this road and the pavement both end at Round Valley — a flat spot of some 30,000 acres, population 1,500. Near the center of that flat spot is the town of Covelo. Ringing the valley and town on all sides are the mountains. The people here speak of anything beyond that ring as "outside."

In ancient times, this valley was probably a lake. There is considerable evidence to prove this assumption. The topsoil in the valley is alluvial, in places as deep as seven feet. In other places, the valley is threaded with gravel from forgotten creeks that once wandered across its bed leaving their trails in gentle curves. A well driller talks of boring through a buried redwood log four feet thick, eighty feet under the valley floor. The oldest residents can remember when parts of the valley, particularly near its drainage, were swampy all year long — the last vestiges of the dying lake. Even now in winter, particularly the wettest ones, there is flooding as the valley receives the run-off from winter rains pouring down the mountains on all sides, and the melting snow from the highest peaks. Winters tend to be cold and wet; and the summers are hot and dry.

For many centuries, this land, and the mountains all around it, was the home of Indian people: Yukis, Nomlakis, Wailakis. Their descendents remain

173

here. The ancient people called this valley Meshakai — the place of tall grass. It is said that in the old days a man could ride a horse through that grass and only the top of his hat would be visible. Times have changed. The native perennial grasses have long been grazed away by cattle, horses, and sheep. Covelo is now a cow and a timber town. And on the sign at the entrance to the valley is the name by which the Round Valley Chamber of Commerce calls the place: "Nature's Hideaway."

In some respects, Covelo is like a great many other small rural communities. Socially, it has seen changes and conflicts over the last decade just as the rest of Northern California has, as urban refugees come on the scene to make their way into the country. In this community, the relations between groups are made more complex by the tensions produced by whites and Native Americans living in close quarters with each group aware of their mutual history. Economically, the town is unstable. Unemployment is chronically high, especially in the winter months when the forest is closed to loggers. The winter nights are long and cold, and the bars seem like the only entertainment for miles around. The dominant economic force in the valley is Louisiana Pacific. Its mill is the largest employer, providing jobs directly for mill workers and indirectly for the loggers and truckers who supply it. Next in size as an employer is the local school district — the town has its own elementary and high school, and after that, the ranches and local businesses provide some jobs, all of them struggling to make ends meet. In contrast with the American suburban standard of two late model cars in the garage, a well-kept lawn, cocktail parties for the grownups, and ballet classes for the kids, Covelo comes up looking pretty bad. But judging by the attitude of the people who live here, and the number of people who drop in at the local Strout office looking for land, the place has a lot going for it.

Partly it is the sheer physical beauty of the place. It is difficult to be unmoved by the great openness of a valley dotted with huge oaks simmering in the dust and heat of a late fall afternoon bordered by blue and purple mountains. It is a heady sight.

But we think it has more to do with that thirty miles separating this place from the "rest" of the world. The separation has certainly had a direct effect on the environment — that is to say, it has placed severe constraints on the impact of the automobile and all that comes with it — as well as on its inhabitants. That thirty-mile trip through the mountains effectively serves to moderate vehicle traffic — and by looking at this valley, you can see how rural America of thirty years ago, untouched by the postwar automobile boom, looked and lived. Here, it is pretty much still that way.

The road into Covelo wasn't paved until sometime in the forties, and the telephone didn't make it over the mountains until a decade later. Television is still a hit-or-miss affair — three channels appearing ghostlike from a repeater on a nearby mountaintop, as though the twentieth century is still some kind of a dream. You keep roads and phones and media out of a place for ten, twenty years, and you've got a place very different from most others. There is some kind of time warp here. People read papers and see the six o'clock news. But it comes in over those mountains. And it doesn't strike with the same resonance

This photograph was taken by Homer Gasquet, which as you may suspect is a pseudonym, but who remains unknown to us otherwise. It is one of the best photographs we have seen of Round Valley showing the savannahlike character of the place.

here that it does most other places. Most of the people who live here know that. And though it isn't usually discussed, it is clear they like it that way.

The oldest white history of this area is spotty. You get it in snatches from old-time residents or their offspring, telling the tales that have come down the years. It is not wise to take it all literally. But it is clear that the people who settled the area did not concern themselves with many of the niceties of life. It was a frontier. A rough and tumble place. You had to know how to take care of yourself. And sometimes frills like civil justice were simply unavailable.

During the first third of this century, Round Valley was home to a reasonably stable white and Indian population supported principally by cattle ranches and farms. The climate proved to be excellent for walnuts and certain hardy fruits. Some of the amenities were still missing, but the people who lived here in those days didn't want for much. There was plenty to eat. Everyone had a garden. There was a grain mill (it remains today as one of the town's major landmarks). There were bakeries, dairies, blacksmiths, and enough other services to make life pleasant, if not opulent. The people had always taken care of themselves and their own. They took — and take — a fierce pride in that fact, resenting as they still do, government intervention in their lives and scorning its "assistance" and those who accept it.

Until the timber boom of the middle fifties, the economy of the area was insular. There is no evidence that anything except cattle and tall tales were exported in any quantity from Round Valley. But as the rest of Mendocino County began to feel the demand for lumber to build the subdivisions of the Bay Area in the postwar years, the fir and pine forests of the Coast Range mountains around Round Valley echoed, as they did everywhere else in this county, to the chainsaw and the bulldozer.

Life in Round Valley was never quite the same again. Some people took jobs in the mills or in the woods. The economy of the whole country was changing, and Covelo was not immune. No longer were goods produced for local consumption. Instead, cheap transportation was making it possible to ship food products, beef, and timber anywhere. Despite its isolation, Round Valley began to feel some of the effects of these changes. Packaged foods began to fill the shelves of the markets in town. The Wonder Bread truck put Round Valley on its route. The gardens got smaller. Less fruit was preserved. The bakeries slowed and finally closed. Little by little, without realizing it, the people here, like those in most other places, depended less on themselves and more on what came over the mountains in trucks. Their incomes came more and more from sources outside the valley: the timber company (Portland, Oregon), the county (Ukiah), the state (Sacramento), or the federal government (Washington, D.C., or San Francisco). Though the pride remained, they were no longer an independent economic unit. They were in fact, the smallest possible part in a large and complex system of interrelated economic units on which they were almost totally dependent. The town's dependency remains so to this day.

Round Valley is designated as one of the prime agriculture areas of Mendocino County, and next to the Ukiah Valley, the largest. Yet the costs of land, property taxes, fuel, feed, seed, fertilizer, and labor are so high that virtually none of the valley's ranches can be said to be profitable.

The mountain country around the valley is well suited as range for cattle. The valley floor is a perfect place to grow high quality feed. Yet for the same reasons, plus a chronically low price of whole beef per pound, ranchers cannot make a living without taking second jobs. Many are on the edge of closing down. Some already have.

Round Valley is surrounded by forests of fir and pine — enough to keep the entire adult work force in the area employed indefinitely. Yet, because employment is controlled by a large corporation which finds it unprofitable to operate except under the conditions of optimum production, no longer possible due to depletion of the resource, lay-offs are inevitable.

Cattle born and raised in Round Valley may not be slaughtered and sold to feed the valley's population unless the cattle are first shipped to be inspected by a government inspector (a distance of some 100 miles) and processed by an inspected slaughterhouse, then shipped back.

Lumber cut from trees taken from the slopes of nearby mountains may not be purchased from the mill by local builders for local buildings. The lumber must be shipped out of the valley to a wholesaler or broker, who then sells it to a lumberyard operator, who then trucks it *back* to the valley where it is purchased at a price that includes transportation and markups.

That is the paradox of this rural town. And its agony. It has entered the twentieth century but finds the price of admission very hard to bear, and all the exits blocked. With a history of independence and self-sufficiency that seems to have ended only yesterday, Covelo is being strangled by regulations and a system of ownership and distribution that prevents it from utilizing its own resources to support its own citizens. If the people here seem to enjoy corny-sounding stories about the past, seem locked in some embrace with their own history, it may be that the memories of their independence are still too fresh and that they are looking for a way to recover some of it.

The pressure is on in this town, as it is elsewhere in Mendocino County and in other small agricultural communities all over. As rural populations increase, there is mounting pressure on agricultural land. Ranchers and farmers are taxed not on the basis of how effectively they can use their land for agricultural purposes, but rather on the "highest and best use" of that land as reflected by its market value. That means conversion to other uses. Property that once sold for $500 an acre now goes for $1,000. It is taxed accordingly and suddenly, instead of an asset, farmland or ranchland begins to seem like a liability. Large ranches are broken up. The smaller units are not as effective as producers, making the job of farming less profitable and even more difficult. The trend is unmistakable. Since 1950, over 20,000 acres per year of California agricultural land has been lost to urban and suburban development.

Into this picture step Covelo's new farmers. Most of them are under thirty-five. They have seen what twentieth-century America is doing to itself and have decided there has to be another way. Some of them have been to college, some have tried corporate life; all of them have decided that their first commitment is to the land. They, and the ranchers who will not give up, are the hope of this small community. And though all the odds are against them, they appear to be the cause of an agricultural renaissance in Round Valley.

There are many farmers in Round Valley. There are even more ranchers and gardeners. We chose Jim Andersen for this story because he is one of the first of the young newcomers in the valley to take up serious farming and one of the few who depend on it as an only occupation and the principal support for himself and his family — part of which is shown in the lower left photograph. Local wisdom has it that farming and ranching is dead here — and in a way that is true. So everyone is watching Jim Andersen, Loren Fisher, Jim Fisher, Johnny Rohrbough, and the others who are crazy enough to do it anyway. A beekeeper has arrived and in addition to providing local honey, presses local apple juice. An orchardist will have several thousand young fruit trees, locally grown, available by next year. The skeptics are right, farming and ranching will never be the same here again. It can't be. It will be farming and ranching of a different kind, and it will be people like Jim Andersen who prove that it can work.

From the road we can see the harvester, back in the middle of the field on one side, maybe a quarter mile from the road. But it is parked. Too early to quit, and besides, we see Jim's pickup parked near the fence back there. We drive through the gate, along the front fence, and then down along the outside of the field of wheat. Eighty acres' worth. The first big stand of wheat this valley has seen in years. We remember last November when they planted this field. Jim decided to do it at the last moment, and they just barely beat the weather. Jim's friends David and Ivan ran that tractor for seventy hours straight, some of the time in the rain. The neighbors across the road couldn't believe it. Those maniacs were out there flogging that old logging cat back and forth across that eighty acres day and night in the pouring rain. When one of them got too tired to drive anymore, the other would take over for awhile. The only time they stopped was to refuel or when something broke. But they got the wheat in.

Now it is September, and Jim is out here with a borrowed harvester, an old green monster past retirement age, and he's supposed to be taking in his crop. Only he isn't. As we pull up even with the machine, we can see a pair of old motorcycle boots sticking out from underneath the harvester, as though the thing had just run him over. A couple of seconds later, Jim unfolds himself from under there, grinning and greasy.

"It quit again." He says it in a matter of fact way, and without a trace of exasperation, though clearly another breakdown is not what he had at the top of his list for this afternoon. He describes the behavior of the machine with a kind of awe, and he admits to being stumped "by this one."

"The last time she quit, it was pretty obvious what was going on." He then describes a bizarre scene in which a part of the front end of the machine came loose and, in a chain reaction too fast to stop and too horrible to imagine, devoured itself, virtually disassembling the entire drive system on the machine's port side. "That one took almost a week to fix," he says wistfully. "I sure hope this one is a little simpler."

He says he began to get frantic when the breakdowns started. He points to a set of bin trailers parked near the fence waiting for the wheat. "The guy who owns those thought I'd have them here for five or six days. That was two weeks ago. For a while there, I was beginning to get a little crazy. Then I decided that wasn't going to help any and I had better make the best of it. I finally came around to thinking that this old machine is giving me a course in farm technology. Everytime I have to fix her, I learn something more."

Jim is twenty-seven. Tall and big boned with a face that opens easily in a huge smile and clear, friendly eyes. Sometimes he wears spectacles. When he does, he gives the impression of a country preacher who might have just stepped off a mule. He comes from Manteca, California, in the Central Valley where his father and grandfather were both farmers.

"Dad took over the farm at the age of thirteen when my grandfather decided that he didn't want to be a farmer anymore and went back to being a stonemason. It was a dairy farm, then later we raised melons and sweet potatoes, then cattle, and finally almonds. All the time I was growing up I was told to get away from the farm. Go to town. Go to school. Get a desk job. I was sort of programmed that way, so that's exactly what I did. I went to the University of California at Davis to major in political science. The first question they asked me was to describe the difference between a liberal and a conservative. Well, I was right off the farm, and I hadn't even begun to think about putting labels on people, and didn't much take to the idea, so I switched my major to ag/business right away. In my last year at Davis, I met my wife, and in the last few days, married her, graduated, and got my first job."

The next three years were a time of great changes for Jim. His first job, in Delano, California, lasted only a couple of months. He was hired to supervise the harvest of 1,700 acres of almonds in 100 degrees heat in the midst of racial and political turmoil surrounding the migrant farm workers of that area. He worked 317 hours the first month for $600, while his new wife was cooped up in a one-bedroom apartment, afraid to go out on the street. Each pay period, the paychecks would bounce, and he'd have to train a whole new crew. The second month he quit. It was his first taste of commercial farming, and he didn't like it.

Next came a short stint with State Farm Mutual Insurance Company. The desk job he'd been told about. It was in the dead files, and the way the insurance business works didn't appeal to him either. That lasted a month. Then Jim and his wife and two other couples embarked on a tour across the country to find the right spot. The idea was that they would buy a farm cooperatively. By this time, having rejected both commercial farming and business, Andersen was considered something of a radical, complete with beard. They found their dream farm in Arkansas, put $1,000 down, and came back to Manteca to find work to pay the rest of it off. Jim took a job with a seed company and for two years learned the agriculture business from the inside out.

"But at the end of two years, I knew I didn't want to be a middleman. I wanted to be down at the farm level and I wanted to be in California." So in October of 1973, they sold their share of the Arkansas farm and moved to Covelo.

"Basically, I guess I came here to be a gardener. We bought this little five-acre place. It had some berries, a big vegetable patch, and a bunch of apple trees. I didn't know how I was going to make a living, but I thought the Lord would show me. We had about $700 in the bank, payments of $185 a month, and an apple crop to pick right away. We somehow struggled through that first year. Everytime we needed a dime, it seemed like it'd show up. I did odd jobs all around the valley. It was important to me to get to know this place. The next spring, in March, Jim Fisher, a long-time resident came around talking about farming. He had forty-five acres of leased land and wanted to get a bunch of people together to work it. We had a go at it, but there were too many people, and it didn't work out. Meanwhile, I put in a huge garden a home. I wanted to find out what would grow here, so I had about sixty different things in my garden. Just about anything you could find in a seed catalog, I had some of it. We still weren't making any money, but we sure did eat good that year!

180

"Then our second child, Jonah, came along and it seems like with the first child you're still pretty free, but once the second one comes you begin to think that you might have to make it on your own. I didn't want to have anything to do with food stamps or any of those programs, but I finally did use them for about six months. I figured that if the Department of Agriculture ought to help anybody, it ought to be a young farmer trying to get started. By that time I had decided that I was going to farm some of this valley, and that things would indeed grow here. But I purposely went slow. I didn't think I could afford to make any big mistakes. That year I helped Jim Fisher [as a co-owner] put a grain crop on that forty-five acres. But the first real big step was that ten acres of row crops I put in. It was my first real attempt at farming. I had a couple of acres of watermelons and three acres of sweet corn. I had canta-loupes and crenshaws on a look-see basis. And I had just six rows of potatoes, 500 feet long."

He also had problems, most of them with his equipment. He was using a 1948 Case tractor with an old three-bottom plow that came out of the thirties. But in spite of that handicap, his crops came up, did well, and by summer, watermelons and sweet corn were finding their way from Jim's field into homes all over the valley and those not eaten in Covelo were being trucked out.

"You know, a dozen ears of corn is like a dozen magic wands. All of a sudden, people I didn't even know were coming up to me on the street telling me how much they liked my corn, or how they just wanted to meet me after having one of my watermelons. It made me feel good. Like I belonged here.

"That next October, we were looking for a place to cut wood. Someone told us there was a lot of down oak over on Ed Phillip's place, so we went over to see. Ed said sure we could cut the wood, but he also asked us if we knew anyone who'd like to lease 160 acres. Well, I began thinking about that while we were cutting wood, and I just couldn't get it off my mind. I had it pictured blocked off into four 40-acre pieces, and by the time we'd finished the wood, I about had myself talked into it. Before I talked to Phillips again, I called the Production Credit Association, the group that had financed me through Jim Fisher, and asked them if they were ready to go with me alone. I told them what I had in mind, and they said yes. So within three days I had my own place, the 10 acres of row crops, the 45 acres with Jim, and now this 160-acre piece. By then it was into November, and the only thing we could put in that late was wheat, so we went to work with that old logging cat of David's. By the twenty-third of November, we had that 80 acres plowed, disked, drilled, and by the first of December, it was all up. It was rough and it was muddy, but we had a stand of wheat in there that wouldn't quit."

Jim Andersen loves to talk about farming. His background in a farming family, his college education, his years with the seed company, his direct pragmatic way, and his optimism make him convincing. He thinks of himself as a learner, open to any lesson that comes his way, but he speaks with con-viction about what he knows. He says sitting on a tractor going a half a mile in one direction, and a quarter of a mile the other direction, six feet at a time, gives you lots of time to think. His plans for that 160-acre parcel are carefully worked out.

"What I plan to do over there is to have a four-field rotation. I'll have alfalfa on the high ground on a five-year rotation, depending on how it works. I may only be able to get a stand to last for four years, or I may be able to get it to last for six or seven. One field will be in permanent pasture. When the low fields are in permanent pasture, they'll be in species such as timothy and rye grass which will stand up to quite a lot of ground water, and the trefoils, which do pretty well, the narrow-leafed ones being the ones for grazing, but also red clover which will stand water, and salina, which is a grazing clover, but has real wet feet. Whether I take a crop of hay off it and then turn my animals in, like a lot of people do, I don't know. I might just do earlier spring grazing.

"The third field will be grain. Either barley on the high ground, or oats on the lower fields, or wheat in rotation. I may have twenty acres of wheat and twenty acres of oats, depending on what the ground looks like. That will supply local feed. Something to run through the mill down there to crack for the chickens, and the finishing out of steers or lambs or whatever. You know, with a couple of pounds of wheat a day, and a good clover pasture in September or October, you can get your cattle to a point where they'll grade choice. And that'll give us another way to market our cattle. Basically, this country's got to go back to grass-fed beef. They're just not going to be able to send 'em to the feed lot. It's not working out.

"Then the fourth field will be in row crops, and that's where my idea of diversification comes in."

Andersen believes that the key to agricultural recovery in Round Valley is diversification. He sees the need for a good cash crop, or perhaps several of them, to compliment the sagging cattle business. He doesn't expect to convince cattle ranchers to go into truck gardening, but he does think that ranching and farming are compatible and that the way of the future in this valley is a strong combination of both. In his own operations, he expects to do well running some cattle and raising hay, grain, pasture, and row crops all on 160 acres. He realizes that this idea would be considered crazy by "traditional" farmers — the ones who for the last twenty years have been farming more and more acres in fewer and fewer crops. As Andersen himself puts it, "The farmer who works a thousand acres in rice over in the [Central] Valley would think I'm plumb out of my mind."

For years in California and elsewhere, agriculture has been busy becoming big business. People in the Bank of America will tell you that unless you can get a quarter of a million dollars and a good line of credit, you might as well forget about starting a farm. The financing, the machines, the chemicals, the labor, the marketing and distribution, all are directed at one or a few crops grown on huge tracts of land, and the highest possible yields, supported by high-energy mechanization and chemical manipulation for maximum profits. The agriculture industry (and especially the businesses that support it, such as petrochemical and food-processing interests) have sold this idea to Americans as the only way to raise the world's food.

It isn't. Andersen thinks it may not even be a good way to raise food, though he stops short of setting himself up in opposition to agribusiness. By the same token, he doesn't consider himself an organicist either, though many of his methods and ideas would be considered "organic." (He refuses to use chemical fertilizers and controls, not just because he thinks they are of dubious merit, which he does, but also because they are too expensive.) He prefers to identify himself with what he regards as a new movement: something he calls "eco-agriculture," which takes the best from both camps. According to Andersen, neither extreme has the answer. As he puts it, "Both are dealing with half a deck. The organicists are right, of course, but they're also impractical. Sure, it's fine to put ten tons of cow manure to the acre. But who can do it? No one's got the animals anymore. And by the time you haul it in, the cost is out of sight." From the industrialists, Andersen says the eco-agriculture movement is taking much improved tillage methods brought about by equipment that works subsoils while leaving topsoils intact. From the other side, they are learning (or relearning) about soil fertility, crop rotations, green manure crops, and control of weed and insect populations without resorting to chemical intervention.

There is another aspect to Jim Andersen's ambition that clearly sets him apart from the proponents of "Big Agriculture." He thinks small. It's not that he is unwilling to work hard. Or that his ambition is somehow stunted. He appears to have every intention of making a good living. It's just that he seems to think of farming as having more to do with the land — and the people — and less to do with business. He identifies himself and his family with this valley — with this community — and if his ambitions have scale, they are for this piece of geography not himself. He thinks of himself as working to help make the valley self-sufficient again. He is optimistic about the possibility.

"Right now, we could supply each and every person in the valley with enough meat of all kinds. But people need more than just meat. We've got a grain mill down there that still has the steam power plant in it, and we can still run that thing by steam. We could run that thing by steam — in a month, if we had to. If everything broke down, and Continental could no longer bring in our white bread, we could do it. In fact, I've got enough wheat down there to supply the whole valley with bread for an entire year. Both red and white wheat. We've got oats down there to roll for breakfast even, and we've got a roller. I mean, as far as bread and meat go, we've got it sacked. The vegetables? Everybody around here can grow a garden or does grow a garden. I see that if everything shut off tomorrow, this valley would be fed, and this valley would be watered. Even when there is a drought in California, we got our thirty inches here. I feel like I was led here and this is the land of plenty. The Lord has been really good to this place, you know?"

He admits that his is probably a simplistic view of what could be done here to make the valley self-sufficient, and that survival and economic independence are two quite different things. He also knows that his own plans for farming — diversity on 160 acres — are plagued by the need for equally diverse equipment which he does not own and could not begin to afford. He believes that his only hope — and implicitly the hope of anyone else who farms in this small place — lies in cooperation between growers, each of whom could afford one kind of specialty equipment and could barter his for the use of others. He also believes that a great deal can be done with older equipment,

183

designed in the days when farming was done at a scale much more like the plan he envisions for Round Valley, and built to last. "You can repair those machines. You can make parts for them. And if you're willing to do without an air-conditioned cab and stereophonic headphones, and don't mind spending a few more hours in the field, they do a pretty passable job."

Which brings us back to the borrowed old green harvester parked in the shade of a giant oak tree late on a hot September afternoon.

Jim has done what he could. It's time to quit. We climb the fence. Jim stoops to a gunny sack lying on the ground and extracts from it a half of a small watermelon. He carves it on the hood of his truck and hands us a big hunk. Now, neither of us is very partial to watermelon, but that afternoon, that watermelon had just about as good a taste as anything we've ever eaten.

ALAN CHADWICK'S SCHOOL FOR GARDENERS

Fifteen acres on the bank of Mill Creek at the north end of the valley. A big, old barn, a house, and a scatter of outbuildings. Forty-six student apprentices and student staff, Alan Chadwick and *the garden*. It is not that people there make visitors unwelcome. Visitors, though they are often an impediment to work, are always treated cordially and with respect. But like any place with a consuming purpose, the garden has an atmosphere that is palpable. Everything there — plants and people alike — is caught up in it. To be there whole is to work there. There can be no other way. You are either in the garden or out of it. Most of us are outside. That makes it hard to write about.

It is also hard to write about because of Alan Chadwick. The man is a sorcerer. He has the capacity to transfix. We have seen him launch into conversation with the most blase visitor on a subject of some obscurity, and weave a spell so complete that in three minutes his audience is struck dumb. But the man is more complex than that. We have seen him hide from visitors; we have seen him ignore visitors and students alike; and we have seen him throw dirt clods — for fun.

It is never wise to dissect magic. The sum of Alan Chadwick's spell is much greater than the naming of its parts. But his effect on students (and visitors) can only be described in terms of the ingredients in his message. For Alan Chadwick is at once mystic, poet, artist, historian, primitive, physician, and consummate student of nature. His power comes not from any one of these roles, but from the integration of them all. His vision is as large as humankind. He believes that our divorce from nature is almost total, and that the only way to save ourselves — to regain equilibrium — is to reestablish through horticulture, ancient ties with God and nature. He is a master horticulturist. His knowledge of plants is encyclopedic. He is possessed by a need to spread the news of the garden to all who will listen. He has evolved a horticultural practice that incorporates an ideology so spiritual that many people think him a madman, with a methodology so enormously practical and productive that agronomists from universities seek him out.

It is probably a good idea, before going any further, to say that Alan Chadwick would not claim authorship of these ideas, nor would he accept a

184

position at the center of the Covelo garden. That place, he would insist, is already occupied by nature herself. He does not even think of himself as a teacher. Though we have never heard him describe his role in so many words, it seems to us that he feels called upon to remind us of ancient knowledge for which we have an instinctive capacity. He believes that he must fire the imagination and spirit, and assist us in finding techniques that are in harmony with the earth's processes. In the last analysis, it is nature who makes the garden; it is the garden that makes the gardener.

He is probably right.

Each year, in the fall, about twenty-five student apprentices come to the garden in Round Valley to learn about plants. Before they are permitted to do this, they must visit the garden and work in it for a period of two weeks during the preceeding spring or summer months. There are many good reasons for this requirement. The work is frighteningly hard to some people unused to physical labor. The hours are long, the life is austere. To be content in such circumstances, one must be highly motivated and dedicated. The garden is also a community. Relationships there tend to be close and, because of the style and purpose of the place, intense. People must get along. Chadwick is often difficult for students to understand. A harsh taskmaster one minute, appearing to be remote and disinterested, or intensely and knowingly concerned the next. The students learn to depend heavily on one another for support.

Apprentices must agree to live in Round Valley and attend the garden for a minimum of one year. There is little time off. They must provide for their own housing and transportation as well as any expenses. The garden supplies food. Instruction is provided without tuition charges in return for the student's investment of time and labor. Students may elect to stay a second year. Some of those who do are given the status of student staff and a small stipend. They must assume commensurate responsibility for the management of the garden and the administration of its instructional program. Some stay longer. At the present time, there are three staff members who have been associated with the garden for four years or more.

The garden in Round Valley is the culmination of something that began almost ten years ago in Santa Cruz, California, at the University of California. There on a hillside covered with rocks and impoverished soil, a garden was made. It was a garden in which ideas grew as lush as the plants — and a generation of students were to find themselves drawn there and somehow altered by it. It was presided over by Alan Chadwick, a tall, tanned Englishman with a shock of white hair, knobby knees, a strikingly eloquent and theatrical manner, and what appeared to be energy without bounds. He spoke of the ideas of the vitalists of the nineteenth century, of Rudolph Steiner, of Goethe, of the market gardens of France, of the poetry of Virgil, and of the influences of the stars and planets on the lives of plants. And he grew flowers and fruits and vegetables in such profusion and of such quality as to boggle the mind. Later, Chadwick left the university, and in a series of steps, began a movement north, through a procession of other gardens, that ended in Round Valley. There he was introduced to a rancher who had his own vision and

185

Alan Chadwick is in the greenhouse with a number of his students examining last year's tomatoes, dried and retained for seed. In the lower photograph you see the students and staff as they looked in the garden's fourth year in Covelo. Some of the old-timers have stayed on to teach or to establish related projects nearby. Others have gone elsewhere. Virtually all remain active in some horticultural undertaking after leaving the Round Valley Garden.

found in Alan Chadwick a powerful ally. It was in this manner that Richard Wilson agreed to assist in the formation of the Round Valley Garden Project. He made land available for the purpose and helped to raise funds necessary to equip and launch the effort. Later he formed a nonprofit group called the Round Valley Institute for Man and Nature to marshal support for the project. Though financially the project has great difficulty, due mainly to its rather radical nature, it has attracted some foundation support, and its founders are hopeful.

Educationally, it is a resounding success. Chadwick and his ideas happen to make good copy. As a result of his University of California days and his lectures and press coverage, the word has gotten out. The project receives as many as twenty-five letters a week from people seeking information, and from would-be apprentices seeking entrance. The institute has set up a membership organization called the Friends of the Garden as a way for nonresident supporters to participate in the work of the project. Membership costs $10 a year and includes a subscription to the garden's occasional publication, *The Dirtman Journal.*

The following description of the garden project and its work is taken from issue number one of the *Journal:*

You can see the dawn coming a long way off. The valley is small enough so that you sense its enclosure by mountains . . . but broad enough to show that the sky is becoming light off in the east above the snow. Down here in the valley the ground is damp. Spring is just beginning. There is some mist hugging the earth in wisps — long strips that hover. There is no wind.

In the garden, everything is still. A rabbit moves silently, like some dream creature, just visible as a soft shape at the far end of the east garden. There is a chill that seems to press all sound into the ground — a nighttime remnant of winter. All is suspended.

The birds can wait no longer. First one, then another begins to speak. As if on signal, a rooster calls from a distance, a final warning to any lingering night creatures. A door slams two fields away. A car motor is heard on the road heading south toward town. The sky is blue in the east and deep purple to the west. The stars in the sun's path begin to fade. So does the rabbit.

By the time the sun lifts its face over the east rim of the valley there are figures moving quietly in the garden. The first students have parked at the end of the east garden and walked to the gate. The others have ridden clicking bicycles to the front of the house and parked them under the maple tree. They walk down the drive to the barn and begin to select equipment for the morning's activity. The hoses, in 75-foot sections, are lifted down from their roost in the rafters. Spades and forks are taken from their places on the wooden tool racks. There is quiet conversation and joking. Everyone has a task, working alone or in small groups of two or three. Instructions are few; work has been organized in advance by student/staff members who answer questions and make simple suggestions as the morning gets under way.

Today there is planting to do in the pear parterre, the berries must be wired and tied, there is to be some field instruction for first-year apprentices on pruning, and there will be a lecture at 9:30 by Alan Chadwick. The lecture will take until about 11 or 11:30. After lunch, work will resume until dark, which at this time of year happens at about 6:30.

For now, work is under way. Movement is steady and gentle. There are no raised voices. But there is laughter. Some of the work is difficult and tiring, but there is no struggling. Extra hands are always available. The pace is even and steady. There is time to do it well.

The 30 or so young people who have come to the Round Valley Garden Project to study are participating in a most unusual educational experience. Under the direction of Alan Chadwick, one of the world's most respected horticulturists, they are committing their energies and possibly their lives to a garden — and to agricultural practices which may have much to do with the future of our species on the planet.

It is a great temptation to describe what is going on here in terms of one world crisis or another. There is little doubt in the mind of any person here that, carried out on a sufficient scale, it could generate forces equal to the problems of human health and hunger. But on a day-to-day basis, the people who teach and learn in this garden are dealing with very immediate questions: How may I spend my life usefully? What may I do in the world that matters? How may I survive by doing the things I believe in and care about most?

Students here are learning the classic traditions of mastery of craft and stewardship of the earth. They are perfecting techniques, already established, by which strong plants, producing healthful food, may be obtained in greater yields, leaving the soil improved rather than depleted, and without resort to chemical intervention. They are working to develop strains of plants that are closer to origin forms in order to restore vigor and hardiness in species weakened by a hundred years of genetic tinkering.

The procedures followed here, and much of the philosophic basis for what is done here, derive from European traditions, and particularly from the work of the German scientist-philosopher Rudolph Steiner. The classic techniques of England, France, and Italy, and much of Steiner's "Biodynamic" philosophy have been synthesized by Mr. Chadwick, who was Steiner's student. Intrinsic to his approach (it is too complex to call a "method") is an integration of meticulous technique and a world view. The parts of this approach which may be called "technique" are intensely practical — centering on the building of soil fertility, the maintenance of productivity, and the creation of environments in which each plant may reach its maximum potential. The result is a radically increased yield of, in the case of edible plants, superior nutritional quality. Inseparable from these techniques, however, is a set of spiritual principles which bind the very life of man with that of plants and all creation. The two are as one — technique and spirit — and in their union is the secret of the enormous appeal of this approach and the key to its potential.

Work in this garden is labor-intensive. Machine power is employed only in those instances where hand labor is unequal to the task, which is seldom. Beds are dug by hand. Field crops are cultivated by hand. Soils are prepared and crops are harvested by hand. The reasons go beyond a simple abundance of student labor. The biodynamic view of things places the human in a special relationship to the plants and creatures in his or her care. It involves

188

obligations which may not be discharged by machinery or from a distance, but may only be properly met by individuals who have finely tuned perceptions, who pay close attention to every detail, and who have direct physical contact with the soil and plants.

It is apparent to any garden visitor that the approach taught and practiced in this garden is enormously productive compared with conventional methods. What is less apparent, and for some harder to accept, is the idea that the abundance of superior fruits, flowers, and vegetables is as much the result of the human spirit acting in accord with the laws of nature, as it is the result of special techniques.

Many of the young people who study at this garden go on to teach others. A number have left Round Valley for cities on the East Coast. Some have gone to Latin America to share their knowledge. Some have stayed in Round Valley, wanting to put their experience to use, and also keeping some contact with this unusual garden school. The most successful alumni of this garden are a formidable lot — at once messianic in intent and as down to earth as tomorrow morning. They have a way of making things happen. Where some are content to talk, these people act. Calmly confident of their skills, and of the value of their experience, they look around them for the best place to put their ideas to work. Steven Decater is one of them.

THE GENTLE QUEST OF STEVEN DECATER

Steven Decater is a young man of twenty-eight years whose present mission in life is simple: he wishes to determine whether or not it is possible for him to learn to become entirely self-sufficient on a small farm in Round Valley. He and a friend, Sue Bolton, are partners in the enterprise, sharing the work and the responsibility of caretaking the place for its owner. Of the farm's slightly more than a hundred acres, Steven and Sue are directly responsible for thirty or forty, though only a little over one of those acres is under intensive cultivation. The balance of the land is used for grazing cattle.

Though Steven's objective may be stated simply, it is more complex than might be imagined. Steven has set conditions on his effort. The first is that only natural methods and materials may be used. The second is that he will be aided in his work by no farm machinery. The only motive power he will permit himself to use beyond hand labor is that of animals. For that purpose he is also becoming involved in the breeding and training of animals — principally donkeys and mules.

Two things about these two young people are important in relation to the agricultural revival taking place here. First, they are both graduates of the Round Valley Garden Project and represent the horticultural influence of that project on the farm community here. In addition, they also represent a growing number of young people whose commitment to the land is deeply personal and idealistic, and who are struggling to succeed on the most practical terms. The hills of this county are filled with shacks and tipis of back-to-the-landers whose ideas were more lively than their ambitions to realize them, or their experience to inform them. Some have taken jobs and

189

stayed on — many of them having compromised their pure intentions with store-bought food on the table while they learn how to do it themselves. Many more have given up and moved to town.

Steven knew enough to know that even with his background in horticulture, one does not shed a lifetime of urban habits like a lizard sheds its skin, and suddenly by dint of burning desire become a husband of the soil. Neither did he deny himself all comforts of this century ar a full stomach while he goes about relearning what our culture once took for granted. He has set himself no absolute time limit, either. Though their caretaking arrangement for the farm is scheduled to last for five years, two of which have elapsed, Steven thinks in much longer terms and seems willing to continue the effort for as long as he thinks they are making progress.

Why? Why would a reasonably intelligent, well-educated and able-bodied person deny himself the relative ease of ordinary employment and instead plunge himself into what appears to be an impossible version of an already difficult enterprise?

Steven Decater is a native Californian. He was born in Sutter, California, a small town eight miles northwest of Marysville, and spent his early years there. When his father died, his mother moved to her family home in Cloverdale, a little farming community in northern Sonoma County where Steven went to high school, did well as a student, and spent his spare time hiking in the mountains around the town. He went to the University of California at Santa Cruz in 1966, just a few months before Alan Chadwick made his appearance there. Steven was interested in metallurgy and physics. He wanted to design a more efficient bicycle. College was a rude awakening for Steven. In his first quarter, he struggled through a world civilizations course, with an omnibus reading list of twenty books. "I thought I had to read every one of those books and remember all of it. I used to study in the hall outside my room in the dormitory, so that if I should fall asleep — which I usually did — the people coming home to the dorm would wake me up. I was getting about four hours of sleep a night, and was thoroughly exhausted. When I took the final, I had it all backwards and flunked it. It was a mind-boggling experience. I thought I had been a pretty good student up until then.

"The next quarter, I was reading for the exam again and dreading it. I had to go to the bookstore to get a book I needed, and while I was there, I got a copy of *Walden Pond* which I had never read. Of course, when I got back to the room, I started reading Thoreau instead of studying for the exam. Everything that he said seemed so clear to me and so correct I decided that I was in the wrong place, and that I was going to get on my bicycle then and there and ride east, learn something about the plants on the way and find out how to survive in a more natural environment.

"Fortunately, I called my mother before I departed, and she told me to not be so upset about the exam and to go in there, and if I had something to write, write it, and if I didn't, not to worry about it, but to go. So I read *Walden Pond* all night, and went to the exam the next morning. It had three questions. The first two I couldn't answer and I said so. The last question dealt with the New Testament books in the Bible. I had been reading the Book of

Mark, with its story about the miracle of the loaves and the fishes, and had decided that it could be interpreted in real life terms. It was interesting to me and I answered that last question with my ideas about how the stories could be interpreted and I passed it! I passed the exam. Here I had worked so hard the last quarter trying to remember everything and had failed, and this time I passed by answering only one question. It was too much for me.

"So after that, when I went to the classes, I asked what are they really saying? What are they proposing that people do? How are they going to change their lives? And I got really distraught because it seemed like everybody came in, and it was almost a social thing. They'd discuss this guy's theory and that guy's theory. It would be a big discussion, and everyone would get up and everyone would go back, and everything was exactly the same. Nothing was changed or different. It was weird. So I began not going to classes. Or I tried to arrange independent studies, and eventually, the next year, this disenchantment led to my leave of absence from college.

"When I came back the next fall, I came back a week early, because I wanted to hike on the campus. I saw the hillside in bloom, I knew that the garden was going to be there, but when I saw it, the hillside was transformed. There were dahlias in full bloom. I saw that and couldn't resist walking in. There was a young fellow I had known before working there in the dahlias. We sat down and had one of the tomatoes from the garden together. When I ate that tomato, it was as if I had never eaten a tomato in my life! I ate it and discovered a completely new taste and texture. It was really wonderful.

"I walked through that garden and it was like a magicland to me, but at the same time it was as practical and as real as anything could be. It was the complete union of those two parts of existence that got me. I started back to my classes, but when I got wound up, I would go to the garden and work for a few hours.

"Eventually, the few hours became more and more hours. I met Alan, and he would see me and he'd say, 'How are you?' And I'd see that he was asking the question, that he was *really* asking, it was not just a social form. And I'd have to say that I really didn't feel too good. Then he'd say, 'Yes, well, perhaps you'd like to *do* something,' and I'd say, 'Yes, I would like to *do* something!' So he'd tell me two or three things I could do. I began to work with the dahlias, and he'd explain what the culture of it was, and what the history of it was, and I began to see that it was a whole world of knowledge and experience. And that it had its roots clear through man's history. It was a whole phase of existence that had never been presented to me — ever — through all my previous education. I was fascinated with it. It seemed to me that I could go along studying such matters for the rest of my time without any trouble at all — and without running out. So I spent more and more time in the garden, and learned more. I eventually asked Alan if a person could grow everything they needed to live on. He said of course! That's the way it always was. Of course it could be done, people have done it for centuries. That's the way it should be.

"When I talked with him about my frustrations with the college, and with that whole scheme of things, he understood. He was the only person I had

191

talked to who did understand. It also seemed that the garden offered a real alternative." For Steven, the garden was an alternative in more ways than one. It was certainly an alternative to the traditional courses of study he had found so arbitrary and unrewarding. But the sum of Henry David Thoreau, the fateful tomato, and Alan Chadwick had far greater implications for Steven than a course of study that made sense to him. For Chadwick was also talking about taking from the earth and putting back. To Chadwick, the farmer is always someone who puts back more than he takes. Which puts him immediately at odds with most modern agricultural practice. The late sixties were the beginning years of ecological consciousness, and Steven Decater began to believe that it was going to be necessary for man to learn how to feed himself without poisoning the earth and without dependence upon energy-intensive methods. He had decided that is what he wanted to do with his life.

"Eventually, that's what led to my leave of absence from the university. I felt like what I wanted to learn was in the garden, so that's where I went." In the middle of his second year at the university, Steven began to work full-time at the garden. He would not attend classes again. His formal education terminated, and his training for what he regards as his life work began.

Except for two full-time but temporary jobs, he has been doing just that ever since the spring of 1968. From October of that year, until March of the following year, Decater worked first on a commercial chicken and egg ranch near Fresno, and then in a factory that makes laminated structural members. In April of 1969, he returned to the campus at Santa Cruz as an employee of the University of California, where he worked as Alan Chadwick's garden foreman and teaching assistant until Chadwick left the university. After that, he spent a little less than a year in a private garden in Palo Alto, and in June of 1972, came to Covelo, after hearing that Chadwick was here to start a new garden. He joined in that effort for one year, then left it in order to begin work on his own farm project.

When asked if he thinks of his current project as a farm or as a garden, he answers, "Neither and both, it has the cultural aspect and approach more of a garden. By that I mean that the cultural methods used are normally associated with gardening. But the range of crops that we deal with are more akin to farming. It's almost like you need a new word for what it is. Because it's not farming in the old sense — or maybe it is, in a pre-industrial sense. The primary objective is not that of producing food commercially because my first purpose is to produce food to support my own existence. If beyond that it is possible ecologically, and physically, to produce an excess for others, I would consider that. And in an economic sense, one does need some kind of crop or product or craft that you can exchange in the economy just to survive presently. Because it does take money. There are still things we need to buy.

"After I had discovered Thoreau, and up until the point I came to the garden, I had been thinking I would go into the wilderness and discover some mode of existence there. But when I encountered the garden and began to understand the culture behind it, I was fascinated with the possibility of man's magnification of nature. I began to see a life in that direction. From that I

We visited Steven Decater's farm/garden early one Sunday morning to take photographs. Though the animals must be fed every morning (in the upper photograph, it's chard for the rabbits), the weekend routine varies somewhat. Sunday is the day Steven works with his donkeys. The pinto you see him leading out of the pasture has been trained to pull a small cart which Steven built of wood and bicycle parts and uses to haul light loads to and from town (about two miles away). He took us for a ride. The donkey wasn't so sure about going — and needed much convincing to maintain progress — but he was very willing to make the run back at a steady trot. In the lower right is a photograph of the farm taken from the east.

decided to be a 'gardener' — but I also have this desire to know what a man has to do with nature to reproduce the support of a human life, and at the same time to leave nature in as fertile or more fertile a condition than when he started. It's a personal quest with me. I regard it as an individual's office to know what is necessary to support a human life — and to be recreative.

"Thoreau, in a sense, didn't do that because he raised a crop of beans and sold his bean crop into the economy. He was a farmer. In his time the economy paid him enough for that crop of beans by hand that he could buy his other food supplies. But today, it's a different situation. If I try to grow a bean crop by hand and trade it into the economy, I'm sure I'm going to come up on the *sub* end. [Laughs] And besides, that really wouldn't answer my question, because the economy I want to know something about is not the economy that says, 'We'll use things up as rapidly as we can as long as it's there, because we've got half a country in timber and can sell wood cheap.' The economy I want to know about is nature's economy — what, in my lifetime, I have to regenerate so that my life is supported, and so that when I'm gone, I will have helped put back what is needed for the next generation. And that's a different economy altogether from the one we consider operative and legal presently.

"My idea here on this land is to provide for my support first, so that I can keep in motion, and then to start regenerating resources — such as planting trees for the kinds of wood that will be needed here for human life — all plants, in fact. Trees are just a simple example. But there is a lag between the time these things are put in and the time they may be used. It's that lag that we have to deal with if we're going to get by meanwhile. When the resources have been removed, as they have here, and I have to go sixteen miles away to bring them in, there are a whole bunch of economic questions that you run into. Should I just go to the store and buy a fencepost, or does it really add up to buy the gasoline and go sixteen miles into the forest and spend the time cutting it and bringing it back here? What really balances? Those questions are confused now because we're dealing with a really confused situation. We've been working within a transportation economy that has completely dispersed the resources. What we need is an economy in which the resources are localized again.

"That's what a farm once was. When man stopped being a gatherer and stopped going back and forth, and in and out, and all over, he became a gardener and began to put the plants that were necessary into his immediate environment. He simplified the transportation problem and gave himself the maximum leverage on the whole support system. I think that's what needs to be recreated. People need to reorganize themselves out of this transportation dependence. It's almost as though we've become hunters and gatherers all over again — only now we've got centuries of technology that are stacked up on that premise. The art and culture of localized resource development has been dropped, and it was dropped about the time petroleum products made it possible to move things all over cheaply.

"For a time, people were really productive on a local basis. In Paris, in the nineteenth century, there were the intensive market gardens that grew in a ring all around the city. They used the by-product of the city's transportation system — horses. They used horse manure as the fertilization and also for the heat energy for this intensive cultivation system. They used raw manure for hot beds, they used a lot of glasswork, and they supplied the population of that city with fresh produce all year long.

"Now the people in the cities are in a sense occupying land way out here. I mean, that the land is being occupied by them because it is required to grow the food and other things they need. But the land isn't being used *intensively*, it is being used *extensively*, with high-energy agriculture and high-energy transportation. Both of which have questionable long-term effects on people and on the environment. And both of which tend to concentrate huge numbers of people in cities, while tying up huge amounts of land to support them. I think that if more people worked on the land and worked without mechanical assistance in an intensive kind of cultivation, less acreage would be required to feed the same number of people, and they'd be better fed. The thing that seems to make sense to me is to work toward smaller concentrations of people, working within an environment which is cultivated to produce the maximum and the most diverse resources possible on a local basis."

Is it working? The question is inevitable. For Steven Decater's whole effort is grounded in the very practical matter of making a living. The answer has to be yes — partly. With a little under one acre in intensive cultivation and a sizable population of farm animals, Steven Decater and Sue Bolton can feed themselves and then some. The "then some" can be sold at the local farmers' market and almost pays for the things they must purchase. They still must raise an additional $50 a month to buy what they need — mostly feed for the animals. The next phase of their plan is the cultivation of a second acre which will be used to grow grain and pasture crops using animal power as an aid in cultivation.

The absence of machinery in Steven Decater's plan has to do with how he wants to feel about his relation with the land. As he describes it, that relation is a deep and intensely personal one, and it is his "feeling" for the land he works that sustains the enormous effort he is making.

"When I get discouraged or get to feeling hopeless about it, I've got to be able to go out there in the field and sit down and be still. I've got to let that feeling gradually seep back in. If I ever go out there, and it doesn't seep back in, then I'll know I'm in trouble!"

Steven Decater does not pretend to think that his is a scheme that very many other people will follow. Nor does he try to convince others. He had to think for several days about whether he should even submit to the interviews on which this part of the book is based. But he believes fervently that what he is attempting is the only way he can live his life.

"I'd rather live in a world that is more like a garden. You can't wait for everyone to make it happen. And you can't talk everybody into trying it. So you just do it yourself. You just start.

"I think we can do just about anything we can imagine. If we put all the energy into this kind of relation with the earth that we have put into the other kind, we'd be in a very different place right now.

"You get what you go for."

195

It would be misleading to suggest that the town of Covelo is uniformly enthusiastic about and involved in a small farm revival. The phrase isn't even used here. We have conjured it as a way of putting a name on something that is beginning to happen in this small community. But in any town, you look for the energy. You listen to the conversation. You look for the people with that certain gleam in their eyes. And unless we have gone blind in our own home town, the signs here point unmistakably to the folks wearing overalls with mud on their boots.

It would also be misleading to suggest that a handful of renegade farmers and ranchers are about to put any kind of economic stability back into a community that has suffered from chronic depression for twenty years. They won't. What they might do, however, is help to restore to this town a sense of purpose and the belief that even though the most powerful forces at work would have it otherwise, it is still possible for rural people to achieve a substantial measure of self-sufficiency and economic independence.

The question is not so much whether economic stability is possible in a place such as this. The real issue is on what kind of terms is it possible? If the residents of this small place choose to sever the links that bind them to a system that exacts a price too dear, they will very likely have to give up much of what that system promises in return. But in reality — this is the irony — the system tends to promise more than it delivers. Most of the people in this and other rural communities live on incomes far below the national average. They accumulate little savings or discretionary income. Their security rests primarily in the land and in their ability to provide for themselves by working it. When that is gone, they have little left.

Perhaps the hardest lesson to be learned by the residents of such a place is the realization that what the American economy and political system promises has little to do with rural or small town life, and that it is necessary to articulate more precisely what it is we value here — then set out to be sure that it cannot be taken away in the name of progress.

The economy and social structure of this rural community is much like that of any other "underdeveloped" country. It is not possible to impose on it a standard of living or a value system that is transplanted from somewhere else. It confuses the natives and destroys the fabric of the local culture. The problem here, as in other places like it, is that people living in small towns haven't yet fully realized that rural communities are fundamentally different from cities, just as we haven't yet admitted that Somalia is fundamentally different from Cincinnati. (Not only have we fooled ourselves, we've also put one over on the Somalis.)

Covelo is a place of land and trees and mountains. What will save this place is a clear understanding of what that means to a gathering of people who live on that land and call themselves a town.

Like Steven Decater says, "You get what you go for."

196

The Power Without

MENDOCINO COUNTY REPRISE

In California the political decisions and, increasingly, the economic fate of small unincorporated towns such as Mendocino and Covelo are shaped by elected officials at higher jurisdictions. In Mendocino County an elected Board of Supervisors, consisting of five members (each member represents a district in the county), runs all unincorporated areas of the county, including all towns except four. It is a large piece of business they undertake — they not only do the duty of properly governing ten or fifteen small towns but also the spaces in between, which amount to an area as big as a small state.

Of course, the board is assisted by the normal county agencies: health, law enforcement, building and planning departments, and so forth. And the county has its own battery of civil servants. But the board consists of men who serve part-time. Each has his own business or profession. That in itself is just as well. But it severely taxes those members who take seriously their responsibility to understand the problems of scattered constituents who may live an hour and a half to two hours and light years in lifestyle away.

To further complicate matters, the state of California has allowed to grow and fester in the State Capitol (for the last fifteen years) an incredible apparatus which at some time in the past was intended to accomplish the paper work of state government, but has now coopted much of the power of elected officials and is increasingly self-serving. We speak of the bureaucracy of the state government — now a labyrinth of agencies that occupy the new high-rise towers in a solid phalanx up Capitol Mall to the State House.

Increasingly, the daily business in the warrens of state government translates into directives and mandates that are a burden on local officials and render these officials helpless to deal with mounting demands for reform from hard-pressed citizens. In effect, the state government, through the administration of its own and federal programs, has usurped the right of local jurisdictions to govern themselves. Uniform regulations are imposed on all municipalities or counties, regardless of size or ability to cope. Seeking alternatives requires time and expertise that most rural communities simply do not possess — not to mention the concentrated support of elected officials at the state level. Sometimes it means going to court.

As we write this, the Board of Supervisors of the county of Plumas is being sued by an agency of the state of California for refusing to put into operation (and in part finance from county funds) the full spectrum of public welfare programs required by the state. Plumas is a rural county located in the foothills of the Sierras, sparsely populated, with a modest economic base derived from timber, agriculture, and tourism. Plumas County officials reviewed the fifteen or more programs required by the state, and decided that Plumas would offer only those required by federal law. The result was a law-suit from the Director of State Welfare against the supervisors, accompanied by fines. The case is in the courts.

Our purpose in mentioning this is not to support the action of Plumas officials, who may or may not have had good cause for taking the action they did. Our purpose is to point out that many rural counties in this state (and we suspect elsewhere) consider themselves unable to cope with government on the scale that is presently in vogue in Washington, D. C., and (at least) in Sacramento.

Politicians and planners all over the state of California have wept over the loss of prime agricultural lands to housing and commercial development, and have repeatedly warned that further depletion of the land resource will threaten our ability to provide such fundamentals as breakfast, lunch, and dinner on the table. And yet, tax laws in this state on real property continue to favor and reward land speculation, since they are based on market value. Farmers who are caught between ceilings on earnings — imposed by a ravenous system of middlemen and retailers on the·one hand and soaring costs of production and taxes on the other — do what anyone who thinks about it for ten minutes would do: sell. When a decent living may no longer be had by farming or ranching, there is no choice. Inevitably, the land, having appreciated in value, fetches a price that reflects the trend up, is developed and resold at a still higher price, and is used as the basis for the next hike in property taxes. Should the county fail to properly assess and levy taxes based on sales activity, the law permits the state of California to intercede and to do so itself, in order that there be no inequity from county to county.

It is all terribly fair and unassailably logical. And it isn't working. At every level, the citizens in small communities, and their elected officials, who are, after all, their neighbors, are drawing the line. Frustration and bitterness have reached their limit, and new pressures are being felt for reform. In some cases, the pressure for change takes the form of outright disobedience. The Plumas County welfare fight and the Mendocino tax strike are examples. Elsewhere the tactics are gentler.

In the little town of Potter Valley (unincorporated), citizens recently completed a five-year battle to recover their own local schools, which had been lost to nearby Ukiah in a unification move. Citizens at the time were willing to believe that unification would lower costs and improve the quality of education. To their dismay, they found the reality far short of the promise and immediately set about to correct their error. They discovered that such things as unification are easier to do than un-do, and in the process were obliged to start their own private high school (and finance it) in addition to paying taxes

198

to support the public schools they were convinced were not working to their standards. In this instance, an official in the State Department of Education assigned to the case actually assisted local people to accomplish their objective — which they did. But they would not have been able to accomplish anything had a handful of parents not been willing to expend huge amounts of time, energy, and money to do what they believed was right.

Elsewhere in the county of Mendocino, property owners dissatisfied with the state building code, waged a long and tiresome fight, first against county officials, and later in the State Capitol itself, for changes which would make it legal to have the kind of homes they wished. Essentially, they were asking to be permitted to build homes without electricity or other amenities which most people take for granted, and which the laws of this state have made into requirements. Eventually, the matter was considered by the governor himself, who happens to be sympathetic, and certain alterations are being made, establishing a new category of construction that will permit deviations from the code for certain owner-built homes.

The point of all this is that the government we have is the one we deserve. It is as simple as that. If most of us are content to appear at the poll every fourth November, and limit our politics the rest of the time to an occasional argument at the local tavern or over the bridge table, we are going to pay the price for it. Power, it would seem, abhors a vacuum. And in the absence of a vigilant and actively responsible electorate, the professional politicians, the career bureaucrats, and the lobbyists with their corporate sponsors, will fill the void.

As you can see by looking at the content of this book, working reform from the streets of a rural town is a tough business. The status quo is always revered. And for the most part, the structure of our system of government makes it difficult for anyone to fuss with the machinery without good cause and extensive agreement. Were it not for that fact, we might now be in a state far worse than we are.

It seems as though the days of a direct democracy are numbered. Except for the Town Meeting in New England, which is itself a fading institution, decisions about most day-to-day matters in government are made by professionals and the experts they hire to advise them, not those who elect them. The public servant is no longer a man who serves out of some sense of duty — a patriot's tithe. The public servant is a career person, and his or her need for personal security and pride in his or her work must be taken into account when one is surveying the resistance in government to the will of the people.

It is not a simple problem. One will not dismantle the apparatus of government simply because it appears to be an obstacle in the way of realizing one's expectations. Yet it is clear that across the land, and in every category of human activity, the limits imposed by government and the relentless hunger of commerce for profits — sometimes separately, sometimes in collaboration — are impinging on the lives of individuals. How does a single person, or a group of residents who may gather in a rural community, deal with institutions so large and so opaque?

199

One begins. Anyplace. If this book has any message, or if the stories contained in it hide any lesson, it is that the power without is never any match for the power within. Again and again we have seen untrained and inexperienced amateurs mix it up with the minions of the powerful — attorneys, government officials — and come out with their prize against all odds. God knows how they do it. Call it pluck, bottom-hard will, or outrageous good fortune. It is all of those . It is a willingness to persist endlessly regardless of all predictions. It is not knowing how, and so inventing tactics that work only because they have never been tried. Maybe it is the kind of terrible fire that boils up in the person who knows he or she must succeed or perish.

It is clear that affairs in this country have long been dominated by those elements in the society which tend to concentrate political power — urban centers and large institutions, principally corporate and governmental. This being the case, it is no wonder that small cities, farming towns, villages, and rural people have been left to their own devices. A population shift such as the one now becoming apparent — away from urban centers, and toward rural areas — is not apt to alter the balance of power in any appreciable way. One can assume that the people who choose to locate themselves away from urban problems will be making political choices as well.

As the density of population in rural areas builds, the problems, indigenous to those areas, will intensify. Unless those who choose a rural environment are willing to become active participants in preserving it, their reasons for the choice are almost certain to be destroyed by the very choice they have made. It is not a cheerful prospect. But, as we have attempted to show in this book, it is certainly not hopeless, either.

Another photograph by the elusive Homer Gasquet. This one shows the mountains of Northern California covered mostly with second growth conifers, except those patches on the far ridge which have been clear-cut. The sight of this mountain "mange" is common here.

The Last Stand

There is no hiding place.

That may be a downbeat finale. It is certainly a bit of intelligence that tends to lie on the mind like a cold stone, and though it isn't news to everyone, it is something most Americans consistently refuse to accept. We don't mean that the words are not acceptable. We mean the notion of limits, spatial or otherwise, is something that until recently, Americans have not had to reckon with in daily affairs. Americans like to believe there is always another place to go.

Raised as we were with the *idea* — if not the fact — of plenty for everyone, the lesson of limits has been slow to reach us. We are a young country. How many adolescents do you know who will accept in their gut that there is something, anything, they cannot do? The correlation is not as far-fetched as it may sound. Human aggregates have personalities and exhibit collective behavior that is every bit as real, and sometimes as frightening, as that of individuals.

They have histories. They learn from experience and can be influenced by the actions of others. They behave in ways that are withdrawn, belligerent, comtemplative. They undergo trauma — on occasion appear to be irrational. In this instance, the analogy helps to explain a state of mind that is peculiarly American.

A nation of have-not immigrants turned loose, we were fed the wide-open spaces with our breakfast cereal, supported in fact by the scale of the territory. Our post-industrial mettle was tested in two World Wars. We didn't run out of anything, though we supplied half the planet with the apparatus of battle. Our national hero is a person (usually male) who plants himself in the wilderness, hacks out an existence, and in the process, makes use of pretty much whatever he needs. Later on, he joins the city council out of some sense of civic duty. But he is essentially a man of independent spirit who views whatever is around him as something that is at his disposal. Anything that he cannot do something with has little value, and there are no limits to how far he may go. If he uses up local resources, or the neighborhood suddenly become

203

undesirable, there is always somewhere else. Moving on is not something associated with giving up but with starting fresh. Our hero is self-made and incorporates all the biases that may be inferred from that label. Chief among these is an imagined immunity from natural cause and effect in a natural order which, in fact, exacts a price (infinite adjustments in a system of balances) for any excursion.

Now that we appear to be running out of *everything,* survival is no longer something that may be taken for granted. The wide-open spaces have shriveled, or are now owned by multi-national corporations. The land has boundaries that are defined not so much by the map as they are by economic and political constraints, which are more real because they are experienced daily. The next frontier doesn't exist. It never did.

What we have come to learn, in the process of writing this book, is that for the most part we still don't know how to live as communities in a world in which constraints, both natural and economic, are given. And the degree to which we chase the old American dreams, ignoring the fact of limits, is the measure of our blindness and our great danger. We have not yet decided, as a people, that the world is a miraculous place — and that the miracles have very much to do with the interconnectedness of things. All things. We have not yet learned that it is not all there — whatever we want — for the taking.

There are painful lessons ahead. They will call for a great readjustment of some ideas that we have long considered the most sacred. Most of them have to do with individual freedoms. We will have to learn something that the makers of this country knew from the beginning — that personal freedom can be defined only within the framework of a system of values that places responsibility on each individual. A teacher we know once put it this way: There must be a structure in all things. You accept it or you don't. If you accept it and adopt is as your own, it is like the bones within you — it holds you up. It is the strength on which you move. If you don't accept it, then it is like a cage. And you are inside it.

It must be one way or the other.

What we started out to show in this book was that small communities are probably the safest places to learn how to rebuild the ideas and institutions that are faltering around us. We still believe that. But what we have learned has shown us that small communities in this country — and especially rural ones — are in grave danger. Economically unstable, politically inept, they are easy prey for the denizens of the city on the prowl in the sticks. In less time than it takes to plant, tend, and harvest a single crop, land purchases and immigration from without can radically alter the patterns of rural activity.

This change can occur, at times, with the best of intentions. It is not always the effect of rapacious land grabbers. Outsiders accustomed to urban standards do not customarily abandon them when they arrive in the country. Instead, they work their expectations on their new surroundings. They convey them to others. And little by little, by direct intervention and in hundreds of subtle consequences caused by indirection, patterns shift — expectations are altered — and the rural conditions so attractive in the beginning, vanish. Some of these changes are the result of simple numbers — public services, for instance. But most of them — by far the largest number and the least visible — are the result of cultural influences. The city and the suburb are cultures that are as radically different from the culture of most rural areas of this country as any foreign cultures would be. The suburbanization of rural countryside is as much an inadvertent result of a way of thinking and behaving as it is a result of land grabbing and speculation.

Small communities anywhere, and particularly rural ones, will be safe only when the people who live in them understand them fully and accept personal responsibility for their protection. It is our conviction that protection of a community must by definition involve accepting self-imposed limits on wealth, choice of goods and services, and freedom of movement. There is no way to have it all — everywhere.

To the readers of this book who live in cities, and who dream of the small town as an escape, we offer a special word of caution. It isn't. The small town is as much a product of the American dream as anything else we have grown up with. To consider it as a place to hide is to consider trading one set of conditions and problems for another. One of our principal concerns in writing this book (and it has been reinforced everywhere) is to dispel the idea that the small community, wherever it is to be found, is any kind of *frontier*. A place for a clean start. There is no such thing as a clean start. There is only one kind of frontier left, and that is the kind that we carry around in our minds.

Resources

Small Towns Institute, P.O. Box 517, Ellensburg, Washington 98926.
Small Towns Institute publishes a monthly newsjournal, *Small Town*, that
brings new ideas and resources to both citizens and professionals in small communities across the country. The Small Towns Institute is a nonprofit organization concerned with finding new solutions to the problems facing small
towns and countryside communities today. Home Membership $15 a year.
Professional Membership $25 a year.

The Town Forum, P.O. Box 569, Cottage Grove, Oregon 97424. The Town
Forum is a nonprofit research and educational organization dedicated to
exploring creative community: land use and the environment, ambient energy
systems, participatory planning, social infrastructures, and new communities.
The publications mentioned in the Cerro Gordo story are available from the
Town Forum: Town Prospectus and First Feedback $2; The Cerro Gordo
Experiment: A Land Planning Package $2; Gathering the Townsfolk $2.

Rural America, Inc., Dupont Circle Building, Washington, D.C. 20036.
Rural America is an important organization that represents the first
citizen-sponsored effort to provide a voice for rural America and small towns.
The organization publishes a monthly newspaper-format report on rural problems: agriculture, rural health care, energy, housing, unemployment. It
sponsors an annual conference to prepare a platform on which to speak out for
or against important political issues affecting rural communities. Membership
and subscription: If your income is below $10,000, send $5; above $10,000,
send $15. Contributions are tax-deductible.

The Institute on Man and Science, Rensselaerville, New York 12147. The
Institute on Man and Science, independent and nonprofit, is an education
center concerned with new approaches to critical social problems. Its activities
include forums and meetings, research studies, and demonstration projects
such as Stump Creek. Readers interested in more detailed information
concerning the Stump Creek Revitalization Project can order the following
publications: Paper Number One: The Project Approach $1; Paper Number
Two: A Community Profile $3; The Revitalization of Stump Creek $ .50.   207

Institute for Liberty and Community, Concord, Vermont 05824. The Institute for Liberty and Community is a nonprofit research and educational organization with principal interests in the following areas: restoration of the small-scale community; individual and community self-help techniques; the preservation of individual liberty in an age characterized by large public and private institutions; and decentralization of concentrations of economic, political, and social power. Recent projects include a publication, "Vermont Citizen's Guide to Electric Power Issues"; a year long symposium on "Economic Empowerment of the Poor"; a major report entitled "Retirement Security Reform: Restructuring the Social Security System"; and two local conferences on "Decentralizing Vermont."

The Institute for Local Self-Reliance, 1717 18th Street, N. W., Washington, D.C. 20009. Although the Institute for Local Self-Reliance was established to investigate the technical feasibility of community self-reliance in *high density* living areas, we have included it here because the organization is also committed to humanly-scaled communities in general. Much of the research that has come out of studying neighborhoods is transferable to small communities and small towns. The newsletter *Self-Reliance* is published bi-monthly. It is filled with information on cooperative housing experiments, appropriate technology, small-scale production systems, the newest developments in politics and economics regarding energy, agriculture, housing, and waste recovery. Subscriptions: Individuals, $6; Institutions, $12. Memberships (includes subscription and 20 per cent discount on other publications prepared by the institute): Individuals, $25; Institutions, $40.